County Companion

GW00703522

Sussex
Hilary Arnold

Cadogan Books London
Century Publishing London

Contents

Writing: Hilary Arnold
Editor: Fiona Jardine
Editorial Assistant: Leone Turner
Illustrations by Alan Chapman,
Pauline Pears
Series design by Information Design
Workshop
Cartography: Line and Line

ISBN 0 946313 20 2

First published 1984 by Cadogan
Books Ltd, 15 Pont Street, London
SW1X 9EH in association with
Century Publishing Co. Ltd,
76 Old Compton Street,
London W1V 5PA

Typeset in Great Britain by
Words & Pictures Ltd. London SE19
Made and printed in Great Britain by
Purnell & Sons (Book Production) Ltd.,
Member of the BPCC Group,
Paulton, Bristol

How to use this guide 4

Complete Guide 6

Places to visit, towns and
villages in alphabetical order

Detailed Maps 104

Sussex Route Map 104
Map 1 106
Map 2 107
Map 3 108
Map 4 109

Town Directory 110

Arundel 110
Brighton 110
Chichester 111
Eastbourne 111
East Grinstead 112
Hastings 112
Hove, Lewes 113
Rye 113

Street Plans

Brighton 110
Chichester 111
Hastings 112

Leisure A-Z 114

Air Sports & Pleasure
Flights 114
Airport 115
Angling 115
Aquarium 127
Archeological Sites 127

Art Galleries 128
Bird Parks 129
Boat Trips 130
Canoeing 131
Caravan & Camping Sites 131
Castles 137
Church Buildings 138
Country Parks 139
Crafts 140
Cricket 142
Disabled 144
Events 145
Farms 147
Gardens 147
Golf Clubs 151
Grass Skiing 157
Greyhound Racing 157
Gymnastics 157
Hill Figures 158
Historic Homes 159
Horseracing 162
Lifeboats 163
Marinas 164
Markets 164
Mills 166
Motor Sports 169
Museums 169
Nature Reserves 175
Other Historic Buildings 178
Picnic Sites 178
Railways 180
Riding 181
Roman Sites 184
Sailing 184
Show Jumping 186
Sports Centres 186
Swimming Pools 189
Tennis 190
Tourist Information
   Centres 191
Unusual Outings 192
Vineyards 194

Walking 195
Water Skiing 198
Windsurfing 198
Women's Institute 200
Woodland 201
Yoga 202
Zoo 202

Acknowledgments 205

How to use this guide

Complete Guide

The first section of the book describes all the major towns and villages of interest in Sussex. They are included, along with outstanding attractions, in alphabetical order. After each name there is a map reference locating the place on one of the detailed maps. Places of interest to be found in the various towns and villages are described in this section but all details of their opening times, charges, facilities and other information can be found in the Leisure Directory. All places of interest in bold type have a listing in the Leisure Directory under the relevant section. For example: **Sheffield Park** (Historic Homes) This indicates that the details for Sheffield Park can be found in the Historic Homes section of the Leisure Directory. **Chalk Pits Museum** indicates that details for this museum can be found under the Museums section of the Leisure Directory.

Maps

A full map of Sussex showing all major roads can be found on pages 104-105. This is followed by four detailed maps of sections of Sussex on which are located all major places of interest and other important features such as caravan parks.

Town Directory

The major towns are listed here with the facilities and places of interest to be found in and nearby those towns. All details about the places to visit can be found in the Leisure Directory. For example:
Museum: Arundel Museum & Heritage Centre (under Arundel in the Town Directory) can be found in the Museums section of the Leisure Directory.

Street Plans of some major towns can also be found in this section with places of interest located.

Leisure A-Z

This section lists activities and places to visit, giving all important details. A full list of the topics included can be found on the Contents list at the front of this book. All entries are in alphabetical order. Where relevant, a map reference is given immediately after the name of the place of interest, locating it on one of the detailed maps. A page reference is given if the place is described in the Complete Guide.

The telephone number of the place is then given, followed by the location and all other details.

Symbols

⊞	caravan park
↲	angling
⌖	golf course
🛈	tourist information centre
🅿	parking
✕	licensed restaurant
⊡	snacks
♿	access for disabled visitors
🛍	shop
⊼	picnic site
⸹	swimming pool
♀	bar
⚓	sailing
∪	riding
⛺	campsite
PO	post office
▼	place of interest

The following opening hours apply to all buildings and other historic monuments which are managed by the Department of Environment. Some buildings and monuments are open for further periods in the summer and these extra opening hours are listed with the entry in the Leisure Directory.

March-April & October:
weekdays 9.30-17.30
Sundays 14.00-17.30
May-September:
Weekdays 9.30-19.00
Sundays 14.00-19.00
November-February:
Weekdays 9.30-16.00
Sundays 14.00-16.00

All DofE buildings and monuments are closed on December 24-6 and January 1. Some of them also close for the lunch hour which is normally 13.00-14.00.

Complete Guide

Aldingbourne Map 1 Bc

This tiny village to the east of Chichester contains many attractive old cottages and larger dwellings, an ancient church and a beautiful mill house standing on the banks of a large pond.

The settlement dates back to Saxon times and possibly earlier. From as early as 1050 it was visited by the powerful bishops of Chichester who built a country retreat here. King John was another visitor. He came to Aldingbourne first in March 1208 and on many subsequent visits in order to relax and enjoy the delightful setting.

When Cromwell's Parliamentary forces sacked the bishops' country retreat here in 1642, the village lost one of its most prestigious and historic buildings. However, St Mary's church still provides evidence of the villages past links with Chichester. Although it was restored in 1867, much to see of its Norman origins remain to be seen, particularly inside. An outstanding feature is a five-bay arcade dating from about 1170.

Alfriston Map 3 Ac

Alfriston is deservedly one of the best known and best loved of all East Sussex villages. It is situated in the magnificent Cuckmere valley, a short drive from major holiday resorts. As a result of this and of its enormous charm, Alfriston attracts large numbers of visitors, especially at weekends in the summer months.

The village was an important Saxon settlement. In the nineteenth century a Saxon cemetery was uncovered at Five Lords Burgh, a hill to the west of the village. Excavations produced an abundance of Saxon utensils, weapons and coins, as well as some Roman finds. All these are on show at the Barbican Museum in Lewes. It is said that in the ninth century Alfred the Great assembled his fighting thanes at Alfriston before one of their many battles in the south of England against marauding Danes. Alfred defeated the invaders on this occasion at 'Terrible Down'.

It is certain that a Saxon fortification was built here and the mound on which it stood now carries the ancient church of St Andrew. The present building dates from 1360. A legend, connected with the location of the church, says that when foundations were originally laid, in a field north of the village called Savyne Croft, each night invisible hands tossed the large stones from this site to the Tye, the mound on which the church now stands. Eventually the villagers gave in abandoning the Savyne Croft site in favour of the Tye.

Another ancient story attached to the church is that of Lewinna, a virgin Christian martyr who was murdered, presumably while defending her virtue, by a Saxon heathen in the seventh century. Lewinna became an early Saxon saint. Until the mid-nineteenth century it was customary for a wreath of white flowers to be laid on the coffin of a virgin who died in the parish. The flowers would later be hung in the church. A guide book published in 1894 tells of as many as 70 of these garlands hanging in the church at one time.

It is a grand church, often referred to as the 'Cathedral of the Downs' because of its spacious proportions. In the same year as the church was built, 1360, a **Clergy House** (Historic Homes) was erected for its priest. It stands by the church today, providing a fine example of a medieval wealden house. This carefully restored building was the first acquisition of the National Trust in 1896 and its excellent condition, both inside and out, pays tribute to the Trust's work. The half-timbered, wattle and daub exterior is topped with a fine thatch. Inside can be seen the basic layout for domestic buildings of the period. A large hall, with an open hearth in its centre, provided the living quarters with no partitions, or privacy, for the occupants. On one side of this was the priest's living quarters, known as the solar, which now contains a permanent exhibition of 'Life in Chaucer's England'. On the other side of the hall was the service wing for the house; a National Trust shop is now housed there. The grounds of the Clergy House have been reconstructed as an Elizabethan knot garden.

Alfriston can boast many other historic buildings, including the outstanding fifteenth-century Star Inn with its

A

fine carvings featuring a depiction of St George and the Dragon. Another old feature of the town is the remaining stump of a medieval market cross.

Four miles north of the village is **Drusillas Zoo Park** with a small but varied collection of animals, including rare breeds of domestic cattle and sheep, a range of small mammals, penguins, flamingoes and an aviary. A beautiful display of butterflies can be seen in the Bennett Butterfly House. In addition, there is a railway and an adventure playground for younger visitors, a cottage bakery and a shop selling pottery and leather goods.

Housed in an old thatched Sussex barn at the zoo park is **Valley Wine Cellars** (Vineyards) where a collection of old machinery used for making wine and cider, and a fascinating variety of antique corkscrews, are on display. Tours of the wine cellars include refreshments which range, according to the time of day and the amount visitors want to spend, from light snacks to gourmet dinners. There is a small vineyard here; each September an English Wine Festival takes place.

Clergy House at Alfriston

Amberley Map 1 Bb

This famous West Sussex village is superbly located on a low ridge above the marshy flats lying between the River Arun and the edge of the South Downs. Until the middle ages river craft could be taken from the sea up the Arun to this point, which accounts for the siting of this ancient settlement. In the last century a canoe dating from the middle ages was found in the area.

The Normans built a manor/castle here and the church, St Michael's, dates from 1160, although most of the existing building is from the thirteenth and fourteenth centuries. Dominating the village are the remains of Amberley Castle, built when the old manor became a country residence for the bishops of Chichester in the fourteenth century. In about 1380 Bishop Rede extended and fortified the manor, adding a great hall, and this house is still occupied. Having seen to domestic comfort, Bishop Rede erected a vast wall and gatehouse, providing Amberley with a stronghold and with one of the most striking skylines in Sussex: the bold castle wall standing out against flat surrounds with the church and a wide variety of old buildings stretching away from it along the ridge.

The last of the Chichester bishops to use the castle was Bishop Sherbourne who made additions to the house in the early sixteenth century. Just over a century later the castle was sacked during the Civil War and has been in ruins ever since. It is not open to the public.

Many of the industries that helped this area of Sussex, and much of the southeast, flourish over the centuries have now disappeared. However, **Chalk Pits Museum**, which opened in Amberley in 1979, provides a fascinating glimpse into these past occupations. The site of the museum is a former chalk quarry and lime works and huge lime kilns are a major feature. Many other 'old' industries can be visited, including a working blacksmith's shop, a printer's, a carpenter's, a cobbler's and a pottery. There are many other displays together with a narrow-gauge industrial steam railway in full working order. It is mainly an open air museum and is closed

A

in winter, though shelter is available for rainy days.

The area around Amberley is delightful. The village, with its cottages in many styles and built from a wide range of materials, is surrounded by fine scenery offering pleasant walks on the downland hills to the south, or through the marshy Amberley Wild Brooks to the north, where the celebrated 'Amberley Trout' abound, recommended by the most renowned of anglers, Izaak Walton.

Angmering Map 2 Ac

This old village, inland and west of the pleasant resort of Angmering-on-Sea, has several historic buildings. The church of St Margaret dates from the twelfth century but little remains of its original features since restoration during the last century. The tower was built by the nuns of Syon (or Sion) Abbey in 1507. An old house dating from the fourteenth century, Pigeon House, was built for one Thomas Pygeun, a merchant. Next to it stand some exceptional old farm buildings.

A more grand home is the old farm house, New Place, which was built by Sir Thomas Palmer in the sixteenth century and stands to the north of the village. His son, Sir Edward Palmer, became the proud father of three sons, all of whom were knighted by Henry VIII. They were triplets but with the rare distinction of entering the world on three successive Sundays. The story is often repeated but with no mention of their poor mother, who, if the tale is true, suffered the rigours of birth for over two weeks.

Like New Place, many of the attractive cottages in the village date from Tudor times; others were built in the seventeenth century. The remains of the oldest building in the area can be seen to the west of the village - a fine Roman villa, built here in the first and early second century. It was discovered in the nineteenth century when excavations uncovered a bath house and hypocaust, an underground heating system.

Ardingly See Wakehurst Place

Arundel Map 1 Bc

Arundel has a long and lively history. The settlement was well established in Saxon times, standing on a natural route by an important river but at a vulnerable point where the River Arun has cut a gap in the South Downs. The Saxons used a fort on a mound to defend their village and its mill, and to prevent visiting marauders from moving inland, since at that time the village was easily reached from the sea. The Normans developed Arundel into a port; it was regarded as important enough to become the seat of one of William the Conqueror's favourite and most celebrated knights, Roger de Montgomery (de Monte Gomerico).

Arundel Castle was built by the knight on the site of the Saxon fort. Over the centuries it was subjected to sieges and sackings and then extensive restorations and rebuildings but elements of the Norman original can still be seen. For over 500 years it has been the home of the Fitzalan family (Earls of Arundel) and of the Howards (Dukes of Norfolk), the two names being combined in 1842. The Dukes of Norfolk are the Earls Marshal of England and their family is one of the most prominent in the country.

Arundel Castle survived early sieges but was severely damaged during the Civil War when the Parliamentary forces took up their position in the ancient church of St Nicholas, bombarding the castle with cannon fired from the church tower. Extensive rebuilding took place in the eighteenth century and then large scale restoration was carried out under the 15th Duke of Norfolk between 1875 and 1900. The castle was again restored in the 1970s.

Part of the Victorian work included the building of a reproduction medieval hall. Earlier, at the beginning of the nineteenth century, the library was constructed, a room of 177 feet made entirely of Honduras mahogany. It contains a sixteenth century Bavarian chest and a seventeenth century Portuguese ebony cabinet. Other rooms house fifteenth-century furniture amongst the fine antiques and the Long Art Gallery displays portraits of the Earls of Arundel and the Dukes of Norfolk in chronological order. Artists represented

A

in the castle's art collection include Reynolds, Gainsborough and Van Dyck.

One bedroom was specially decorated and furnished in honour of a visit from Queen Victoria and Prince Albert in 1846 and another outstanding interior can be seen in the domestic chapel which, in the early twentieth century, was refurbished in mock-Gothic style.

The Fitzalan-Howards are a Roman Catholic family, and this has given an unusual aspect to the Anglican parish church of St Nicholas, in that it has a Roman Catholic chapel, the Fitzalan chapel. The church was rebuilt in 1380 and contains medieval wall paintings. In 1544 the chancel was sold to the Duke of Norfolk for the use of his family and the chapel was later created there. The chapel was closed down during the Reformation under Henry VIII and it was damaged during the Civil War when Parliamentary soldiers used the chapel as a stable. It was restored in 1886 and, until recently, a wall separated it from the main section of the church. A lawsuit, brought by the parish vicar in 1880, claimed the chapel was part of the church and not owned separately. The vicar lost the case but, as a result, the Duke of Norfolk was impelled to divide his family chapel from the Anglican church. This wall has now been replaced by a glass screen.

The same Duke of Norfolk, the 15th, built the magnificent **Arundel Cathedral** (Church Buildings) to a design by Joseph Hansom, inventor of the hansom cab. It was completed, in the French Gothic style, in 1873 but did not become a cathedral until 1965.

The vast majority of buildings in the town are from the Victorian era but with some notable Georgian exceptions including the old coaching inn, the Norfolk Arms, in the High Street. **Arundel Museum and Heritage Centre**, housed in another of the town's fine Georgian buildings, has displays of the town's history. The informative exhibits cover over 300 years, showing how the settlement changed during Celtic, Roman, Saxon, and Norman occupation and during the medieval and later periods.

A more unusual museum in Arundel is the **Museum of**

Curiosity which contains the extraordinary life work of Walter Potter, a Victorian taxidermist and naturalist. His stuffed creatures are set in amusing tableaux, depicting scenes such as the Kittens' Tea, the Rabbits' Village School, Death of Cock Robin and the Guinea Pigs' Cricket Match. **Arundel Toy and Military Museum** can be found in a Georgian cottage, the Dolls House, in the High Street. Its collection of old toys, games, dolls, and small military exhibits provide a wonderful outing for children and anyone who enjoys toys.

The town has a 1000-acre landscaped park attached to the castle. In this beautiful setting is **The Wildfowl Trust** (Bird Parks). Carefully created environments provide 55 acres of natural habitat for a magnificent collection of over 1000 birds, including ducks, geese and swans. Hides overlook several ponds, reed beds and a wader scrape. The visitors' reception hall, which has a wide viewing gallery, has won design awards. There is also a lecture theatre, a natural history bookshop and a gift shop as well as an exhibition area. It is one of the few places where the general public can see these beautiful wild birds in a safe and controlled yet natural environment. The Trust attracts many professional ornithologists and is an important centre for research and study of the many species found there.

Battle Map 4 Ab

On 14 October 1066 the course of English history changed when William, Duke of Normandy, defeated the Saxon King Harold in the best-known conflict ever fought on English soil. William the Conqueror built a church on the battle site in memory of his victory. Later, an abbey was established here and the small town of Battle grew up around it.

Battle Abbey (Church Buildings), with its grand gatehouse, still dominates the town. Today, when passing through the gateway, it is hard to envisage the awful violence of that battle in 1066, but close by is the field where the two huge armies of skilled fighters stood facing each other as the sun went down. On his deathbed, Edward the Confessor had named Harold his successor, yet William, a first cousin of

B

Edward, also claimed the throne, and had even extracted Harold's support. He brought his army to fight what he saw as a holy crusade for his place as the King of England. Despite an earlier promise of support for William, Harold was equally determined to maintain that position. The English army had hastened towards the south coast from London, having, only days before, defeated another invasion attempt in the northeast. Because of that battle the coast facing Normandy had been left undefended and William landed at Pevensey unopposed with 700 ships of the Norman fleet. After hastily fortifying Pevensey and then Hastings, he led his knights and soldiers on route for London.

The rise beside the main ruins of the abbey is what was once called Senlac, and it was here that the English army took up a strong defensive position. The Normans stood their ground on the hill visible about 400 yards to the south and it is believed that William commanded his army from a position near the railway bridge on the road which skirts the abbey. After unsuccessfully attacking the English army the Normans retreated to regroup and Harold is said to have made his fatal mistake by following them. Quickly rallying his forces, William turned back to attack and broke through the English line. Harold was killed by Norman knights and the bloody battle continued, with the English army inflicting further serious defeats on sections of the Norman army before the Normans finally took the day. A model of the two armies' line-up for the battle can be seen at the abbey.

The altar of the church which William founded here was placed on the exact spot where Harold is believed to have fallen, his death blow, according to legend, coming from an arrow through his eye. Nothing remains above ground of that church but the altar is marked by Harold's stone, placed there in 1903. Excavations are now taking place in order to reveal the foundations of this historic church.

Benedictine monks built the abbey, later enlarged in the thirteenth century. Much of the building from this period still stands, in particular the refectory. The gatehouse dates from about 1340. After the dissolution of the monasteries, the buildings were handed over by Henry VIII to his Master of the King's House, Sir Anthony Browne. He destroyed the church and adapted the abbey for his own domestic use. Much of this was again rebuilt as a Gothic mansion in 1857. This mansion, the first building to be seen on passing the gatehouse, now houses a girls' school.

On the street side of the gatehouse is the Pilgrim's Rest, which dates from the fifteenth century and is one of the town's most historic buildings. There is another church dating from the Norman period, St Mary's, which was founded in the early twelfth century and has been largely rebuilt and restored over the centuries. However, a Norman arch can still be seen there, in St Catherine's chapel.

Langton House, which dates from the sixteenth century, is the home of the **Battle Historical Society Museum**. Interesting displays provide insight into the history of Sussex from prehistoric times to the present day. There is a particularly good exhibition on the local iron industry. For those interested in Battle and its historic associations, there is a replica of the world-famous Bayeux Tapestry, a half-size version made in 1821, and also a diorama showing the Battle of Hastings.

Bayham Abbey Map 3 Ba

These majestic ruins stand in the beautiful Teise Valley, on the border between Sussex and Kent. Premonstratensian monks founded the abbey in the thirteenth century and created an imposing building, the outlines of which are still visible, as is some of the finely decorated stonework. Apart from the magnificent ruins here, the area is also known for superb trout. Confusingly, there is another Bayham Abbey, across the river in Kent, and not an abbey at all but a Victorian mansion built for the Camden family.

Bentley Wildfowl Reserve Map 3 Ab

Over 100 species of wildfowl can be seen here in the lovely setting of formal gardens and woodland. The 23 acres of park have been designed to create environments close to the birds' natural habitats. If visitors are confused by the enormous

B

range of wildfowl, paintings in Bentley House will help identification. The house also contains some fine antique furniture.

A vintage and veteran car museum can also be visited here and there is a play area for children.

Beachy Head see Seaford

Bexhill-on-Sea Map 4 Ac

Until the last century Bexhill village was a small and insignificant settlement, situated on a rise inland but overlooking the coast. Its nearest neighbour, Little Common, was reached across empty downland and travellers between the two were wary of smugglers and brigands. Today, the old church of St Peter, Norman in origin, still dominates the upland where the old village stood. Attractive, weatherboard cottages, a Georgian house and the old manor are located nearby.

In 1894 Augustus Hare wrote in his guide to Sussex that 'A new seaside resort is rapidly springing up , one and a half miles from the old village, under the name Bexhill-on-Sea'. Neighbouring Hastings and Eastbourne were, by then, well-established resorts but development of the coast near Bexhill had not begun until the 1880s when the earls of the manor, the De la Warr family, started the resort. Bexhill has remained smaller and quieter than its neighbours despite a strong following amongst daytrippers and holiday makers who come to enjoy the fine beaches, sandy at low tide, and excellent amenities of the town. The town is also a popular for retired people and commuters.

The grand promenade was originally created for cyclists who could enjoy riding their new-fangled machines along the coast. The first seaside entertainment complex for an English resort was commissioned for a major site on the promenade in 1935-6. An important, progressive building was the result, designed by architects Erich Mendelsohn and Serge Chermayeff, who were associated with the Bauhaus movement. The De la Warr Pavilion still dominates the front at Bexhill and is a popular venue with its terrace bar, theatre, banqueting suite and ballroom. Each summer a music festival is part of the programme here.

Visitors can enjoy a wide range of activities in the area, including bowls, golf, riding, sailing and excellent fishing, from the sea or from the River Rother nearby. There are two museums in the town. **Bexhill Manor Costume Museum**, housed in the old village manor house, is set among pleasant gardens and contains costumes worn between 1740 and 1960, as well as other historic exhibits. **Bexhill-on-Sea Natural History Museum** has a small display of the area's geology, natural history and archeology.

Bignor Roman Villa Map 1 Bb

This important Roman site was discovered in 1811 when a section of mosaic, depicting a woman dancer, was uncovered east of Bignor village during the annual ploughing. Later excavations revealed the remains of a substantial house, built

The De La Warr Pavilion at Bexhill

B

to a grand design and probably occupied by a prominent and wealthy Roman between the first and fourth centuries. The magnificently decorated villa was set around large gardens with covered walkways leading off to domestic rooms, farm buildings and servants' quarters. It was built on a rise overlooking extensive farmland which, it is believed, was connected to the villa.

The remains are protected by a traditional Sussex building of stone and thatch. The fine mosaic pavements include the longest one found in Britain which stretches for 80 feet along the north corridor. A mosaic dating from the first century AD is also on show. The hypocaust (underground heating system) is shown and explained in cross-section.

Bishopstone see Seaford

Bodiam Castle Map 4 Ab

During the One Hundred Years' War against France the Sussex coast was particularly vulnerable. In 1377 Rye was subjected to a devasting attack and three years later Winchelsea was also a point of invasion. Inland, the village of Bodiam, settled on the banks of the River Rother which flows to the sea at Rye, nervously awaited a possible attack up river by the French. The village was the home of a brave and famous knight, Sir Edward Dalyngrigge (or Dalyngrudge) who had won fame on the battlefields of Crecy and Poitiers. He applied to King Richard II for permission to build a castle in order to defend the village.

Bodiam Castle was completed, a massive stronghold, in 1385. Today it is no more than a shell yet this does not detract from its imposing character. The vast structure is rectangular, surrounded by a wide moat. The thick walls of the keep, six feet in width, rise up sheer from the moat to a height of over 40 feet. High towers stand at the corners and the impressive portcullis gatehouse has twin towers over 60 feet high. The visitor enters over the moat, crossing what was once a drawbridge. The serious grandeur is heightened by the castle's setting in the gentle countryside of the Rother valley.

Sir Edward Dalyngrigge's stronghold was never really put

to the test. The Hundred Years' War ended without the French invading Bodiam; later, the owners of the castle were to allow it to be taken twice, without a fight. During the Wars of the Roses, in the 1480s, the Lewknor family occupied Bodiam against Richard III and the Yorkists. When the King's troops attacked, Bodiam soon surrendered. In 1645 the owners supported the King against Cromwell and a Parliamentary force led by General Waller gained easy access to put an end to the alliance.

Following the Civil War, Bodiam Castle was sadly neglected, and has never again been occupied, although it has passed through various wealthy hands. The castle was a decaying ruin when Lord Curzon took it on in 1917. He restored it to the excellent condition in which it can now be enjoyed. After Lord Curzon's death, Bodiam Castle became the property of the National Trust.

Bognor Regis Map 1 Bc

This is a homely resort which provides all the fun of the seaside: miles of sandy beaches, lots of activities to amuse children, a large and popular holiday camp, and delightful parks.

In the 1790s, a wealthy London hatter, Sir Richard Hotham, chose the area around the tiny village of Bersted as the site for his dream resort - a grand and fashionable watering place to rival Bath and the newly developing Brighton. His spa, which he wanted to name Hothampton, never managed to attract the most fashionable elements. The Prince Regent, whose patronage ensured success in the late eighteenth century, came to Bognor only once for a brief visit. However, the seaside amenities developed alongside the grand Regency buildings and Bognor became a relaxing seaside town. Queen Victoria called it 'dear little Bognor' and, after convalescing there in 1929, King George V conferred on the town its Royal suffix, 'Regis', which means 'of the King'. In fact it was during the early twentieth century that it reached its height of fame as a seaside resort.

Today, with a large commuter and retirement population and a steady stream of visitors, Bognor Regis continues to

B

thrive. Among the many attractions is **Zootopia** situated in the beautiful grounds of Hotham Park. Bognor has long been known for its zoo and the animals, of which there are still a wide and entertaining variety, are now shown among fantasy creations and fairy-tale settings which thrill young visitors. There are also 'spectaculars' to watch, such as trapeze performances, and a visit provides a full day out.

The village of Felpham, now a part of Bognor but once a tiny and idyllic hamlet, was the home from 1800-4 of poet and illustrator, William Blake. A cottage, which is still in existence, was rented for him by William Hayley, a poet of some fame at that time. Blake was extremely enthusiastic about the place, using descriptions such as 'a dwelling for immortals' and 'heaven opens here on all sides her golden gates'. However, Blake's time in Felpham ended with a court case in Chichester following an argument with a soldier.

Bosham   Map 1 Ac

A Victorian traveller said of 'Bozzum': 'The people... are remarkably handsome. It has a well-to-do fishing population of evident foreign extraction, who stand aloof from their neighbours, seldom marry out of place, and keep their good looks to themselves.' An exotic and sophisticated atmosphere still clings to this delightful seaside village, although today the fishing folk have been superseded by the sailing set. Bosham's cluster of pretty cottages line a bustling harbour against a backdrop of hills. It is undoubtedly one of the most attractive and unspoilt villages on this coast.

Bosham, referred to in one ancient text as 'Boso's Meadow', was an important Saxon settlement. Holy Trinity church stands on Roman foundations and there is plenty of Saxon work to be seen inside, including a magnificent arch. A small stone tomb is said to contain the remains of one of King Cnut's daughters who drowned in about 1020, aged eight. Cnut, King of England, Norway and Denmark, is said to have lived here at various times and many claim that it was on the beach at Bosham that he failed to turn back the sea.

The church is depicted in the Bayeux Tapestry, the

ancient embroidered account of the Norman Conquest. It was from Bosham that Harold sailed to France in 1064 before he became king. He was captured and taken to William, Duke of Normandy, who extracted from Harold an oath to support William in his claim for the English throne. For Harold and the English this was later seen as a trick and the oath was ignored when Harold succeeded to the English throne. For William and the Normans the breaking of the oath became the basis for an invasion of England. After the Conquest, Holy Trinity church was enlarged and has some fine Norman features.

Bramber   Map2 Ab

The old village was established on an important defensive site beside the River Adur where it functioned as a port until the river silted up in the middle ages. In about 1090, the Normans built a stronghold, **Bramber Castle**, on a natural mound to defend the valley. The castle was besieged and sacked by Parliamentary forces in 1644 during the Civil War, and the resulting ruins are now under the care of the National Trust. St Nicholas church also dates from the Norman period but has been rebuilt and restored over the centuries.

St Mary's (Historic Homes) was first built to house monks in the fifteenth century. After extensive alterations in the seventeenth century, when it became a private home, it was restored to its original design in the nineteenth century. The exterior is timber-framed and inside there is elaborate wood panelling. One room was specially decorated for Elizabeth I and the King's Room is said to be where Charles II stayed immediately before he fled to France. The house has some exceptional antiques and rare books and one of its most interesting features is the entrance to a tunnel which once led to Bramber Castle. There is also a rather gruesome tableaux showing medieval torture techniques. The **National Butterfly Museum**, housed here, is one of the largest private butterfly collections in the world.

The owners of the **House of Pipes** (Museums) describe it

B

as the 'world's most unusual exhibition'. Unusual it certainly is. It contains over 35,000 objects connected with smoking. They come from 150 countries and some are as old as 1500 years.

Brightling Map 3 Bb

Brightling is a charming village located in an area of beech forest and hills. It is closely associated with Jack Fuller, squire of the manor there at the beginning of the nineteenth century and immortalised by his own eccentricities as Mad Jack. Fuller was a Member of Parliament for Lewes, whose great wealth came partly from the slave trade. Yet Fuller's discerning interest in fine art led him to collect Turner's paintings long before Turner was recognised as a great artist, and he also saved Bodiam Castle when it was threatened with demolition. Mad Jack made certain that he would be remembered after his death by erecting several extraordinary constructions. His most famous folly is a 60-foot obelisk on the highest point in the area, at Brighting Down, 650 feet above sea level. Excellent views of the Rother valley can be enjoyed from the site. In the grounds of his home, Brightling Park, Fuller built a domed observatory as he was also a keen amateur astronomer. Another of his creations is Sugar Loaf, a strange conical folly. Fuller is supposed to have bet a friend that he could see the spire of distant Dallington church from a point on his property but, on realising this was not possible, he built the Sugar Loaf to give the impression of such a spire. History does not relate if he did so to win the bet or merely to satisfy a whim. And in 1810, 24 years before his death, he built a massive pyramid in the churchyard at Brightling to serve as his own mausoleum. Any local will confirm that Mad Jack is buried there, sitting upright, with his top hat firmly on his head and a glass of claret in his hand. It seems likely that Fuller himself invented the story before his death.

After gazing in disbelief at the pyramid in the churchyard, St Thomas Becket church itself should be explored. It dates from Saxon times with much Norman work in evidence and contains a section of thirteenth-century glass and some medieval tombs. There is also a bust of Mad Jack here, on the wall. The rector of Brightling in 1362 was William of Wykeham, who went on to become Bishop of Winchester and Chancellor of England.

Brighton Map 2 Bc

The liveliest resort in southeast England and the largest town in all Sussex was no more than a small, undistinguished village until the middle of the eighteenth century. That village was Brightelmstone, ravaged by storms over the centuries and supporting an insubstantial fishing community. The dramatic change in its circumstances is usually attributed to two men: Dr Richard Russell and the Prince Regent.

Russell was no mere doctor. He was a great publicist of his own ideas and at a time when the richer members of English society were looking for new forms of amusement and new cures for their ailments, he found a solution for both and became a famous and celebrated man in the process. In 1753, *Dr Russell's Dissertation concerning the Use of Sea Water in Disease of the Glands* was published. He argued that coastal areas offered the perfect climate and that the sea was an essential element in obtaining good health. And he particularly stressed the qualities of Brightelmstone, the village to which he had moved from Lewes. Visitors began to pour in during the 1760s and 1770s as his ideas became popular amongst those who could read and travel. The nobility were among them and it was not long before the man who was to become an arbiter of fashion in his age, the Prince of Wales (later Prince Regent), duly took the journey down from London to Brightelmstone. He first visited it in 1783. By the time he died, as King George IV in 1830, he had spent the vast fortune of £500,000 on the place, and Brightelmstone village had become the fashionable and thriving seaside resort of Brighton.

At the age of 22, so taken by the place, the Prince decided to live there but it was a few years before he permanently

B

settled in Brighton. In 1785 he secretly married Mrs Fitzherbert and placed her in a house in Brighton. By 1786 he was renting a farmhouse on the Steyne (now Old Steine), named after the rocks then there, called the Stane, over which local fishermen had dried their nets. Then, in 1787, he commissioned a prominent architect, Henry Holland, to build him a grand villa near the same spot.

Brighton Royal Pavilion (Historic Homes) was originally designed as a classical country house with a rotunda and dome. Its elegant simplicity is hard to imagine now since it was much changed in the following decades. First the interior was refurbished in extravagant Chinese style. Exotic, eastern designs were fast becoming fashionable as these areas were opened up anew by travellers and colonialists. By 1815, the Prince had decided he wanted his villa transformed to look more like an Indian Moghul palace and he hired his favourite architect, John Nash, to carry out his desires. By 1822 the building was an extraordinary Regency fantasy, with onion-shaped domes, spires and minarets. It caused quite a stir. Sydney Smith said of it that 'the dome of St Paul's has come down to Brighton and pupped', while William Hazlitt described it as 'a collection of stone pumpkins and pepper boxes'. In the *Buildings of Britain*/ series, Nikolaus Pevsner had to admit that 'As a matter of fact it is vulgar - there is no denying it'.

Its flamboyance on the outside is matched by magnificently rich decor inside. The huge Banqueting Hall has a ceiling 45 feet high and hand-painted to represent the sky in the East at night. A gilded dragon hangs from its centre and from the claws of the dragon hangs an enormous glass chandelier which weighs almost a ton. During the Regency Exhibition, held here each summer, the table is laid with priceless china and Londonderry silverware. Also in the summer, the Music Room is set up as if for a small concert of the sort enjoyed there by the Prince and his entourage. In the King's Apartment, many of his personal items can be seen, and the Queen's Bedroom is laid out as it was when Queen Victoria visited the Pavilion. There is also the Great Kitchen to explore with its iron columns designed like palm trees and a vast 'batterie de cuisine'.

Although Queen Victoria stayed there many times she did not share the tastes, or pursuits, of the Pavilion's creator, the Prince Regent. Her public annoyance with the place was that it offered no privacy and in 1845 she stopped going there. By 1850 she had sold it to the town. When she left, she took with her many of the outstanding pieces of furniture and other items. These were later retrieved from various royal houses, including Buckingham Palace and Windsor Castle, and more has been permanently loaned by Her Majesty Queen Elizabeth II. It is now restored to its former glory and recieves more visitors than any other building in Britain.

Most of the elegant Regency terraces and squares of Brighton and Hove were built in the first half of the nineteenth century. Lewes Crescent, Royal Crescent, Clifton Terrace and Kemp Town, named after Thomas Read Kemp, the local lord of the manor who rented the farmhouse to the Prince, remain largely intact. There is still a small area of older streets, The Lanes, around Brighton Square. Antiques

The Lanes, the oldest streets in Brighton

B

shops, pubs and cafes are now housed in what were fishermen's cottages in this maze of paved alleys. Of the many churches in Brighton, the most impressive are St Bartholomew's and St Peter's. The first was built in the early 1870s at the expense of H.M. Wagner. He was vicar of Brighton from 1824 to 1870 and was responsible for several churches. St Bartholomew's is extremely grand, though built in simple brick. Its nave is higher than that of Westminster Abbey and its intricate ironwork reflects the Arts and Crafts movement which Wagner supported. St Peter's was designed by Sir Charles Barry, later famous as the architect of the Houses of Parliament. He won a competition to build this church before his thirtieth birthday and it was completed, in the Gothic style, in 1828. St Nicholas Church is of Norman origins and has sections dating from the fourteenth and fifteenth centuries. In the churchyard lies Martha Gunn, Queen of the Dippers. Her role, in the heyday of Regency Brighton, was to assist women bathers in modestly entering and leaving the sea. She was a favourite of royalty and her portrait hangs in Buckingham Palace.

The Dome was built in 1806 as stables for the Pavilion. This was the first Indian-style building in Brighton. It was converted to a concert hall in 1935 and seats over 2000 for its varied programmes. Another fine old entertainments venue is The Theatre Royal, built in 1807 and with a sumptuous, red-plush interior. The theatre is used mainly for plays, including West End productions which are often seen here before they reach London.

A grand old house can be seen at **Preston Manor** (Historic Homes). It is Georgian, built in 1738 on the site of a medieval house, and contains a large collection of antique furniture, paintings, rare porcelain and silver. Its finest treasures are laid out in a museum room. The grounds include a delightful croquet lawn, lily ponds and rose gardens.

Brighton offers an enormous variety of activities to supplement its famous resort pleasures such as bathing or strolling along the famous promenade. The Palace Pier stretches out to sea for over a quarter of a mile and provides every essential of seaside fun. There are deck chairs to bask in and fresh shell fish to eat, a helter skelter and ghost train to ride, and the inevitable amusement arcades. The **National Museum of Penny Slot Machines** is housed in the Pier Pavilion and, understandably, will not admit unaccompanied children. Inside is a wonderland of vintage one armed bandits, pin tables and slot machines. Old pennies are provided for those who cannot resist trying their luck and guided tours are available, except in the high season. Near the entrance to the pier is one of Brighton's most famous attractions, the **Aquarium and Dolphinarium**. It was built in 1869 and has spectacular, underground, Gothic-style galleries. It remains the largest aquarium in the country. Thousands of species of exotic tropical, marine and freshwater fish can be seen as well as seals, sealions and turtles. The Dolphinarium seats up to 1000 for its popular and regular shows of the charismatic and delightful performing dolphins.

Brighton's Palace Pier

B

Brighton Art Gallery and Museum is close to the Pavilion, and built in the same style, in what was originally intended to be a tennis court for the Prince Regent. The Fashion Gallery has over 100 costumes, including the extreme styles of each era, presented in period settings. A fine collection of Art Nouveau and Art Deco furniture and furnishings, from 1890-1940, is shown in another gallery. Brighton's colourful early history is explored back to the pre-historic Whitehawk Camp which was established nearby in 3000 BC. The collection includes the early-Bronze Age Hove Amber Cup and a Sussex Folklore room. There are wax busts of some of the famous personalities of the Georgian and Regency periods. The paintings on show include many by English and Continental masters. The Willet Collection is of unusual pottery and porcelain from the eighteenth and nineteenth centuries.

Another important museum is the **Hove Museum of Art**, housed in a nineteenth century mansion in the centre of Brighton's elegant neighbour town. Here the famous Pocock Collection of ceramics is kept as well as important modern ceramics. Other exhibits in this wide-ranging museum include Roman and other coins, medals and byegones, old toys and games, and model ships and dolls' houses. The Hove Collection is of modern British paintings and drawings.

The British Engineerium (Museums) provides a rare opportunity to appreciate a fascinating aspect of our industrial past. It is housed in a magnificent, nineteenth century, water pumping station. Part of its excellent restoration includes its 1876 Beam engine which is put under steam on Sundays. There are hundreds of full size and model engines, including railway engines and fire engines from the past. The story of electricity is vividly explained and the collection includes a wide range of hand tools.

The **Booth Museum of Natural History** is quite different again. E.T. Booth studied and collected over 500 species of birds which are mounted in special displays to show their natural habitat. The butterfly gallery also has a wide-ranging collection of species from all over the world. Another interesting feature of the museum is the large gallery containing the skeletons of rare and extinct animals. These include a 20-foot killer whale. A display entitled 'Unnatural History of an English County' looks at the effects which human beings have had on the Sussex landscape and its threat to conservation of the natural environment.

In recent years a new and exciting development has been the massive project of the **Brighton Marina**. The two expansive breakwaters enclose 126 acres of land and sea providing a yachter's paradise with over 2000 moorings. The marina is Europe's largest. As well as private yachts, there are historic boats and exotic craft from around the world. It is a major centre for water sports with facilities for jet skiing, water skiing, windsurfing, and bumper boats. Harbour boat trips can be taken and fishing charters leave from here. There is a thriving boatyard and fish farm as well as cafes, and major water events take place including power boat races and yachting regattas. One highly enjoyable way of reaching the marina is by the old **Volks Electric Railway** which runs along the front from the Aquarium. It is claimed to be Britain's first public railway, and was opened in 1883. Some carriages which travel the mile and a quarter track are open.

Brighton has diverse sporting facilities. **Brighton Racecourse** (Horseracing) has seventeen meetings each year. Greyhound racing can be seen regularly at the **Brighton Stadium**. The town's famous football team is Brighton and Hove Albion, and cricket enthusiasts can enjoy matches at the Sussex County Cricket Ground. There is a modern sporting complex in the King Alfred Leisure Centre and another recent addition to local facilities has been the Prince Regent Swimming Pool. A vast modern building on the seafront houses Britain's largest conference auditorium, the Brighton Centre, which seats up to 5000.

North of Hove is the **West Blanchington Windmill** (Mills), a hexagonal smock mill standing on a flint tower and connected to old barns. It was built in the early nineteenth century and purchased, for preservation, by the Hove Borough Council in 1936. It contains the original machinery, last used in 1897. There is a small museum display showing the machinery and tools used by the millers.

B

The University of Sussex was founded in 1961 in part of the ancient estate of Stanmer, north of Brighton, and is one of the 'new universities'. **The Barlow Collection** (Museums) is kept here. It depicts 3000 years of Chinese civilisation, through ceramics, bronzes, jades and other items. **Stanmer Park** (Country Parks) was purchased by Brighton Corporation in 1947. The fine Palladian house, built in the 1720s, and its extensive parkland, was the home of the Earls of Chichester, members of the famous Pelham family who have longstanding connections with the county. Henry Pelham, of Lewes, bought the estate in 1714. When the university first opened, the house was used as an annex but it is now undergoing restoration.

The parkland has been used for various purposes since it was taken over. Much of it is abundant farmland. Sections are used as the large municipal nursery and over 40,000 trees and shrubs are grown here each year. There are glasshouses where Brighton's summer flower displays are raised. A training centre gives horticultural instruction to young people aiming to make a career in public parks and recreation. Much of the remaining area is open for sports, such as cricket and football, and as a country park. There is extensive landscaped parkland to wander, as well as mature woodland and beautiful gardens.

The village has avoided development and is a rare example of a rural manor and its outbuildings. Next to the house is the church, rebuilt in 1838 but originally fourteenth century. Around it are old farm and service buildings. The village is being restored by volunteers from the Stanmer Preservation Society who also run the **Stanmer Village Rural Museum**, which incorporates some of these buildings. A forge, originally in Falmer village, has been reconstructed. On show is a wide collection of agricultural implements such as a donkey wheel and a horse gin. There are blacksmith's and wheelwright's tools, and other rural and domestic byegones.

On the coast to the east of Brighton, beyond the Marina and Roedean girls' school, is the village of Rottingdean. Despite its close proximity to a very large town, it has managed to preserve its own character. Its village pond and pretty green are enclosed by attractive houses, a short walk from the clifftops where the South Downs meet the sea. The pre-Raphaelite artist and active contributor to William Morris's Arts and Crafts Movement, Edward Burne-Jones, lived here at North End House from 1880 until his death. Several of the stained glass windows in St Margaret's Church were designed by him. This Norman building, with much Early English work, was renovated in the mid-nineteenth century but retains many of its earlier features. The old vicarage, now the **Grange Museum and Art Gallery**, is an early Georgian house, remodelled by Edwin Lutyens. Part of the National Toy Museum is housed here, a delightful collection including old rocking horses, toy soldiers, clockwork toys, Jack-in-a-Boxes, model theatres and much more. A display about the history of Rottingdean and the local area has been mounted by the Rottingdean Preservation Society. There are also paintings and other art exhibits. An important feature is the collection of memoriabilia of the

Rottingdean's village pond

C

writer Rudyard Kipling. Kipling was the nephew of Edward Burne-Jones and he came to love Rottingdean when staying with him. In 1897 he moved into The Elms, which overlooks the green. He wrote the *Just So Stories*, *Stalky & Co.*, and *Kim* when living here. The Grange has a Kipling room with letters and documents belonging to the writer, portraits of him and early editions of his works. Kipling was a famous celebrity at the end of the nineteenth century and many sightseers came to Rottingdean to catch a glance of the writer. In 1902 he moved to a quieter part of Sussex and to a more secluded house, in Burwash.

Burwash Map 3 Bb

Rudyard Kipling lived at **Bateman's** (Historic Homes) from 1902 until his death in 1936. The house, now a National Trust property, is outside the village, approached through old iron gates beside the large yew trees of its lovely garden, developed by Kipling. This was originally the home of a local ironmaster, built in 1634 with tall chimneys and fine Jacobean panelling inside. It has been left as it was when Kipling and his family lived there. His study is dominated by the cluttered, ten foot-wide desk at which he wrote such books as *Puck of Pook's Hill* and his unfinished autobiography *Something of Myself*. Visitors can wander at ease to inspect the personal documents and manuscripts of the writer, and other items such as his Nobel Prize. His Rolls Royce stands in the garage and in the garden is the water mill, now restored, which he installed to generate electricity.

Burwash was a centre for the iron industry, established in the area from 50 BC and later developed by the Romans. The beautiful High Street has seventeenth and eighteenth century houses. St Bartholomew's Church has a basically Norman tower and nave but was largely rebuilt in Victorian times. Inside is a fine fifteenth century brass memorial. A tablet commemorates John Kipling, the son of the writer, who died at Loos, in France, in 1915, during the First World War.

Camber see Rye

C

Chanctonbury Ring see Washington

Cissbury Ring see Worthing

Chichester Map 1 Ac

The county town of West Sussex is one of Britain's most
long-established towns. Regni and Belgae tribes were settled
there when the Romans entered this area of England in AD
43. They met no resistance from the locals and chose the site
where Chichester now stands to first make camp. Later the
Romans created an administrative centre and market town,
Noviomagus, there. The local tribal chief, Cogi, was
bestowed the rare honour for a non-Roman of being made
Imperial Legate for the district. His Roman name was
Tiberius Claudius Cogidubnus. In 477 the Saxons, led by
Aella, landed nearby and took advantage of the remains of
Noviomagus and set up camp there, driving the Britons into
the forests around. The name Chichester derives from 'Cissa
ceasta', the camp of Cissa. Cissa was a son of Aella and took
charge of the area.

In 681, St Wilfred landed at Selsey and established a
Christian centre there. In 1075, soon after the Norman
Conquest, the see was moved to Chichester. A major
Norman town developed around the cathedral and castle they
built. The castle was destroyed in the thirteenth century. In
the middle ages the town was an ecclesiastical and market
centre. Wool was a major local industry, and later the export
trade developed. Chichester continued to thrive, with new
development in the eighteenth century when it was a
fashionable place to live. Since then it has remained a
peaceful and beautiful country town.

Bishop Ralph Luffa directed the building of **Chichester
Cathedral** (Church Buildings). Its spire rises above the
landscape for miles. Work was continued by Bishop Seffrid II
after extensive damage was caused by fire in 1187. The
additions and alterations have continued and the building is a
harmonious blend of Norman, Transitional, Early English,
Decorated and Perpendicular styles. It has a rare feature in

C

its detached bell tower, built in the fifteenth and sixteenth centuries. The spire dates from the early fourteenth century. During heavy storms in 1861, it collapsed, with the tower. Photographs of this disaster can be seen in the south transept.

The finest treasure inside is a twelfth-century Romanesque stone carving depicting the arrival of Christ at Bethany and the raising of Lazarus. It was originally brightly coloured and studded with jewels. There is fine stained glass and ancient monuments. One of the modern windows was designed by Marc Chagall. Other twentieth century additions include paintings by Graham Sutherland and Hans Feibusch, and a tapestry by John Piper. During restoration in 1932, the heads of 15 prominent men were carved on the exterior. They include Ramsey Macdonald, Stanley Baldwin and George V. Guided tours of the cathedral can be arranged and the old Treasury can also be seen.

Another outstanding Chichester landmark is the market cross, built to an intricate Perpendicular design in Caen stone. It stands to 50 feet and was presented to the town by Bishop Story in 1501.

A bookshop is now located in St Olave's, a thirteenth century church. The oldest domestic building in the town, The Chantry, also dates from the thirteenth century. Vicar's Hall is even older, with parts dating from the twelfth century including the vaulted undercroft. And Vicar's Close is a row of houses from the fifteenth century. **St Mary's Hospital** (Other Historic Buildings) belonged to the Greyfriars, Franciscan monks, until 1269. The Hospital of the Blessed Mary, in existence since before 1229, then moved into the building and it was converted to a typical medieval hospital: a long, single-roofed building with a main infirmary and chapel block. It was completed in about 1290. It is the only building of its kind to have survived in England. By the beginning of the seventeenth century, it was becoming more of an almshouse than a hospital. During the Restoration period the area which had once been lined with beds was converted into separate chambers where the needy could live. Today they have been enlarged and modernised and about fourteen elderly people live there. It is a delightful building with a low, sloping roof and tall, seventeenth century chimneys. Inside the main hall is a fine display of tie-beamed roof timbers, with the old chapel at the end.

Georgian Chichester is centred around the Pallants district. One of the outstanding buildings is **Pallant House Gallery** (Art Galleries), built in 1712 and a fine Queen Anne town house. Its local nickname is 'Dodo House', so-called because of the strange birds mounting its entrance posts. The prosperous wine merchant who built the house specified ostriches, but the creatures which resulted, based on drawings of the time, look nothing like ostriches. Pallant House has two outstanding art collections, the Bow Collection of porcelain, and the Walter Hussey Collection of paintings and art objects, presented as a gift by the former Dean of Chichester. There is also a typical Queen Anne period kitchen, Shippham's Kitchen, taking its name from the local firm famous for its fish paste.

The **Chichester District Museum** is closeby, in Little London. The building is eighteenth century, and once a cornstore. It contains the history of the district including finds from the Roman town, Noviomagus, and geological exhibits. Nearby at Priory Park, in a medieval Priory church once used by the Greyfriars, is an extension of the museum, **Guildhall Museum**.

Another notable Georgian building is the Town Hall, built in 1731 by Roger Morris and later extended by James Wyatt. The outstanding modern building is the Festival Theatre, completed in 1962. It is an hexagonal theatre 'in the round', with 1374 seats. No seat is more than 66 feet, the length of a cricket pitch, from the stage. The wide-ranging programme presented here, particularly interesting during the five-month summer festival, includes opera, ballet, jazz, orchestras and virtuoso artists.

The Romans are believed to have landed, in AD 43, near Fishbourne and set up a military base there. About thirty years later a magnificent villa was erected, **Fishbourne Roman Palace**. It is believed to have been built for the local King, Cogidubnus. When it was first discovered, during the laying of water pipes in 1960, it was thought to have been a smaller villa, but as excavations continued it was realised that this was the largest Roman villa yet found in Britain. There is a fascinating museum display explaining the history and layout, with audio visual programmes. The mosaic floors are of high quality. The courtyards and corridors can be identified, and there is a bath suite and hypocaust system of underground heating. A dining room has been reconstructed as it was in AD 100, and most of the remains are under cover. The palace had abundant gardens, with plants bought from Rome. A section has been laid out as it was in the first century, using plants believed to have been grown then. There is a picnic area and refreshments are available.

North of Chichester is the enormous estate of Goodwood, home of the Dukes of Richmond. **Goodwood House** (Historic Homes) was designed by James Wyatt and built at the end of the seventeenth century. He incorporated an earlier, smaller house on the site, built in 1720. This had been enlarged in the 1760s by the architect Sir William

Festival Theatre in Chichester

Chambers. The fine stable buildings near the house were part of his work at that time. Despite the grandeur of Goodwood House, it has a flint facing, insisted upon by the Third Duke of Richmond. He died before the building was completed and Wyatt's grand design was only partially carried out. Lord March, heir to the Ninth Earl of Richmond, continues to live there and administer the estate.

The house contains a famous and extensive art collection, including paintings by Canaletto, Van Dyck, Kneller, Reynold and Stubbs. There is antique English and French furniture, a collection of rare Sevres porcelain and fine tapestries. Queen Victoria's Faberge walking stick and her Coronation cushion can be seen. The First Duke of Richmond was the son of Charles II and his French mistress. An emerald ring he gave her is displayed.

The extensive landscaped grounds contain **Goodwood Country Park**, a protected area of outstanding natural beauty. **Goodwood Racecourse** (Horseracing) is perhaps the most attractive course in England. It was laid out in 1802 and has 15 meetings a year. Pleasures flights can be taken from **Goodwood Airfield** where there is also a flying school. The 12,000-acre estate also contains a grass ski slope, a golf course and a riding centre. **Goodwood Motor Circuit** was once world famous as a venue for grand prix racing. It is now serving the motor industry as a test track and is used by the Motor Sports Club for members' meetings and competitions.

The 50-mile coastline of Chichester Harbour spreads out below the town. It is often filled with sailing craft, using its 17 miles of navigable channels. Many of the attractive coastal villages have become yachting centres. There is no direct access between Chichester and the harbour. The canal which connected them, built in the early nineteenth century, is now unused. From Roman times the harbour was used for exporting goods from the area, including hides and wool in medieval times. In the eighteenth century it was a flourishing boatbuilding centre. Today it is a peaceful haven with virtually no commercial traffic.

Footpaths provide waterside walks and ferry boats cross the harbour. Boat trips can also be taken around it, run by

C

Chichester Harbour Conservancy (Boat Trips). In winter, 30,000 birds migrate here to escape the bitter winter of the north. Species include shelduck, Brent geese, and many wildfowl and waders. **Pagham Harbour** (Bird Parks) is an extensive bird reserve on 1000 acres of tidal mud flats. There is an information centre at Sidlesham where leaflets are available for a nature trail.

Clayton see Poynings

Coolham See Shipley

Crawley Map 2 Ba

This the only New Town to have been developed south of London. In 1947, Crawley had a population of less than 10,000. It is now a a much larger, thriving town, noted for its modern architecture and planning. Yet the centre still contains buildings dating back to the fifteenth century. St John the Baptist Church is from this period and has earlier features. London's second international airport, **Gatwick Airport**, is north of Crawley. The busy air traffic can be viewed from a spectators' gallery.

Crawley has fine leisure and park facilities and lies close to two extensive Wealden forests, Tilgate and St Leonards. **Tilgate Park** (Country Parks) is to the southeast of the town. Its 400 acres include lakes, woodland, lawns and ornamental gardens. There is a golf course here as well. An important animal reserve is located within the park. Tilgate Park Nature Centre has a wide variety of animals and birds. Rare breeds of livestock are gathered in large paddocks and include impressive White Park cattle, Soay and Wensleydale sheep, and Lop pigs. Smaller mammals, such as pygmy goats, rabbits and guinea pigs, can be seen. The birds on view include wild and domestic fowl, aviaries of British birds, including owls and crows, and a large colony of water birds living on a section of Titmus Lake. The centre was established in 1966 to conserve rare and endangered domestic animals and to provide sanctuary for wild animals. It is a fascinating collection and the animals are easily seen despite their large paddocks. An exhibition room explains the work of the centre and provides information on the animals and birds as well as the environment of the park.

Worth is an attractive old village on the eastern outskirts of Crawley. It has one of the most famous of all Sussex churches. St Nicholas dates originally from the eleventh century and is a large, simple Saxon building of great beauty and atmosphere. It was carefully restored in 1871, leaving the impressive Saxon arches, which include a fine chancel arch.

Cuckfield see Haywards Heath

Ditchling Map 2 Bb

This pretty village has a long association with arts and crafts, a connection which lives on in the area today. In the 1920s the artists' colony here included Eric Gill, the sculptor and designer, and Frank Brangwyn, the painter. Its most famous inhabitant today is Dame Vera Lynn. The church of St Margaret has many thirteenth-century features; sections are even older. Of the many delightful old houses in the village, including one with attractive geometric tile facing in red and black, the outstanding example is the rustic sixteenth-century Wings Place, also known as Anne of Cleaves House. It is one of the homes given to that queen by Henry VIII but she is not believed to have even visited it.

Ditchling Beacon (Nature Reserves), near the village, is the third highest point on the South Downs and stands at 813 feet. In the past it was used as a site for a burning beacon to warn of activity in the English Channel and on one occasion a fire was lit to give word of the approach of the Spanish Armada. A Roman camp is believed to have been established on this easily defended hill, and before that it was the site of an iron age hill fort. Today walkers on the downs stop on the summit to take in the spectacular views of the coast and surrounding countryside. This area of downland scarp is protected and many rare chalk-loving wild flowers and insects can be seen on the grassland and scrub. Another protected area is **Ditchling Common** to the north of the village where there is a one-and-a-half mile nature trail through scrub land. A leaflet can be obtained describing the trail. A well-known local landmark is **Ditchling Cross**, south of the village near the beacon. This large chalk cross carved in the downs is believed to be connected with the Battle of Lewes, where Simon de Montfort defeated Henry III in 1264. The cross may have been the work of the monks of Southover and is best seen from the north.

Easebourne see Midhurst

Eastbourne Map 3 Bc

This relaxed family resort is known for its south-coast sunshine, well-kept streets and abundant flower gardens. The long, three-tier promenade is packed with holiday-makers throughout the summer. The fine weather can be enjoyed on three miles of shingle beach, where safe swimming is enjoyed

Wings Place at Ditchling

under the watchful eye of the lifeguards and deckchairs are always to hand. Military bands entertain crowds of over 3000 people in the grand bandstand beside the sea. For children there are the special facilities of the Treasure Island play centre, with big model jungle animals set among the paddling pools and sand pits. The elegant pier was opened in 1870. Despite a battering by storms and crowds, it remains in excellent condition. Eastbourne offers everything that is traditionally associated with Sussex by the sea.

Evening entertainment takes place at four major venues. The Congress Theatre has spectacular summer shows and concerts throughout the year. The Royal Hippodrome, an Edwardian Theatre, also provides summer shows and celebrity concerts. The Winter Garden has such events as wrestling and dancing, while the Devonshire Park Theatre is the place for popular drama and comedy plays. Three 18-hole golf courses are within easy reach of the town centre, and bowlers, sailors and anglers are also well catered for. Lovely Devonshire Park is host to major tennis tournaments and county cricket.

One of the best art galleries in the south, **Towner Art Gallery**, contains the work of many outstanding British painters of the nineteenth and twentieth centuries. There are sculptures by Henry Moore and Elizabeth Frink and a delightful look at Eastbourne's past through the Victorian sketches of Louisa C. Paris. The gallery is housed in an old manor built for the Gilbert family in 1734. This manor is at the centre of the oldest section of the present town. Nearby is St Mary's church which dates from the twelfth century and is well worth exploring. Its Tudor parsonage, next door, has underground passages which surface under another of the old buildings in the area, Lamb Inn, which dates back to 1240. The purpose of the tunnels is not known but many believe they must have been used for smuggling.

At the end of the eighteenth century three hamlets stood in this area, East Bourne, South Bourne and Sea Houses. Between them was the splendid stately house, Compton Place, home, in the nineteenth century, of the Duke of Devonshire, and regularly visited by royalty, including our

E

present Queen. Earlier, the area was popular with those who had adopted the fashion of taking the sea air and bathing from the coast: King George III sent his children here for their holidays on more than one occasion. When the nation was gripped with the fear of an invasion by Napoleon's French army, towers and forts were built along the coast as defences. This particular stretch had four Martello Towers and a redoubt fort. One of the towers still stands and is now known as **Wish Tower 73** (Museums), the 73rd Martello Tower in the chain. The tower gets its name from its proximity to marshy ground, traditionally called 'wash' from the old English *wisc* meaning 'wet place'. A maritime museum, with particular emphasis on the defence of England's south coast, is now housed in the tower. Under the tower was the old lifeboat house which became the first permanent **Lifeboat Museum** in the country in 1937. In 1822 Eastbourne became the second place on the south coast to be given a lifeboat station. The present station is not open

Wish Tower 73 on the cliffs at Eastbourne

but the turntable and short slipway by which the *Beryl Tollemache* reaches the sea can be seen outside.

The other remaining coastal defence against Napoleon, the **Redoubt Fortress** (Museums), built in 1804-12, also offers displays on the coastline and defences. Here, too, is the Sussex Combined Services museum. The fort is a circular, sunken brick building which was once enclosed by a dry moat. It was equipped as a gun installation and housed troops and supplies. The parade ground in the centre is the setting for open air concerts in the summer, notably the exciting '1812 Night'.

The two major landowners in the district, William Cavendish, Duke of Devonshire, and Carew Davies Gilbert, began to develop Eastbourne as a major resort from 1851. Planning was careful; even today no shops can be opened along the seafront so as to preserve the grand facades which line the promenade and maintain the Victorian character. However, some things have changed. Until 1871 mixed bathing was not allowed from the coast in town, and only women could enjoy the bracing water.

Among Eastbourne's many lovely gardens is a semi-tropical creation which is the home of the **Butterfly Centre** (Unusual Outings). Among waterfalls and exotic plants, is a magnificent display of live butterflies.

From the pier, boat trips can be taken to see **Beachy Head** (Nature Reserves) which dominates the coastline to the west of Eastbourne. Its dramatic cliffs tower to a height of 575 feet above the sea, and energetic visitors can enjoy walks along the clifftops here. Care should be taken not to go near the cliff edge since it is not stable. The other danger presented by this massive outcrop is, of course, to sailors. Before the first lighthouse, called Belle Toute, was built 400 feet up the cliffside in 1834, many boats were wrecked on the rocks. Sailors only survived if they were able to cling to the rocks above the water level. So regular were the wrecks here that the local vicar, in the early eighteenth century, hacked out a staircase and cavern from the chalk, known as Parson Darby's Hole, to which sailors could climb and find refuge. A new lighthouse was built at the base of Beachy Head in 1905.

E

The area has now been designated a nature reserve and there is a nature trail, with accompanying leaflet, and a natural history centre with information on the flora and fauna of the headland.

Four miles north of Eastbourne stands **Polegate Windmill,** built in 1817 and restored to full working order in 1967. Adjoining the mill is the old storeroom which has been converted to a small milling museum, with displays of old milling machinery and other bygones.

East Grinstead   Map 3 Aa

East Grinstead, within easy reach of London, has a large commuter population and has grown rapidly since the war. Yet its High Street has one of the loveliest stretches of charming old buildings to be found in a county full of such pleasures. Some of the historic, timber-framed houses date back to the fourteenth century and there are equally fine examples from the fifteenth to eighteenth centuries.
Sackville College (Historic Homes) is an almshouse founded in about 1609 and completed a few years later by Robert Sackville, Earl of Dorset. He built the living quarters and chapel to house 31 of his family's old retainers - 21 men and 10 women. The lovely stone building remains a refuge for the elderly. There are guided tours of the common room, dining room and chapel; of interest is the courtyard and the antique oak furniture.

Another old home to visit in the area is **Standen** (Historic Homes), built in 1894 by Philip Webb. Webb was influenced by the Arts and Crafts movement, and, in particular, by William Morris whose original wallpaper and textiles were used in the rooms. In his guide to Sussex, Oliver Mason points out that unlike many Victorian creations, this is a 'light, modest, and restrained' building. Fine furniture, pottery and paintings of the period are on show, together with a delightful conservatory, elegant billiard room, and, a rare feature, the original electric light fittings. Standen is managed by the National Trust. A hillside garden can be visited separately.

Another attractive garden at **Kidbrooke Park** (Gardens) was laid out by Humphrey Repton, the renowned landscape gardener. This parkland on the edge of Ashdown Forest is located in the grounds of an eighteenth-century mansion, now a private school. Its position offers splendid vistas; the grounds include weir ponds, a valley field, a wild garden, a bog garden, terraces and a pergola.

Gravetye Manor (Gardens) is Elizabethan, bought in 1885 by William Robinson who enlarged and replanted the lovely gardens. The house is now a hotel and country club and there is only limited access but the gardens can be viewed. Close to East Grinstead is an interesting Victorian convent, St Margaret's, built in 1865. Here an embroidery school produces intricate vestments and other church embroidery. St Swithun's Church was largely rebuilt to a design by Georgian architect James Wyatt in 1789 after the tower had collapsed in 1785. It contains old brasses and monuments. **East Grinstead Town Museum** has an informative exhibit entitled 'Story of Our Town' and other displays of crafts and bygones from the area.

Etchingham Map 4 Ab

This village on the confluence of the Rother and Dudwell rivers has a famous parish church in the Decorated style, dating from about 1366. It has a grand central tower. Inside, among the ancient brasses, is the now headless memorial to the church's founder, Sir William de Echyngham, the oldest, dated brass in Sussex. Another old feature of the church is the weathervane, probably original and, if so, one of the oldest in England.

Haremere Hall (Historic Homes), nearby, is an early seventeenth-century manor containing a wide range of antiques, including a collection of beautiful rugs and with some intricate Jacobean wood carvings. The stable block for the house was once important since Haremere Hall was the home of the Master of Kings' Horse to the Prince Regent in the early nineteenth century. Now they are once again an important equestrian centre, home of the **Sussex Shire**

F

Horses (Unusual Outings). Heavy, working horses have been reintroduced to the estate's farms so the breeding operations have a practical side. A magnificent shire stallion and other fine horses, such as two Ardennes working mares, can be seen. Cart rides are available for children and there are regular demonstrations in the stable courtyard, showing how these delightful animals work and are trained. This is also a training centre, with courses for handling working shire horses.

Fletching Map 3 Ab

The church of St Mary and St Andrew dates back to pre-Norman times and the building, despite restoration, still has some thirteenth century fragments. Inside, fine monuments include a fourteenth-century brass, a grand tomb for Richard Leche, High Sheriff of Sussex, who died in 1596, and the mausoleum of the Sheffield family.

John Baker Holroyd, 1st Earl of Sheffield, bought the estate near Fletching in the mid-eighteenth century. **Sheffield Park** (Historic Homes) was remodelled for him by James Wyatt in 1775-8, and was the architect's first major country house in neo-Gothic style. King Harold's father had lived here in the eleventh century and the house was greatly extended in the Tudor period when Henry VIII visited it. One of the outstanding features of this beautiful house is its situation, amidst **Sheffield Park Garden** which is run by the National Trust. There are lakes with lovely waterside plantings and exotic giant trees in full maturity. The rhododendrons and azaleas are the main attraction in the early summer; during the autumn the trees and shrubs are spectacular. Two famous landscape gardeners were responsible, in the years immediately prior to the remodelling of the house, for the garden's design: Capability Brown and Humphrey Repton.

Sheffield Park Station, in the estate, is one of the terminals for the **Bluebell Railway**. The track, through delightful countryside, carries vintage steam engines pulling old carriages. Journeys are from Sheffield Park to Horsted Keynes. Part of the station at Sheffield Park contains a small museum.

G

Glynde Map 3 Ac

The large country estate of Glynde was divided in 1589 when its owners, the Morley family, moved to a new house. This was **Glynde Place** (Historic Homes), built in 1569 for William Morley. The fine Tudor building was created around a courtyard and faced west - an important detail because today the entrance is by the east-facing wing. The house shows signs of drastic alterations which took place in the mid-eighteenth century, when many wealthy landowners were giving their properties a Georgian facelift. Richard Trevor, Bishop of Durham, who had inherited Glynde Place, went further than a facelift, he turned his house around. What is today the back is still recognisably, and originally, Tudor and includes the great hall, typical of houses of that period. The front, however, is Georgian, where three rooms were converted into one large front hall and a new entrance was built. The driveway was rerouted to the other side of the house and taken through a new stable wing. Further alterations took

Glyndebourne

place during the nineteenth century when the Victorian owners, in keeping with the taste of their time, reinstated Tudor elements. But despite these changes, the building is impressive and retains a certain harmony. Inside is a wide variety of art treasures and objects of interest.

Next to his house, Bishop Trevor built an unusual church. It aroused mixed feelings among Victorian commentators. One described it as being 'in very bad taste, the style called Grecian', while another was touched by this 'pretty little Grecian church'. It is, in fact, in the Palladian style, complete with classical features and Italianate decorations both inside and out.

Up the road from Glynde is Glyndebourne, the home of the Morleys until 1589, and now world famous as the venue for the Glyndebourne Festival Opera. The house was greatly rebuilt in the nineteenth century in a revival of its original Tudor style. It stands in magnificent gardens. In 1934, Audrey and John Christie fulfilled their dream and attached an opera house to their stately home, providing a unique setting for opera and one which captured the imagination of music lovers and performers alike. The Festival Opera has thrived, and each summer season it attracts internationally renowned singers, conductors, directors and designers who combine their talents to stage critically acclaimed performances. Visitors to the opera are obliged to wear evening dress and this, with the traditional picnicking from sumptuous hampers on the expansive lawns during the long supper break, has given the whole event its atmosphere of formal indulgence. A restaurant has now been built which incorporates part of the mature gardens. Oak trees emerge through its roof.

Goodwood see Chichester

Hailsham see Michelham Priory

Hastings Map 4 Ac

Of all the resorts of Sussex, Hastings is undoubtedly the most important historically. It was to this ancient port that William of Normandy sailed in 1066. He had chosen the Saxon settlement, named after the Hastingas who lived there, because of its safe, natural harbour, its proximity to the Norman coast and its easily defended position. His fleet was blown off course and landed at Pevensey, but since the English forces were engaged in fighting off an invasion in the northeast, he marched unhindered on his original target and quickly fortified the town. The birth of a new England took place here following the Battle of Hastings. **See Battle**

Hastings Castle was the first Norman castle built on English soil. The original erection was a prefabricated wooden fort, bought from Normandy in sections. This was soon replaced by a sturdy castle and, under the command of Robert, Count of Eu, it became the Norman headquarters for the south coast and their main port. The castle ruins, high on Castle Hill, consist of part of the curtain wall and church. The prefabricated fort stood on a high mound, built up from earth scooped out to form a deep, defensive ditch. This mound is known as the Mount and it is well worth climbing to its summit, perhaps taking the **West Hill Cliff Railway** for the first part, in order to take in the panoramic views it offers of the south coast and across to France.

Hastings, then, was established as an important centre by the time of the Normans and it thrived over the next centuries. When the Cinque Ports were created, giving certain strategic ports and towns privileges and prosperity in return for allegiance and fighting forces for the King, Hastings was the most important of them. But although it was then one of the major towns in southern England, its future was doomed. King John dismantled the castle in 1216 to avoid it being taken and used by French invaders. A decade later, Henry III refortified the castle but this did not prevent devastating French raids on the town in 1339 and 1377. By that time the port was also facing another enemy. The sea was eroding areas of the cliff, while at the same time the town's greatest natural asset, its harbour, was silting up. By the end of the thirteenth century the thriving Cinque Port had lost its prominence and for the next 600 years Hastings was to remain a small fishing settlement.

Since it was established so early, and was so prosperous in

the early middle ages, Hastings has a large and very interesting Old Town which luckily has not been affected by the eventual development and expansion of the town into a seaside resort. In a relatively small area, between Castle Hill and East Hill, lies Old Town, with its streets lined in historic half-timbered and weatherboarded buildings. There are narrow alleyways and ancient inns, and it is not difficult to imagine it as the centre of a salty fishing port. With the original harbour gone, the fishermen hauled their boats up the beach; they continue to do so as they have for centuries, although today hauling is done with the help of motor winches. Several attempts were made to build a new harbour and the sweeping breakwater now standing at the east of town was the result of the last attempt in 1893. One of the most attractive elements of old Hastings is the weatherboarded net lofts on the beach, which were first there in the sixteenth century. The tall, tarred and narrow lofts were designed to save space since their owners had to pay ground rent. You can still see nets being mended outside them. Many of the lofts are very old, although some

Fishing boats on Hastings beach

were built quite recently to exactly the same style.

The fishermen had their own chapel built in 1854 but it was never consecrated. It is now the **Fisherman's Museum,** on the Old Town front called Rock-a-Nore. This was the site of a shipbuilding industry until early this century, and the museum houses the last hauling lugger built here, the *Enterprise.* There are many other local fishing mementoes in the museum.

Old Town contains two historic churches. St Clement's was rebuilt after French raids in about 1377 and the Perpendicular building required extensive restoration after it was bombed in the Second World War. Dante Gabriel Rossetti was married there in 1860. All Saints dates from the same period as St Clement's, built in about 1436, and again on the site of a church destroyed by the French. It contains many interesting features including, a medieval wall painting called 'The Doom' and showing the Last Judgement with Jesus depicted on a rainbow. There are also ancient monuments and brasses in the church.

Another feature of Old Town is **St Clements Caves** (Unusual Outings). These natural caverns, once the haunt of smugglers and outlaws, were greatly extended by a Mr Golding in the nineteenth century. He also made sculptures in the rock which have been added to in more recent times. There are guided tours of the caves; they can also be hired for private functions.

While medieval Hastings is Old Town, the present centre erupted in the last century when Hastings became a resort. Not everyone was pleased to see the little town change as it was developed. Nineteenth-century essayist, Charles Lamb wrote: 'I love town, or country; but this detestable Cinque Port is neither. There is no sense of home in Hastings... It is the visitants from town, that come here to say that they have been here... that are my aversion... All is false and hollow pretension. They come because it is the fashion, and to spoil the nature of the place. They are mostly stockbrokers...' The oldest remaining part of that new resort is Pelham Crescent, built by Joseph Kay for the 1st Earl of Chichester in 1824. By then the open countryside which divided Hastings from its neighbour, St Leonards, was beginning to see developement

H

and in 1828 plans were made to create a major resort at St Leonards. Wealthy London builder, James Burton, acquired the estate with its seafront and, inspired by the success of Brighton, set about creating a Regency style resort. His son was the renowned architect, Decimus Burton, and he was responsible for St Leonards' beautiful buildings. The centre of the development was the building now housing the Royal Victoria Hotel, with colonnaded terraces either side.

Sadly the overall effect has been interrupted and dominated by the 1930s creation Marina Court. But beyond this, to the west, is more of the Burtons' St Leonards. Decimus Burton's own villa was built as part of an attractive group including an Assembly Room, now the Masonic Hall. South Lodge and North Lodge, nearby, are also his work, as are the villas of Quarry Hill and Maze Hill which echo his designs for buildings in London's Regents Park. St Leonards was further extended during the nineteenth century, notably at Warrior Square, and the space between the twin towns narrowed until they virtually became one.

Modern Hastings continued to flourish as a major resort, with its long promenade, pier and wide-ranging facilities for visitors. James Burton is the subject of a special display in **Hastings Museum and Art Gallery**, which also contains Lord Brassey's collection of oriental art and Pacific ethnology, brought back from the South Seas aboard his yacht *Sunbeam*.

Hastings Museum of Local History is in the old Town Hall and has exhibits on the Norman Conquest, local history from the stone age on, the architecture of Old Town, and much more. The **Hastings Embroidery** (Unusual Outings) was commissioned from the Royal School of Embroidery to commemorate the 900th anniversary of the Battle of Hastings. It is an intricate work of applique with 27 panels containing 81 pictures depicting major events in English history. The embroidery is 243 feet long and 3 feet high. It is housed in the Town Hall alongside a scale model of the battle and a collection of dolls in period costume. White Rock Pavilion, built in the style of a Spanish American mission in 1913, has a theatre and concert hall where summer spectaculars and other entertainments are provided.

Nearby, in White Rock Gardens, is the **Hastings Model Village** (Unusual Outings). This delightful miniature shows a Tudor village and is set in landscaped gardens of the same scale. The **Lifeboat House** (Museums) contains the two 37-foot lifeboats which are launched from its site on The Stade to carry out sea rescue in the English Channel. Guided tours are available, including inspection of a lifeboat. There are various exhibits and displays on the history of the Hastings lifeboat and its past crews.

Hastings has a long, shingle beach and is well known for angling. Each year a major sea-angling festival is held in early autumn. Another annual event to note is the Town Criers' Contest staged each August.

High on the cliffs to the east of town, which can be ascended in the **East Hill Cliff Railway**, is **Hastings Country Park**, established in 1971. The park comprises 500 acres of downland and scrub near the village of Fairlight and contains several marked nature trails, all with accompanying leaflets obtainable from the visitors' centre, explaining the topography and plant and wildlife in detail.

Haywards Heath Map 2 Bb

Towards the end of the nineteenth century, Augustus Hare described how the land around Haywards Heath was being 'cut up and sold in small portions by the Sergisons, and is now a colony of cockney villas'. That colony has certainly grown, for the old market town is now almost a postwar new town with a large commuter population and extensive modern housing developments. But Haywards Heath remains an agricultural centre and its cattle market is the largest in Sussex.

Two lovely villages have almost been drawn into the town, yet both have maintained their character. Cuckfield, to the west, was the home of those Sergisons who were selling the land. They lived in a beautiful Elizabethan mansion, Cuckfield Park. From 1627, Charles Sergison lived at **Legh Manor** (Historic Homes) near the village. This sixteenth century manor was restored by Edwin Lutyens in the early part of this

H

century after it was bought from the Sergison family by Sir William and Lady Chance in 1917. The large main hall and three other rooms can be viewed. The garden is also delightful with fine views over the south downs. It was restored and replanted from 1918 with the help of famous gardener, Gertrude Jekyll.

The church in Cuckfield was started in the thirteenth century but was heavily restored in the nineteenth century. One good result was a stained-glass window by a highly respected artist, responsible for many of the finest examples of Victorian stained glass in Sussex, Charles Kemp.

Kemp lived in the other Haywards Heath satellite village, picturesque Lindfield. His home was the sixteenth century Old Place, near the church, which he altered to his own designs. This is just one of the village's extraordinary array of fine, historic buildings. Its High Street has been described as 'without any doubt the finest village street in East Sussex' and it gets many visitors in the summer. There are Tudor houses, old wealden cottages, handsome Georgian homes and the church built in the fourteenth century. Another noted inhabitant of the town was William Allen, a Quaker and reformer who was part of Robert Owen's co-operative movement and a campaigner for the abolition of slavery. He settled in Lindfield in 1824. On the West Common the cottages he built to house local 'distressed workers' can still be seen.

Haywards Heath is surrounded by magnificent gardens. To the north is **Borde Hill Garden,** large and rambling with a magnificent collection of rare trees and shrubs. It is crossed by paths and there is a picnic area. Further north is **Nymans** (Gardens) which is run by the National Trust. This is a delight to visit at any time but its colourful flowers and shrubs are at their most spectacular in midsummer. The house, built by the man who designed the gardens in the early part of this century, was destroye by fire in 1928 and the ruins still stand, rather attractively, amidst the blooms and magnificent mature trees. Nymans offers spectacular views and a wide range of small gardens within its boundaries, including a sunken garden, old rose garden and heather garden.

To the west of Haywards Heath is **Leonardslee** (Gardens),
situated in a small valley which it fills with its flowering
shrubs and mature trees. A stream completes the picture and
there are several small lakes. Finally, to the south west, is
Heaselands (Gardens) where there is an unusual and
delightful water garden which attracts water birds to its lakes.
Birds are a feature here, with a collection of wildfowl and
aviaries containing other unusual birds. Heaselands has lovely
flowering shrubs, fine mature trees and woodland in its 30
acres.

Heathfield   Map 3 Bb

Now a modern, lively town, the old part of Heathfield remains
as pretty as a small village. This settlement grew up as a
centre for the local iron industry. In 1450, Jack Cade was
killed here and his memorial stands in Cade Street. He was a
famous rebel who led the yeomanry of Kent and Sussex in
their struggle against crippling taxes. Petitions which Cade
organised were sent to the King setting out the veiws of
commoners, but they were ignored. Cade proved to be a fine
soldier when he and his followers defeated King Henry VI at
Sevenoaks not long before he died. They then marched on to
London but met with no success for their cause.

In 1607, Roger Hunt, vicar of Heathfield, set sail to help
establish the first permanent colonial settlement in America, at
Chesapeake Bay. A stained-glass window in Heathfield's
thirteenth century parish church commemorates the event.

Henfield   Map2 Ab

The lovely leafy village of Henfield, now almost a small town,
is a centre for market gardens. **Henfield Museum** is in the
New Village Hall and has an interesting collection of local
history and archeology. South of the village is **Wood Mill**
built in the eighteenth century. This watermill now houses a
countryside exhibition including small mammals and fish, as
well as an open beehive. There are also audio-visual
programmes about Sussex wildlife and nature reserves

organised by the Sussex Trust for Nature Conservation who have their headquarters here. The 15-acre nature reserve adjoining the mill has a woodland nature trail and a pond from which children can net specimens of pond life.

Herstmonceux Map 3 Bb

The name is pronounced 'Herstmonsoo' and derives from the Monceux family, Normans who acquired the manor in the late twelfth century. Crafts such as wood-carving and basket-making have been the traditional industries of this area. Herstmonceux is particularly known for trugs - boat-shaped gardeners' baskets which were first made in the mid-nineteenth century. **Thomas Smith Trugs** (Unusual Outings) was founded in 1858 and trugs are made there in the traditional way by skilled craftsmen. Every stage of their creation can be seen and a guided tour can be taken.

The village is a harmonious mixture of old and new with its most historic section now somewhat separated to the south of the main village. Here is the Early English church of All Saints, built in the late twelfth century. It contains two fine memorials. A brass in memory of Sir William Ffiennes is dated 1402 and is in remarkably good condition. A grand, canopied tomb was erected in memory of Lord Dacre, who died in 1534, and his son, Sir Thomas Ffiennes. The sculptures which decorate it do not portray these two men but, it is believed, were taken from Battle Abbey at the time of the dissolution of the monasteries.

Herstmonceux Castle was restored to its former glory in the first half of this century and now stands as a superb example of a fortified manor house. The building has all the elements of a fairy-tale castle, with its turrets and towers reflected in the wide moat. Sir Roger Ffiennes built it in 1440 in a revolutionary material for the time, red brick. In 1777 it was partially dismantled and those fine red bricks used to build nearby Herstmonceux Place. After the castle had been completely rebuilt it was taken over by the **Royal Greenwich Observatory** (Unusual Outings) in 1948. Their telescopes and other installations are contained in the magnificent grounds of the castle. The 200 acres contain woodland, formal gardens and grassland, crossed by paths and a marked nature trail, with accompanying leaflet. Large lakes are home to various fish and waterfowl. An exhibition about astonomy can be seen in the two large rooms of the castle which are open to the public. Also here is an audio-visual programme on the history of Herstmonceux Castle and displays of local flora and fauna.

Hickstead see Hurstpierpoint

Horsham Map 2 Aa

The name of the town could be derived from the Saxon *Horsa*, giving some indication of the age of this settlement. Horsham has long been an important agricultural centre and, more recently, a prospering modern development. The town retains delightful pockets of its past, represented by fine old buildings. Like Oxford, Horsham's main crossroads is called Carfax. Here is the old Town Hall, built in the seventeenth century and restored in the early nineteenth. Pump Alley, a narrow, pretty passage, leads through to the Causeway which is a full street of historic buildings dating mainly from the fifteenth and sixteenth century.

Causeway House is one of these, now containing the **Horsham Museum**. It is a truly wide-ranging collection, incorporating many important elements of Sussex rural life as well as other aspects of the history of Horsham and the local district. The Albery collection consists of old manuscripts connected with local parliamentary history. In sharp contrast are the agricultural displays and replicas of a saddler's and a blacksmith's. There are toys from the past, period costumes, veteran bicycles and civic relics. Some of the more barbaric aspects of the town's past are reflected in the reconstructed prison cell and whipping post from the old county goal; here also is the Horsham stocks and the bull ring.

Horsham's many important buildings include St Mary's church, dating from the twelfth century. It has a Norman doorway, a restored fifteenth-century fresco, a fourteenth-century Trinity chapel and several outstanding monuments. Southwest of the town is Christ's Hospital, the Bluecoat boys' school. The school was established in 1552 and moved to Horsham from London in 1902. The mock-Gothic building has elements from the school's London premises which were demolished when the school moved.

Hove see Brighton

Hurstpierpoint Map 2 Bb

This pleasant village contains many attractive buildings from the seventeenth and eighteenth century. The Holy Trinity church was built in 1845 to a design by Sir Charles Barry, who was the architect of the Houses of Parliament.

South of the village is **Danny** (Historic Homes), an Elizabethan manor, whose design is based on the letter E, in honour of Elizabeth I. She bestowed this estate on George Goring, who later became the Earl of Norwich. He built Danny in 1582-93. A second main entrance bears the date 1728, when Danny's owner Henry Campion extended the building. The house has long belonged to the Campion family and contains many items associated with them. During the

Danny house at Hurstpierpoint

First World War, Danny was used as a meeting place for the War Cabinet presided over by Prime Minister Lloyd George. It was here that the terms of the 1918 armistice were drawn up.

North of Hurstpierpoint is **Hickstead All England Show Jumping Course**. Through the spring and summer, major national and international show jumping championships are held here. It is said to be the finest show jumping arena in the world and many believe that Hickstead's excellent courses were partially responsible for raising the standard of riding in this country.

Lewes Map 3 Ac

This was until recent years the county town of all Sussex but now of East Sussex. Lewes is a small but impressive and historic settlement. Daniel Defoe said, 'Lewes is in the most romantic situation I ever saw' - it stands on the River Ouse surrounded by outstanding downland scenery. Its long, long recorded history tells of an important Saxon settlement here, established at a crossing place on the river. The Normans developed the town, recognising its important defense position at a gap in the downs. There is some dispute about the original **Lewes Castle**, built by William de Warenne before the end of the eleventh century. Most experts say it was wooden but others insist it was flint. It did not stand long before a sturdy stone castle was erected, the ruins of which can be explored today. From as early as the mid-fourteenth century the castle fell into disrepair but was saved by the Sussex Archeological Society who continue to run and maintain it, as well as many other important buildings in Lewes and elsewhere. The ruins consist of part of a Norman keep, restored in the nineteenth century, and the imposing Barbican gateway built in the fourteenth century and one of the largest of its kind in England.

William de Warenne and his wife Gunrada, who some believe was a daughter of William the Conqueror, established a religious centre when they invited Cluny monks to build a priory. Lewes Priory was a magnificent building including the

L

church, St Pancras, over 450 feet long. It was finished in the late eleventh century. Little is left of it now except fragmented ruins near Southover, now a part of Lewes but once a separate village to the south. The church of St John the Baptist at Southover was originally one of the outbuildings at the gates of the priory. It contains monuments to the priory's founders, William and Gundrada de Warenne, found in the nineteenth century and believed by the discovers to contain their bones.

The Battle of Lewes in 1264 was to have important results for England. Simon de Montfort led an army rallied to defend his, and other barons', demands more representation. After his forces met those of King Henry III in a terrible fight which left over 5000 dead, de Montfort won the battle and gained the added bargaining power of a captive King and his heir, Prince Edward. The treaty which resulted from the battle is regarded as the basis on which our parliamentary government was established.

Lewes was a thriving medieval town and became a Protestant centre which paid the price of many martyrs during Mary Tudor's bloody anti-Protestant rule. During the eighteenth century it was still thriving and an important administrative centre as well as a fashionable place to live. Today the overall atmosphere of the place is Georgian, a period in which Lewes was still an important port on the Ouse and before it was overwhelmed by the development of the little village of 'Brightelmstone, near Lewes', later to be known as Brighton.

The Castle, built on a steep hill, is the best place from which to survey the town, the valley of the Ouse and the surrounding countryside. The narrow High Street contains many Georgian-fronted shops, often disguising far older buildings. The whole is somewhat dominated today by the large County Council building. Opposite is the mid-sixteenth-century Shelley Hotel, with a Georgian facade including geometric tiles, a decoration often repeated on the buildings of the town. The **Bull House** (Other Historic Buildings), a medieval inn, dates from the fifteenth century, with much of it added in the sixteenth. Here lived Tom Paine, the famous eighteenth-century radical and author of *Rights of Man*. Paine was an excise officer in Lewes, sacked, it is said, because he campaigned against for better working conditions and pay in his job. He married the daughter of the Bull's landlord but they later separated and Paine crossed the Atlantic to join the revolution in America.

St Michael's church is known for its round tower, one of three to be found in the Ouse valley. The tower dates from the thirteenth century but most of the church is eighteenth century with a notable fourteenth-century arcade. Inside, the fine stained glass can be enjoyed and a monument to the Pelham family can be seen. Sir Nicholas Pelham was a great soldier. One of his many courageous deeds occurred when he fought off a French raiding party at Seaford in 1545, and the victory is remembered in an inscription on the memorial. The family lived for many years at Pelham House, an Elizabethan building with a Georgian facade. Another historic church is St Anne's, Norman originally and with a fine twelfth-century south arcade.

The Elizabethan building, **Barbican House** (Museums),

Harvey's Brewery in Lewes

L

standing opposite the Castle gates, is the home of the Sussex Archeological Society's museum. The museum has exhibits of local history from prehistoric times, with fascinating displays of how life was lived in the ancient past. Reconstructions of early tools and machinery include an iron age loom.

The Society has another museum in the Southover district of Lewes, **Anne of Cleaves House Museum**. Anne, who was Henry VIII's fifth wife, was given several properties in Sussex as part of her divorce compensation, including this house and Lewes Priory, following its dissolution. The house is another half-timbered, early sixteenth-century building incorporating an Elizabethan farmhouse at the back. Several rooms are furnished as they would have been in the seventeenth and eighteenth centuries. The museum has a wide range of local byegones including domestic implements, games, toys and Victoriana. The outstanding feature is a large display of Sussex ironwork from the seventeenth and eighteenth centuries, much of it intricately decorative. There is also a gallery showing the history of Lewes from the time of the Norman Conquest.

Another important old building in this area is Southover Grange, a sixteenth-century home now used as a public building and set in delightful public gardens. The seventeenth-century diarist John Evelyn lived here for part of his childhood and attended Lewes Grammar School, founded in 1512, although its present building, in the High Street, is Victorian.

Another small collection of historic interest can be seen at the **Military Heritage Museum** which contains displays showing aspects of Britain's military past.

Litlington Map3 Ac

This charming small village on the South Downs near Alfriston has a lovely Norman church with a white, weatherboarded bell tower. It was first built about 1150 and retains many original features. The village has flint-faced cottages and some more substantial old homes including Clapham House at which Mrs Fitzherbert is said to have lived before she secretly married the Prince Regent in 1785 and moved to Brighton.

South of the village is **Charleston Manor** (Gardens), described in Nikolaus Pevsner's series, *The Buildings of England* as 'A perfect house in a perfect setting'. The south wing dates back to Norman times, about 1200, and there are also Tudor and Georgian elements. Two lovely Sussex barns stand by the house as well as a dovecote said to have been built in medieval times. Charleston was built by a prominent Norman, William the Conqueror's cup bearer. The house is not open to the public but its delightful gardens can be visited. Fine yew hedges follow the line of the south downs, forming a striking background to the gardens. It has a wide selection of climbers and roses, rare chalk-loving plants and an orchard.

Charleston Manor featured prominently in the lives of the writers and artists who made up the Bloomsbury group earlier this century. Artists Vanessa Bell, her son Quentin Bell, and Duncan Grant, lived there. The village church at Berwick, north of Alfriston, was decorated with paintings by these artists during the Second World War, depicting biblical scenes set in Sussex scenery. The much-restored thirteenth century

Part of old Litlington

M

church has clear glass windows, looking on to real Sussex landscape.

Just south of Charleston Manor is Westdean, another delightful village nestled in the South Downs and surrounded by Friston Forest. The Norman church contains some interesting old monuments and a modern bronze head by Epstein. To the east of Litlington is tiny Lullington church, regarded as one of the smallest churches in England. It is in fact the restored remains of a much larger medieval church, and what stands now is part of a fourteenth century chancel.

Littlehampton   Map 1 Bc

This pleasant resort has been known for its peace and relaxation since it first attracted visitors in the early nineteenth century. It never developed into a major resort so its coastline has remained unspoilt, attracting writers in search of solitude rather than fashionable socialites. Coleridge and Byron were among its nineteenth-century visitors, and John Galsworthy, who later owned a country house at Bury north of Arundel, enjoyed working holidays there in the early part of this century.

Littlehampton has an excellent coast for sailing and angling, an attractive golf course and is set in beautiful countryside. **Littlehampton Museum** contains maritime and local history exhibits, including old maps and paintings, Roman finds and models of ships built here.

Mayfield   Map 3 Bb

Standing high on a ridge in the Weald, Mayfield's lovely old buildings reflect its long history. As much of the village was destroyed by fire in 1389, its oldest buildings date from the fourteenth century but it was an important settlement for centuries before this. The hills of the region were rich in iron and Mayfield was a centre for this ancient industry. 'Restless, reckless and inflexible' St Dunstan, Archbishop of Canterbury from AD 959-88, built a church here. One of the many legends connected with him claims that he shoved the church into place with his shoulder when he discovered it was not correctly aligned. He was said to have been skilled in iron-making, and to have had a forge next to his church. He later became the patron saint of ironworkers. The most popular St Dunstan legend relates how Tunbridge Wells came to have its chalybeate springs, the reason for its development as a spa. St Dunstan, working one day in his forge with his red-hot tongs in his hand, was paid a visit by the devil disguised as a beautiful young woman. The devil found his nose firmly pincered by Dunstan's tongs, causing him to leap across the Weald and plunge his nose into a spring.

On the site of St Dunstan's church, a palace was built for the archbishops of Canterbury to use as a country retreat. 'St Dunstan's tongs' can be seen at the old palace to this day. The fine building probably dates back to the tenth century but the oldest remaining parts are thirteenth century. It has a remarkable great hall, built by Archbishop Islip in 1350. Yet another Mayfield legend has it that the Archbishop used so much wood for his extravagant country retreat that he was punished with a fall from his horse and died, in Mayfield, from the injuries. The hall is nearly 70 feet long and 40 feet wide. Another important feature of the old palace is its Tudor gatehouse, added after the palace had been given to Henry VIII by the Archbishop Thomas Cranmer in 1545. During the Elizabethen period it was owned by Sir Thomas Gresham, founder of the Royal Exchange, and Elizabeth I is believed to have visited. The building was dismantled in 1740 but over a century later, in 1863, the Roman Catholic Duchess of Leeds bought its ruins and paid, with other donations, for its complete restoration and conversion to a convent. The great hall became the convent chapel.

Mayfield has many other historic buildings, including fine, half-timbered fifteenth and sixteenth century houses and attractive weatherboarded and tiled cottages. The church of St Dunstan was rebuilt in the Perpendicular style after the fire in 1389 but it has parts which date from the thirteenth century.

Michelham Priory Map 3 Bc

Two miles west of Hailsham, a town established by the Normans and for centuries an important agricultural centre, is **Michelham Priory** (Church Buildings). It was founded for

M

Augustinian monks in 1229 by Gilbert de Aquila of Pevensey and is approached through a handsome fourteenth-century gatehouse and over a ancient bridge across the Cuckmere River. The priory was dissolved in 1536 and what was left of it by the end of that century was incorporated into a stately Tudor home, built by Herbert Pelham in 1595 and home of the Sackville family from 1605 to 1897. The large moat which surrounds it was originally 12 feet deep, covers an area of seven acres and is a mile in circumference. Inside, the priory's treasures include antique furniture and musical instruments, fine stained glass and exhibits of Sussex ironwork. The lovely grounds contain a restored Tudor great barn in which a display of old farm machinery and a reconstructe wheelwright's and forge can be seen. There is a craft shop and the priory's original water mill has been restored to working order. Art exhibitions and music festivals are held here.

Midhurst Map 1 Bb

The atmosphere of the ancient market town is one of mellow prosperity and it is surrounded by some of loveliest scenery in Sussex. The town's history certainly goes back as far as Saxon times and probably further. It has many fine old buildings of historic interest. Of its inns, two are particularly noted. The Angel is one of the many places in which the Pilgrim Fathers rested between Southampton and Portsmouth when leaving for America; the Spread Eagle dates from the fifteenth century but has a later facade, dated about 1700. Its annex, once stables, dates from the sixteenth century. The Norman parish church was largely rebuilt in the 1880s and its fine memorials were moved to the little church at nearby Easebourne. In West Street is the old doorway which led into the Commandery of the Knights Hospitallers of St John until it was destroyed in 1811. The Market Square has amongst its historic buildings an Elizabethan house. At one end of the attractive South Pond is the bridge which once spanned Midhurst Canal. That, like the railway line, has now gone. Midhurst Grammar School was founded in 1672 and its ex-pupils include H.G. Wells, the writer, Richard Cobden who fought for free trade, and the geologist, Sir Charles Lyall.

Cowdray Park is a large estate which borders the town. It is now known for the polo matches regularly played there and for the ruins of its stately home, **Cowdray House** (Historic Homes). The house, now no more than a shell, portrays magnificently the richness and grandeur of English Tudor architecture, having avoided Victorian restoration. The substantial ruins have been well restored and maintained. Inside, one intact section contains the kitchen and, above it, a small museum with exhibits detailing the history of the estate and its owners.

Cowdray House took over 60 years to build. It was begun by Sir David Owen who inherited the estate in 1492. He sold it close to his death to Sir William Fitzwilliam who continued the work, followed by his brother Sir Anthony Browne. Both brothers were in favour with their monarch, Henry VIII. Browne received several fine monastic buildings at the time of the dissolution, including Battle and Bayham Abbies in Sussex. His descendants, the Viscounts Montague, continued to live at Cowdray, but both that family line and the house were doomed, some believe cursed. Legend relates that a priest, on being forcibly removed from Battle Abbey, said that Browne's home would be destroyed by fire and water. It was when the last Viscount Montague, the 8th, was away that Cowdray House burned down and just over a week later the Viscount too was dead. He drowned in Germany during a dangerous escapade in which he attempted to shoot some spectacular rapids on the Rhine. So ended Browne's house and family line, by fire and water.

During the nineteenth century, after further disasters befell those who had inherited the estate when the two sons of the last Viscount's sister were drowned at Bognor, the estate was eventually purchased by the 7th Earl of Egmont. He built the present house there, an attractive Victorian mansion. Then, in 1908, it was bought by Sir Weetman Dickinson Pearson who restored the ruins. He was made 1st Viscount Cowdray in 1927 and his family have continued to live on the estate since.

The ruins are said to be haunted by the ghostly figure of the White Lady of Cowdray. A lady dressed in flowing white robes

N

is supposed to wander in the house late at night. This could refer to the wife of one of the owners of Cowdray. He is said to have spent fifteen years in hiding in a priets' hole, only emerging at night to take a walk with his wife. This was the 5th Viscount Montague, a man of violent tempers who shot his chaplain one day when he arrived for mass but found the service over.

Easebourne is a tiny village on that estate. Its restored church, once used partly as a priory church, contains memorials to Sir David Owen and Sir Anthony Browne. In the early thirteenth century a priory for Augustinian canonesses was founded here and what remains of the original building now forms the basis of a house attached to the church.

North of Midhurst, the **Hollycombe Steam Collection** (Unusual Outings) is in the grounds of an old house and surrounded by its woodland gardens. There are two steam railways, a steam saw mill, steam tractor and other steam farm implements. Among the wide-ranging steam-powered exhibits is a film projector showing an early film made in 1896.

Newhaven Map3 Ac

The River Ouse was gradually changing its course during the 1560s away from its outlet to the Channel at Seaford. A particularly violent storm in 1570 caused the river to form a new estuary near what was then the village of Meeching and over the next decades the river continued to alter its course slightly but remained stable enough for Meeching to be given a new name, Newhaven, and for a port to be established there in the mid-seventeenth century. This was still small and rather insignificant in the mid-nineteenth century but in the next decades it was developed fully, with new breakwaters, landing stages, docks and shipyards. Augustus Hare wrote in his guide to Sussex, published 1894, that it had become 'an ugly, dirty, little town and smoky little port, with dangerous drinking water, and a long pier at the mouth of the Ouse, whence steamers cross to Dieppe in four-and-a-half hours'. Newhaven is no longer that unpleasant-sounding port but its ferries have not beaten the Victorian steamers' time to Dieppe. Besides remaining an important cross-Channel car-ferry terminal, the port still handles cargo, has a fishing fleet and boatyard and, in recent years, a modern yacht marina has been established.

St Michael's church dates from the Norman era, twelfth century, and has a fine beamed roof. It is worth exploring the churchyard for the gravestone of a certain Thomas Tipper, who died in 1785 and was a prominent member of the community, being the local brewer. His 'Newhaven Tipper' was a potent brew made with brackish water. On his gravestone a delightful rhyme, by T. Clio Rickman, 'an emminent politician of his day', refers to this beer as 'best old Stingo', and the verse of praise for its creator ends: 'Reader, in honest truth, such was the man; Be better, wiser, laugh more if you can'.

The Bridge Hotel dates from the seventeenth century and it was here that King Louis Philippe of France and his queen took refuge after fleeing France during the 1848 revolution. The *Illustrated London News* of March 4, 1848 reported that 'The King and Queen proceeded to the Bridge Hotel, where they ordered beds and intend to recover in some measure the

The Fort at Newhaven

N

alarms and fatigues of the week....The King has not so much baggage as he could carry in his pockets, in fact he had not a change of clothing'.

In 1864 Lord Palmeston ordered 72 coastal forts to be built, one of which was to protect the port of Newhaven. **The Fort** (Unusual Outings) was used as a training base and garrison until 1914 and during the Second World War it was refortified. Afterwards, it became a peacetime garrison until 1956, and then was allowed to decay until restoration started in 1981. The Fort, the largest fortification of its type in Sussex, can now be seen in its former condition, covering 10 acres with a large central parade ground, deep dry moat and gun implacements. A museum area contains displays on the fort, including audio-visual presentations and underground rooms.

Another museum to visit is the **Local and Maritime Museum** with its unique collection of old photograph of the Newhaven area and port in its heyday, with other exhibits of local and maritime history. The museum was created by members of the Newhaven and Seaford Historical Society.

Northiam Map 4 Ab

This large old village has many attractive cottages with white weatherboarding. Standing on the green is an oak said to be 1000 years old. Sheltering beneath it during a break on her journey to Rye in August 1573, Elizabeth I changed her high-heeled, green silk shoes. After dining and dancing she left her shoes as a memento for the village and they can still be seen at **Brickwall House** (Gardens), one of Northiam's finest historic houses. The lovely timber-framed Jacobean building dates from the early seventeenth century but on the site of a much older home. Inside the outstanding features are magnificent seventeenth-century stucco plaster ceilings and a grand staircase. The formal gardens are entered through terracotta entrance gates and include an eighteenth century bowling alley, a sunken topiary garden and fine yew hedges. A chess garden is at present under construction. From 1616, Brickwall was the home of Northiam's most prominent family, the Frewens, lords of the manor and rectors of the parish.

Acceptable Frewen, born in Northiam in 1588, became its Puritan rector. Surprisingly, he was also a staunch royalist and chaplain to Charles II during his exile in France. At the Restoration Acceptable was repaid for his loyalty and services and made Archbishop of York.

The Frewen family mausoleum and chapel was built in 1846 next to the old church of St Mary. The church tower is believed to date from the early twelfth century and the spire is sixteenth century. There is also much fourteenth and fifteenth century work to see.

An outstanding medieval hall house stands just outside the village. **Great Dixter** (Historic Homes) was built in the second half of the fifteenth century and contains one of the largest and most beautifully preserved great halls in the entire country. This is largely due to the devotion of its owner in the early part of this century, Nathaniel Lloyd, who commissioned the architect Edwin Lutyens to restore and extend it. Great Dixter is regarded as perhaps Lutyens' greatest domestic work - his additions and restorations blend perfectly with the original house, the extentions including a sixteenth-century hall house brought section by section from Benenden. Only the original fifteenth-century house and its superb gardens are open to visitors. The great hall originally had a central hearth, around which would have lived the retainers of the owner. The solar, or owner's domestic quarters, is on the first floor, reached by a fine Lutyens wood staircase. A tiny window from the solar allowed its occupant to keep an eye on events in the hall. The parlour can also be seen. The simple, uncluttered house provides fascinating insight into the way of life in medieval times, and contains furniture carefully chosen by Nathaniel Lloyd to complement the house. There is also some fine needlework, much of it by members of the Lloyd family.

The gardens, laid out by Lutyens under the close direction of Nathaniel Lloyd, are set out in distinct sections, some formal, some wild. Despite careful maintenance and well-planned beginnings, the overall effect remains one of lovely informality.

The atmosphere of Great Dixter is refreshingly personal and relaxed, due, no doubt, to the fact that the Lloyds continue to

P

live there and care for both house and garden.

Four generations of one Northiam family, the Perigoes, have run a builders and undertakers business in the village. **Perigoe Workshop Museum** has five rooms of their workplace, just as they were in the past. The tools they used are on show as is the Northiam parish hearse, drawn by pony or by hand, and bought in 1897 to commemorate Queen Victoria's Jubilee.

Just west of Northiam is another lovely village, Ewhurst, meaning 'the village of the yew forest'. It stands high on a ridge offering good views and some of its lovely weatherboarded cottages are brightly painted. The church is Norman, with much twelfth- and thirteenth-century work despite rebuilding in 1837 after the central tower collapsed. The churchyard has an impressive collection of trees, including many North American species, and it is now a private garden.

Pagham Harbour see Chichester

Parham Map 2 Ab

One of Sussex's outstanding stately homes, **Parham House** (Historic Homes), lies three miles south of Pulborough. The entire effect of the estate is firmly in period, 'a Tudor house in a Tudor landscape'. The house itself is open only by appointment and is expensive to visit but the landscaped **Parham Gardens** are more easily accessible.

The Palmer family obtained the estate, originally a grange of Westminster Abbey, from Henry VIII after the Dissolution of the Monasteries. The splendid new house was started in 1577 with a foundation stone laid by two-year-old Robert Palmer. He later sold the estate to the Bysshops and this family occupied it until 1922. After changing hands this century, it is now cared for by the Honourable Mr and Mrs Clive Gibson. Over the years the estate was altered but today it again looks much as it did originally, thanks to the careful restoration carried out this century. The panelled Great Hall has a beautiful plaster ceiling and is hung with portraits and hunting pictures - part of an extensive art collection in the house. The Long Gallery is 160 feet long and has a ceiling by Oliver Messel. Another of the rooms on view is the Great Parlour, the Palmer's private living room. Apart from the fine paintings, the house also contains rare needlework, antique furniture and carpets.

The garden was redesigned by Mrs Gibson with Peter Coats. It includes a herb garden, Elizabethan garden, an orchard and a delightful Wendy house built into a stone wall. And in the parkland is St Peter's church, dating from medieval times. Its lead font is fourteenth century.

Penhurst Map 3 Bb

Penhurst is a tiny, unspoilt hamlet consisting of a lovely Perpendicular church, a seventeenth-century farmhouse and lodge, and some mellow farm buildings. Ashburnham Park is nearby and the Ashburnham Furnace, the last ironworks in Sussex, is next to the lodge. It closed in 1825.

Petworth Map 1 Bb

A delightful town to rival its neighbour, Midhurst, Petworth's maze of narrow streets are lined with historic buildings, including many around the Market Square. There is fine architecture of every period from Tudor to Georgian, and the few Victorian additions also blend well. The parish church of St Mary dates from the fourteeth century. It was largely rebuilt in 1827 when its crooked lead spire was removed. A local rhyme says, 'Proud Petworth: poor people, High Church, crooked steeple'. Sir Charles Barry, architect of the Houses of Parliament, replaced it with a another but this, too, proved insecure and was removed in 1947.

The town is dominated by the great estate of **Petworth House**, the walls of which stretch for 13 miles and border the town. Since Norman times the estate was in the hands of the Percy family. In the seventeenth century, the Percy heir was Lady Elizabeth who lost two husbands before she was fifteen years of age. Lady Elizabeth's second husband, Thomas Thynne of Longleat, was murdered in London's Haymarket, she was bequeathed to Charles Seymour, 8th Duke of Somerset. The stately house which now stands was built under his direction in the late seventeenth century. Its front is 320 feet long and the house contains some of the finest carvings and one of the largest art collections in England. Standing in a superb, 3000-acre park, landscaped by Capability Brown and complete with deer, it is now administered by the National Trust.

Two outstanding woodcarvers worked on the interior of Petworth. One was the famous Grinling Gibbons, whose Carved Room in the house is regarded as amongst the finest examples of his work, with extraordinarily intricate panels and frames. The other was John Selden, the estate carpenter, who helped Gibbons, learnt from him and himself became a master. His work is everywhere, including the entrance hall and chapel. Selden is said to have died trying to save some of Gibbons' carvings from a fire.

In the early nineteenth century Petworth was inherited by George Wyndham, 3rd Earl of Egremont and he, too, had a great impact on its interior. A skilled art collector, he acquired many of the extensive range of paintings now hanging in Petworth. Turner was a personal friend and much admired by Wyndham. The artist often visited Petworth and enjoyed fishing in its park. As well as paintings by Turner, there are works by Holbein, Rembrandt, Van Dyck, Reynolds and Gainsborough.

South of Petworth is **Burton Mill**, a watermill built in the eighteenth century. It has been restored and produces wholewheat, stoneground flour. Next to it is Burton Pond and nature reserve. The pond is believed to have been a hammer pond when the iron industry flourished in Sussex during the sixteenth and seventeenth centuries. A nature trail starts from the mill and fishing permits can be obtained there for angling in the pond.

Pevensey Map 3 Bc

Pevensey once had a natural harbour, lying in a bay now containing the Pevensey Levels, an area of marshes. There is an extensive bird reserve there. When the Romans were faced with the threat of marauding Saxons attacking the south coast of England, they built a line of forts around what they called the Saxon shore. Pevensey was the last of these to be built, in the third century. The fort was called Anderita, named after a vast and impenetrable forest, called Andred's Wald by the Saxons, which stood nearby. Bede described it in Ad 731 as being infested by wolves and wild boar. Because Anderida was later incorporated into Norman **Pevensey Castle**, much of it still remains. The massive walls of the fort are 12 feet thick in places and reach up to 30 feet high. Along the wall are Roman towers, or barbicans, which were partially restored in the eleventh century by the Normans. The wall enclosed an area of 10 acres containing timber huts to house the Roman garrison. Local Britons moved in once the Romans had left but eventually the Saxons, led by Aella, made a savage assault in about AD 480 and ancient historians relate that not one Briton was left alive.

William of Normandy landed at Pevensey in September 1066. He had chosen Hastings as the landing site for his invasion army but the fleet was blown off course. Pevensey's natural harbour and, by then, ruined Roman fort, were

Pevensey village from the castle gate

P

undefended since the English army was fully occupied in the northeast, fighting off another invasion attempt. After his success in the Battle of Hastings, William divided Sussex into sections called 'rapes', and gave the rape of Pevensey to his half-brother Robert de Mortain. Using the Roman fort walls as a basic outer defence, a stone castle was eventually built, either by de Mortain or by his successor, Richer de Aquila, in the southeast corner of the Roman outer wall. Over the next 300 years it was twice besieged and fell, due to starvation rather than assault. Twice it withstood sieges. The first such occasion was when the retreating army of Henry III held out there against the forces of Simon de Montfort after the Battle of Lewes in 1264. By that time Pevensey had become a corporate member of the Cinque Ports but despite its strategic position never reached any great prominence. The second siege to be withstood by the castle occured when supporters of the future Henry IV, led by Lady Pelham whose family occupied the castle, held out against the armies of Richard II in 1399. One of the earliest surviving letters written in this country was sent by her, during the siege, 'to her trew lorde'. The castle had been restored during the the fourteenth century, but was not to see military action again, although it was refortified to some extent in 1587 to meet the threat of the Spanish Armada and centuries later it was to prove useful during the Second World War. At this time pill-boxes were built on the keep and in some of the Roman bastions but they are brilliantly disguised and have to be searched out. One is among the ruins of a fallen Roman wall. The castle was used by British, Canadian and United States troops, with the medieval towers becoming a garrison, and was also a base for the Home Guard.

The village of Pevensey, once a small town, has some Tudor buildings. The Old Mint House was greatly altered in the Tudor period and Edward VI visited it, but the house was originally built in the fourteenth century. It takes its name from the fact that it stands on the site of the Norman mint which produced coins in Pevensey until the mid-twelfth century. The Parish church of St Nicolas dates from the beginning of the thirteenth century and contains a fine alabaster monument of John Wheatley who died in 1616.

Playden see Rye

Plumpton Map 3 Ab

The name of Plumpton is associated with a racecourse for most people but the little village, lying under the steep scarp of the South Downs, is worth visiting in its own right. A church here was mentioned in the Domesday Book which indicates that the present building, dating from the Norman period, was probably built on the site of an earlier, Saxon church. It is an attractive flint church with a thirteenth century tower. The inside was quite heavily restored during the nineteenth century, but very old wall paintings are faintly recognizable.

Plumpton's setting in lovely, gentle countryside, makes it a perfect base for walks. There are two beautiful private homes nearby, both with twentieth century alterations by Edwin Lutyens. The grounds of Plumpton Park can be seen from a footpath. The other big house is Plumpton Place which is not

Plumpton Racecourse

P

accessible but is a lovely moated mansion which dates from the sixteenth century, built on the site of a house mentioned in King Alfred's will. It was part of the dowery given by Henry VIII to Anne of Cleves and was later the home of the Mascal family. Leonard Mascal, who wrote about the pursuits of country gentlemen in Tudor times, is believed to have introduced carp into England by cultivating them in the moat here. An old proverb says 'Turkeys, carp, hops, pickerel, and beer, Came into England all in one year.' Pickerel are young pike.

An ancient bronze age settlement was established on Plumpton Plain, south of the village, and its outlines can still be identified. It is one of the best examples of such ancient traces to be found in the English landscape. **Plumpton Racecourse** (Horseracing), to the north of the village, is an important venue for National Hunt racing with about seventeen meetings each year, enjoyed in delightful surroundings.

Poynings Map 2 Bb

Poynings is an ancient settlement. A charter of AD 962 which lists the lands of the Saxon King Edgar, mentions Puningas, now Poynings. An even earlier settlement was established in the iron age on the hill above the village, which, with its deep scarp, is known as Devil's Dyke. Local legend has it that the devil, in the dead of night, intended to allow the sea to enter the Weald through this hollow and so destroy the churches of the area. But an elderly lady carried a candle to her window and the devil fled, thinking he had seen the rising sun.

Poynings church of the Holy Trinity is a fine Perpendicular building. Michael of Poynings, who died in 1369, left provision for its creation in his will. The font is extremely old and could be the original one; in the south transept one of the attractive windows, mostly dating from the fourteenth century, is said to have come from Chichester Cathedral in the mid-seventeenth century.

Downers Vineyard nearby on high ground, offers spectacular views from Walstonbury Hill to Chanctonbury

Ring. The present six acres, planted with Meullar-Thurgau vines, is to be extended to cover 18 acres and other grape varieties are to be introduced. Tours can be arranged and 'Downers Wine' can be purchased at any time. A little further north of Poynings lies **Newtimber Place** (Historic Homes), a lovely seventeenth century moated house which is still inhabited. Among its attractions are Etruscan-style wall paintings and a delightful garden.

The village of Clayton, northeast of Poynings, should not be missed. The Norman church of St John the Baptist contains some of the most magnificent wall paintings to be seen in an English church. They date from the mid-twelfth century and have been carefully preserved.

Clayton also has two nineteenth century mills, **Jack and Jill Windmills**. Jill is the white one and a post mill originally built, in 1821, on Dyke Road in Brighton. In 1852, using 86 oxen, the mill was transported across nine miles of the downs to Clayton. Jill last worked in 1906 but is now undergoing extensive renovation by the Jack and Jill Windmill Preservation Society and it is anticipated that it will be grinding corn again in a few years. Jill can now be explored inside on certain days by arrangement. Jack is a black tower mill built in 1866 and is no more than a shell. It is also situated on private land and is not accessible.

Ringmer Map 3 Ab

This village is now developing into a small town but still retains much of its rural charm, particularly close to the green. Standing in magnificent countryside, the village is an ideal base for walks. The church, originally Norman, has been restored but retains many thirteenth- and fourteenth-century features. Some of the modern internal features, including the gallery and the organ, were provided at the expense of John Christie who did much for the area and founded the Festival Opera at Glyndebourne. The Springett Chapel is dedicated to a prominent family in the district who lived close to Ringmer.

Guilelma Springett is one of two seventeenth-century Ringmer women remembered on a commemorative sign. She married William Penn here, who was to become one of the

R

most prominent of settlers in the new American colonies. The other woman, Ann Sadler, also married a man who later made his name across the Atlantic. He was John Harvard, a founder of Harvard University.

Gilbert White, the eighteenth-century naturalist and author of the classic *The Natural History of Selbourne* regularly spent holidays with his aunt Rebecca who lived at The Delves, near the church, and was the wife of Ringmer's vicar, Mr Snooke. Many of Gilbert's studies for his great work were undertaken in this area. Mrs Snooke's tortoise, Timothy, was of particular interest to the naturalist and she bequeathed her pet to Gilbert White when she died in 1780.

South of Ringmer is **Raystede Centre for Animal Welfare** (Unusual Outings). Here, beside a lake and in the peace of the country, is a 25-acre sanctuary for unwanted and threatened animals, both wild and domesticated. There is a badger sett and a rabbit village, some exotic birds and monkeys, as well as dogs and cats, donkeys, goats and horses.

Robertsbridge Map 4 Ab

The village, on the main A21, has a main street with a fine collection of old cottages and other buildings, featuring much attractive weatherboarding. The surrounding hills and valleys are dotted with oast houses and hop growing is still important in the area. Another notable local industry has been the making of cricket bats by the Gray Nicols company, established in 1876. A bat with which the legendary cricketer W.G. Grace is said to have scored over 1000 runs, was made there.

Robertsbridge Aeronautical Museum is just north of the village. It contains a wide selection of aircraft engines and components, documents and uniforms connected with the RAF and the aircraft industry, and other associated items such as log books. Over 60 types of aircraft are represented, from the First World War to the present day.

To the east of the village, on the banks of the River Rother, a Cistercian abbey was founded in the twelfth century by Robert de St Martin, after whom the village is named. After the Dissolution the abbey formed the basis of a farmhouse.

Across the Rother from here, in the beautiful valley, stands the little village of Salehurst with its delightful old church, dating mainly from the fourteenth century.

Rottingdean see Brighton

Rye Map 4 Bb

Perched on a steep ridge overlooking the Romney Marsh is one of England's best-preserved old towns. Its narrow, cobbled streets are lined with historic buildings, creating picture-postcard scenes usually only found in tiny pockets of towns or the occasional small village. Yet here there is a small and perfect town, compact and unmarred by modern development. Naturally, throngs of visitors are an unavoidable aspect of Rye too. But since Rye was as popular in the Victorian era as it is today, the old town seems to have been able to absorb sightseers without compromising its charm to commercial vulgarity.

Rye flourished as a member of the Confederation of Cinque Ports from the late thirteenth century. When the Cinque Ports were first established by Edward I in 1278, Rye was one of the 'Two Ancient Towns' which were limbs of the head port of Hastings, the other being neighbouring Winchelsea. But in the late thirteenth century massive storms changed both the course of the River Rother and of Rye's history. The river's estuary had been at the port of New Romney, a major Cinque Port. The Rother, after the storms of 1287, forced a new outlet to the sea near Rye, giving the town an important estuary and great new potential as a port. New Romney gradually declined in importance and as this happened so Rye grew in prominence and became a head port of the Confederation in its own right in about 1336. Its strategic situation had long been recognised but so had its vulnerability because of its situation on the English Channel coast. In those days the sea reached Rye. After raids against the settlement by the French in the early thirteenth century, Henry III made Rye a Royal Manor and ordered that a castle be built there. All that remains of this is **Ypres Tower** (Museums), so named because it was the home of John de Ypres from 1430. Its use as a

R

major defence for Rye was relatively shortlived since serious French raids continued through the thirteenth and fourteenth centuries, at a time when Rye was becoming more and more important. As a result, the town was walled and fortified. Ypres Tower was no longer the main bastion and it became the Court House and later a gaol, as well as being a private home for a while. It now houses a popular museum, containing fascinating and well-designed displays of local history and the history of the Cinque Ports is included.

From 1329 the town was given grants to enable a strong wall to be built for fortification but this did not prevent further French raids. In 1377 the town suffered its worst attack and was left devastated. Following this the strong walls were quickly completed. Parts of them remain and the Land Gate, in the northwest corner of Rye, was once one of the entrances through the wall and had a portcullis. The town would have been surrounded by a deep trench on this landward side, crossed by a drawbridge. The town's defences were again revised in the Tudor and Elizabethan periods, when the question of the security of the south coast of England was once more in doubt. In the Gun Garden beside the Ypres Tower, on the very edge of the steep ridge which drops away to the River Rother and marshland beyond, once stood six brass guns presented to Rye by Elizabeth I in gratitude for the town's loyalty and action during the period of threat from the Spanish Armada. Elizabeth I visited Rye and was known to be fond of the town she called 'Royal Rye'. The Gun Garden now contains three new cannon made in Rye and placed there in 1980 to mark the 80th birthday of Her Majesty Queen Elizabeth the Queen Mother, Lord Warden of the Cinque Ports.

It has often been said that somehow Rye is not typically English, despite its half-timbered buildings and elegant Georgian facades, its ancient rustic inns, charming hotels and tea houses. Perhaps this is because it is so compact, clinging to a hillside like a Mediterranean mountain village. Its medieval walls are now mainly gone but the town still has the feeling of being enclosed. The best, in fact the only, way to enjoy it is to wander its lovely little streets and alleys, pausing to appreciate its wealth of architecture and history. Probably one of its most famous features is the turret clock of St Mary's church, seen not from the Church Square but from the top of Lion Street, near a tea shop, the birthplace of seventeenth-century dramatist John Fletcher. This is said to be the oldest turret clock in Britain. But the big attraction is not its age or its lovely painted face, but the Quarter Boys who emerge on every quarter-hour, except the hour itself, to strike the bells. St Mary's, like Rye, suffered severely from French raids in its early history. It was built first in the Norman era and has alterations, repairs and additions from almost every architectural period which followed. That turret clock still has its original working parts, made in Winchelsea in 1560. The church bells were once looted and had to be retrieved, with other treasures, from France.

Many of the buildings are extremely old, dating from as early as the fourteenth century. In the small open area at the top of Lion Street is a delightful group incorporating The Flushing Inn, dating in part from the thirteenth century, and Ye Olde Tucke Shoppe which is late fourteenth century. Here also is the Town Hall, built in 1743. One of Rye's mayors in the Georgian period was James Lamb. Lamb had a lucky escape from a murderous butcher named Breads who stabbed the mayor's brother-in-law to death one dark night. The poor victim was mistaken for the mayor, who was ailing in his bed, because he wore his cloak. Breads' body was publicly exhibited in a gibbet cage after his execution in 1743 and the cage can be seen in the Town Hall.

Lamb House (Historic Homes), James Lamb's lovely home, is believed to have been rebuilt by him from an existing house in the early eighteenth century. It later became famous as the home of American novelist Henry James. James came first to Playden, a village north of Rye, in 1896, seeking solitude and a change from London. He soon moved into Rye and in 1898 he bought Lamb House where he lived until his death in 1916. H.G. Wells, one of many writers who visited James in Rye, said of the house that it was 'one of the most perfect pieces of suitably furnished Georgian architecture imaginable'. After James's death, another novelist, E.F.

R

Benson, owned the house. And while James was there a contemporary of his, another American writer, Stephen Crane, also lived in Rye. Both the Lamb House and its pleasant garden can be visited.

The house stands close to Rye's best-known road, Mermaid Street, steep, cobbled and atmospheric. Smuggling was important to Rye through much of its history, helping to keep it affluent although never openly condoned by its respectable inhabitants. The Mermaid Inn was a haunt of smugglers. It dates from the fifteenth century, with sixteenth-century additions, and it is easy to imagine the revelry which took place there. It is only one of many buildings from that period which line this street. 'The House Opposite' the Mermaid Inn is so called because its owners grew weary of enquiries for the inn.

Other outstanding buildings, among so many, include the Grammar School, built in 1636; the George Hotel, with a Georgian facade disguising a fifteenth-century half-timbered original; the Austin Friars, known as the Monastery, which is the chapel of an ancient friary established in Rye in the fourteenth century; and the old Apothecary's Shop in the High Street, with its elegant eighteenth-century bow windows.

Rye Art Gallery has an impressive permanent collection of paintings, selections of which are shown in a varying display. It also has regular exhibitions. Across the courtyard from the gallery are the **Easton Rooms** which form an extension. Works, including local arts and crafts, are on sale here.

Apart from its strategic importance, charm and smuggling activities, Rye also flourished because of a substantial influx of wealthy Huguenot refugees who fled France in the sixteenth century to settle in Rye. Rye survived against many odds, not least the natural enemy, the sea. Its port was not stable but subject to silting and the harbour is now some distance from the town. There was, however, a thriving shipbuilding industry here as late as the end of the nineteenth century but by then Rye had been in decline for some time. The town was probably at its height in the early years of the nineteenth century when the port was full of ships and the lovely medieval town, showing the fresh impact of Georgian style, was thriving. **Rye Town Model and Light Show** (Unusual Outings) recreates the town as it was in this period in intricate and fascinating detail. The story of the town is told using light shows and clever sound effects against a painstakingly accurate model of Rye based on the first ordnance survey map of the area.

Another interesting view of the past can be seen in Playden, north of Rye. **Cherries Folk Museum** is devoted to showing how life was lived in rural Sussex before 1946. Agricultural and domestic displays depict life on the farm, a blacksmith's and a saddler's, old-fashioned schooling practises and much more.

The River Rother, and the Royal Military Canal which joins it north of Rye, are both important for anglers. Iden Lock is particularly popular. Nearby also is the pretty old town of Winchelsea and the pleasant little village of Icklesham with a fine old inn. Camber Sands, to the east of Rye, provide a popular destination for those seeking wide sandy beaches and undulating dunes, backed only by marshland and grazing sheep. **Camber Castle** lies in ruins but is at present being renovated and made safe for visitors. It was part of a vast network of south-coast defences against the French built by Henry VIII in about 1540.

St Leonards see Hastings

Salehurst see Robertsbridge

Seaford Map 3 Ac

The Saxon, Aella, who led raids against the south coast of England and eventually created settlements there, is recorded as having landed on one occasion in the fifth century at Mercaedesburn, a settlement on the banks of a river where it met the sea. It is believed that the river was the Ouse and that the ancient settlement stood at what is now Seaford. Town records only go back to 1562 but by then Seaford already had a long and colourful history. Its grand Norman church of St Leonard bears witness to the town's former

S

prominence. The nave pillars are said to show signs of having been burned and there are apparent scorch marks. Such a fire would have occurred during one of the ferocious raids against the town by the French which took place in the fourteenth and fifteenth centuries. A celebrated Sussex hero at this time was Sir Nicholas Pelham. He carried out his most famous exploit at Seaford when he organised a local army against Claude d'Annabant, High Admiral of France, who was making repeated raids against the port. He used the River Ouse as an escape route to Lewes having thrashed the invaders. His monument in St Michael's Church, Lewes, carries the inscription: 'Wot time the French thought to have sack't Sea-Foord, This Pelham did repel'em back aboord'.

Having survived the ravages of storms and the raids of the Hundred Years' War, Seaford reached its height in the sixteenth century as a bustling port, the Ouse then entering the sea at what is now Splash Point. In 1544 the port was a late recruit to the Confederation of Cinque Ports but its prominence was shortlived. In about 1570 a terrible storm, and

The Seven Sisters

probably more than one, caused the River Ouse to break its banks at the little village of Meeching. The mouth of the river at Seaford dried and Meeching gradually became established as the port of Newhaven, literally providing a 'new haven' for shipping. With its port gone, Seaford became a quiet town.

Seaford was, however, briefly the cause of some concern when Napoleon threatened invasion at the turn of the nineteenth century. One of the line of south coast Martello Tower defences was built here. Only part of **Seaford Martello Tower** (Museums) still stands due to heavy storms, especially in recent years. It has been converted to a small museum containing information on the area and with exhibitions relating to maritime Sussex.

By the mid-nineteenth century Seaford was on the verge of becoming a popular seaside resort but overshadowed by such prestigious neighbours as Brighton and Eastbourne, the resort never developed but remains peaceful and unpretentious.

Seaford is situated close by some of the loveliest coastal and hinterland scenery in East Sussex. Its own Seaford Head, known for its golf course and bracing walks, towers above the town. Further east lie the Seven Sisters, seven ridges meeting the coast to form curved cliffs. And beyond them is Birling Gap, another feature of this dramatic stretch of coast. **Seven Sisters Country Park** offers nearly 700 acres of down and marshland on the clifftops, with activities such as fishing and canoeing. A nature trail has been marked and an accompanying leaflet is available from the visitor centre.

Inland a short distance from Seaford are some well-known villages, such as Alfriston and Westdean. Bishopstone is smaller and less significant but its church should not be missed. The village has a modern extension standing against the marshy sweep between Newhaven and Seaford and the old section is on the hill behind. It contains one of Sussex's most ancient surviving churches. St Andrew's was first built in Saxon times, the early eighth century, and traces of the original can still be seen. There is far more in evidence of the Norman additions. The font is Norman and there is a twelfth century stone tomb lid in excellent condition, still bearing its original carving.

Sedlescombe Map 4 Ab

The village is known for the Pestalozzi Children's Village which was founded in 1959 in a large mansion nearby. Here, refugee children from all parts of the world are cared for, attending local schools but able to maintain their own cultures. Sedlescombe itself is extremely attractive. Its central street spreads out to a lovely green which is lined with sixteenth- and seventeenth-century houses, built at a time when the village flourished as a centre for the iron industry. The old pump on the green dates from 1900. St John the Baptist Church, originally built in the fourteenth and fifteenth centuries, but heavily restored, has an unusual, early sixteenth-century font cover.

An interesting day can be spent nearby at **Nortons Farm Museum and Farm Trail**. The museum shows the agricultural period during the age of the carthorse. Exhibits include old carts, ploughs and handtools. The farm trail takes in this fruit and arable farm on which cart horses are still

St Leonard's at Seaford

employed. The trail is marked and there is an accompanying leaflet.

Selsey Map 1 Ac

In ancient times Selsey was an island and an important settlement, most of which has been completely washed away by the sea. It was here that the Saxon Aella landed in AD 477 and made his forays inland, taking Chichester, then an abandoned Roman town, and establishing the kingdom of the South Saxons. In 681 another memorable landing took place here when St Wilfred arrived to bring Christianity to the district. He established a see in Selsey and built a fine church. For nearly 400 years this was the Episcopal centre for the south of England, with a line of 24 Bishops of Selsey. But the encroaching sea led the Normans to move the Episcopal centre to Chichester in 1075 and Selsey's ancient cathedral is now buried beneath the waves. Along with it went most of the important Saxon settlement.

Selsey remains a delightful village, famous for its excellent bathing and sailing and its close proximity to the bird reserves of Pagham Harbour. The village's church was situated at Church Norton for centuries. Church Norton is now a secluded and delightful chancel, standing by itself on the coast. The rest of the church, which dated from the twelfth to the fourteenth centuries, was removed in the Victorian period to the village itself and used as the basis for St Peter's Church.

Near the West Sands Leisure Centre is **Medmerry Windmill**, a circular tower mill built of brick in about 1750. The sweeps have recently been replaced making it a fine sight. The ground floor is now used as a toy shop.

Seven Sisters see Seaford

Shipley Map 2 Ab

The village of Shipley is on the banks of the Adur River in beautiful countryside. Its Early Norman church of St Mary's is believed to date from about 1125 and is a fine example of

S

that period of architecture. It is delightfully decorated inside with ancient carvings and there is a thirteenth century wooden box in the north wall of the chancel. It has Limoges enamel and is described by Nikolaus Pevsner as 'a marvellous thing'.

Kings Mill is a magnificent smock mill next to the church. It has been known for some time as **Belloc's Mill** since it was the home of Hilaire Belloc, the writer, from 1906-53. It contains a small museum showing details of his life and work and the mill has been restored, since 1957, as a memorial to him.

In the small village of Coolham is a delightful listed building, **Friends Meeting House** (Other Historic Buildings). This was a Quaker meeting house founded by William Penn over 300 years ago. He left England to be a prominent founder of the American colonies. The house has a delightful, large and peaceful garden with an orchard.

Shoreham-by-Sea Map 2 Ac

Shoreham is an unusual combination for this area of Sussex. Most of its neighbours are either lively resorts or quieter residential seaside towns but here there is modern development and industry as well as an atmospheric ancient town. Shoreham also is a resort and a popular one; offering superb facilities for sailing and angling, and safe swimming from its shingle beaches.

Old Shoreham lies to the north of the modern town. The Saxons settled here certainly as early as the fifth century and probably before. The Romans had established a port at the mouth of the River Adur, Portis Adurni, and this was later to become the town of New Shoreham, founded by the Norman, William de Broase, who died in the early thirteenth century and was a notorious and violent man. He is once believed to have lured several powerful people to his Welsh castle in Abergavenny where he murdered them. His family were lords of the manor of Shoreham and Lords of the Barony of Bramber.

The narrow streets of old cottages and attractive buildings, not quaint or pretty but simple and practical, reflect

Shoreham's past as a busy shipping centre. The town grew in importance through the middle ages. The River Adur, beside which it stands, was until the late middle ages navigable to Bramber, then an inland port. But as the river silted, Shoreham's natural harbour was put to more and more use. By the eighteenth century there was a major shipbuilding industry here.

With two centres established at different times, the town has two churches, both very old. In Old Shoreham is St Nicholas, which still has Saxon traces but is distinctively Norman despite its restoration in Victorian times. Even more impressive is St Mary de Haura in New Shoreham. Both churches were built by the de Broase family and both were given by them to the monks of Saumur Abbey, on the Loire in France. Records of St Mary's go back to 1103 when it was mentioned in a deed drawn up by Philip de Broase on his return from the First Crusade, but most of what is now standing originally dates from slightly later than this. The choir is the outstanding feature of this fine and grand church. It has lost most of its nave bays, with only one remaining, part of the destruction it has suffered over the years from French raids, the Parliamentary forces during the Civil War and from the ravages of storms. Yet it remains one of the most impressive churches in the county.

Another important old building in Shoreham is **Marlipins** (Museums). It is originally from the twelfth century and was probably another building put up by the de Broases. Deeds for it date back to 1347. Its delightful chequerboard front is made of alternating flint and stone. The name Marlipins is believed to refer back to the Norman times when the building was probably used as a warehouse and customs shed. 'Marl' is believed to have been a Saxon word meaning 'tax' or 'levy' and 'pins' were barrels. Marlipins is now owned by the Sussex Archeological Trust who purchased it, using money raised from the public, in 1928. It houses a museum of local history showing industrial and maritime Shoreham through the ages.

The National Trust administers a large area of farm and downland northeast of Shoreham, **Shoreham Gap** (Country Parks). It covers 596 acres and contains traces of extensive iron

S

age, ancient Briton and Roman field systems. Not all of it is open to the public but Southwick Hill and Whitelot Bottom are two areas which can be explored.

Singleton Map 1 Ab

This handsome village consists of delightful flint cottages lining narrow lanes. Its Norman church of St John the Evangelist has a tower believed to have been originally Saxon. Inside are fifteenth-century pews and an eighteenth-century gallery. **West Dean Gardens**, near the village, consist of 35 acres of beautifully landscaped parkland. It has fine lawns, interesting and attractive specimen trees, a 300- foot pergola and a summer house. The walled garden is at present being restored and there is a lovely wild garden area. A museum has been created here which provides a history of gardening and displays old garden tools including an antique lawnmower. West Dean College now occupies West Dean House, which is surrounded by these gardens. It was established in 1971 as a centre for the teaching of arts and crafts. The grand rooms of the mansion have been converted to large workshops and the courses are open to anyone over the age of 16.

Singleton's major attraction is the **Weald and Downland Open Air Museum**. In a lovely 40 acre pastoral setting, the museum provides a sanctuary for important rural buildings which have either been left to fall to ruins or have been threatened with demolition. Here they are re-erected and preserved. The collection is already wide ranging and each building has been carefully sited to show it to its full potential. A medieval house, a working watermill and a fine Tudor market hall are among the rescued buildings brought here from all over the south east. Carpenters', blacksmiths' and plumbers' workshops have been recreated and there is a charcoal-burners' camp and a sixteenth century treadmill. The museum also has temporary exhibitions and demonstrations of rural crafts and trades. The delightful grounds contain a millpond, woodland walks and picnic sites. The museum is a non-profit-making company, registered as a charity. Money from entrance fees does not begin to cover the expenses of running this admirable project, and it depends on the support of many individuals and trusts. Those who would like to donate contributions or to take part in the work of the museum should contact its director.

Southease   Map 3 Ac

This tiny hamlet between Lewes and Newhaven is no more than a few pleasant buildings and a pretty green. The church is one of three in this valley of the Ouse river which has a round tower. *See Lewes.* The original Saxon building and its surrounding group were granted to the abbots of Winchester by King Edgar in AD 966. It remained a monastic centre up until the Dissolution. There is little in evidence of the Saxon church. The flint tower is basically Norman, as are the windows. Inside are Jacobean pews and traces of thirteenth-century wall paintings. The church bell also dates from the thirteenth century and is one of the oldest in Sussex.

Stanmer   see Brighton

Stopham   Map 1 Bb

Where the Rivers Arun and Rother meet they are crossed by an outstanding medieval bridge. Stopham Bridge was built in 1423 and all but one of its stone arches are original. The extended central arch was rebuilt in 1822. The tiny village is basically an ancient manor house with its church and farm cottages. The Barttelot family were lords of the manor from Norman times and lived at Stopham from 1420. The brasses inside the sturdy and well-preserved Norman church are in memory of members of that family.

The impressive stone farmhouse of Stopham Manor has also survived the centuries largely intact. It is believed to date from the fifteenth or sixteenth century but was partially dismantled and rebuilt in the seventeenth.

Ticehurst   Map 3 Ba

There is some dispute about the origin of the name Ticehurst.

U

One theory is that is means 'the wood of the fairy Tys' while others believe it comes from the Saxon 'ticen-hyrst' which means 'the forest hill where goats feed'. What is certain is that there has been a settlement here since at least 1180 and it has a large proportion of old weatherboarded and tile-hung cottages amongst its buildings. St Mary's Church is fourteenth century and contains the small brass effigy of a knight of the same century, although it is inscribed to John Wybarne who died in 1490. There is also a fine monument to George Courthope who died in 1714. The Courthope chapel is dedicated to this prominent local family who lived at Whiligh, a country house nearby. Records show that the timbers used in London's Westminster Hall were taken from the grounds of Whiligh in the late fourteenth century.

Uppark   Map 1 Ab

The grand house of **Uppark** (Historic Homes) was designed by William Talman and built at the end of the seventeenth century for Sir Edward Ford. It is a handsome, solid red-brick building in a lovely downland setting and high on a hill, offering fine views. Inside are the original wallpapers and curtains of its extensive refurbishing in 1750.

It was then owned by Sir Matthew Fetherstonhaugh and later passed to his son, Sir Harry, described by Oliver Mason in his guide to *South East England* as 'gay and dissolute'. Through him, two famous characters of the period became associated with Uppark. They were the Prince Regent, a friend of Harry's, and Emma Hamilton. Long before she became known as the mistress of Lord Nelson she lived with Harry Fetherstonhaugh at Uppark. She arrived there when only 15 years old and with her first child. After bearing Fetherstonhaugh a child, history relates that he abandoned her. She eventually married William Hamilton and started her liaison with Nelson.

On his death in 1846, Harry left Uppark to his wife, whom he married late in life. Her sister, Frances, who had lived with them, later assumed the name Fetherstonhaugh and inherited the estate. H.G. Wells was also associated with the house - his mother was the housekeeper there in the late nineteenth century. Wells lived at Uppark from the age of 13 for a few years and later wrote about Uppark house as 'Bladesover' in *Tono-Bungay*.

The Saloon was created in 1750 and is the most magnificent room in the house, which is now owned by the National Trust. Most of the rooms are open and furnished in style. The bed which the Prince Regent used can be seen, as can the table on which Lady Hamilton is said to have danced. There is also a large Victorian kitchen and a Queen Anne dolls' house. The landscaped, extensive grounds were designed by Humphrey Repton.

Wakehurst Place Map 2 Ba

This stately home was built in 1590 by Sir Edward Culpepper on the site of an earlier house. The estate had been owned by the Wakehurst family since the early twelfth century, and the Culpeppers lived there from the mid-fifteenth century until the

Chanctonbury Ring

W

seventeenth. In the mainly fourteenth-century church of St Peter in Ardingly, the history of the owners of Wakehurst is told by the brasses on the floor. There is one to Richard Wakehurst who died in 1454, and a brass to his wife is beside it. Their granddaughters, Elizabeth and Margaret, both married Culpeppers, which can be seen from their brasses alongside those of the 10 children born out of the marriages. The Culpeppers were one of the most prominent families of that era. Writing in 1657, John Philipot noted of Wakehurst that 'at one time there were twelve knights and baronets alive in this house together'. However, the last Culpepper to live there, Sir William, lost much of the family fortune in gambling and was forced to sell up for only £9,000 to a clerk from the Chatham dockyard.

In 1902 it was purchased by Gerald Loder who later took the title of First Lord Wakehurst of Ardingly. He did much to establish its now famous gardens. His successor was a wealthy London tailor, Sir Henry Price, who made a fortune from his 'Fifty Shilling Tailors' and bought Wakehurst in 1938. He continued to develop the grounds and on his death, in 1963, he bequeathed the estate, and £200,000 for its upkeep, to the National Trust. In 1965, mainly because of the magnificent mature parkland and the fine local conditions for plants and trees, **Wakehurst Place Gardens** were taken over by the Royal Botanic Gardens at Kew. It was the perfect site for an extension of Kew since here in Sussex the soil is rich, the climate is kind and Wakehurst offered enormous potential for experiment and expansion. Of the 462-acre estate, over 100 acres are cultivated and most of the rest is woodland. It is particularly noted for its fine trees and flowering shrubs. Many of the rhododendrons were originally planted by Gerald Loder. There is a water garden and a walled garden, planted in memory of Sir Henry Price, as well as a Himilayan garden and pinetum. An attractive water course links a series of pond and lakes. Yet despite its splendour and grand scale there is much here to inspire ideas for even the smallest garden. The house is not open but there is a restaurant in an elegant, oak-panelled ground floor room and an exhibition room showing the geology and ecology associated with the estate.

Washington Map 2 Ab

The village is noted for its wide variety of building materials
and styles involved in its single lane of cottages. They lead up
a hill to the flint church, rebuilt in the nineteenth century.
From here **Chanctonbury Ring** (Archeological Sites) can be
seen, with its distinctive ring of beech trees. A small, oval iron
age fort was established on this high crest of the South Downs.
The trees were planted around it in 1760. The southwest
section of the ancient fort is the area most easily recognisable.
There are also the remains of two Roman buildings here,
occupied in the third and fourth centuries.

Westdean see Litlington

West Firle Map 3 Ac

East of Lewes is the attractive village of West Firle. The
church of St Peter has a Norman doorway, the only remaining
feature of the original early-thirteenth-century building. Most

St Peter's at West Firle

of the building dates from later in that century with additions dating from up to the fifteenth century. The outstanding family of Firle was the Gage family who lived here from the fifteenth century. Many of the fine brasses in the church are in memory of them. There is also an excellent monument to Sir John Gage who died in 1557.

The lovely stately home of **Firle Place** (Historic Homes) was built for Sir John Gage in the mid-sixteenth century. He was an influential man in his day, a commissioner for the Dissolution of the Monasteries under Henry VIII and holding many other prestigious posts for that king. Later he was Mary Tudor's Chamberlain and, as Constable of the Tower of London, he took charge of the execution of Lady Jane Grey. Yet, despite these roles in administering the break with the Roman church and carrying out anti-catholic practises, Sir John remained a catholic. Tudor Firle Place was given a Georgian front, in Caen stone, and extensively altered in about 1730. Inside the magnificent Great Hall reveals the Tudor core of the house.

The Gage family have continued to live in the house over the centuries. In the eighteenth century, General Thomas Gage was the Commander-in-Chief of the British forces at the beginning of the American War of Independence. Documents from this period concerning the war can be seen in the house. There is an extensive art collection, including works by English and European Old Masters. The English and Sevres porcelain is another important collection and there is also fine antique furniture.

West Hoathly Map 3 Aa

Expansive views across the South Downs can be enjoyed from this fine old village. There are several notable buildings. The Norman church of St Margaret has parts dating from the thirteenth century; standing opposite is a seventeenth-century stone manor. Beside this is a medieval **Priests House** (Historic Homes) built in the early fifteenth century for Lewes Priory. The construction details of this delightful building have been exposed to show its timber frame and wattle-and-daub filling as well as the Horsham slab (stone tiles) roof. Inside, the furniture is mainly eighteenth and nineteenth century. It now houses a museum of local history containing byegones and needlework.

Wilmington Map 3 Bc

The village is best known for its large hill carving the **Long Man of Wilmington**. Its origins are unknown. Local legend says that it is the figure of the Giant of Windover Hill who was killed by the Firle Beacon Giant and lies here where he fell. It is surrounded by ancient barrows and flint mines which add weight to the theory that it was cut in the bronze age. It has also been claimed that the figure was cut by either Saxons or Vikings. However, records of its existence go back only to 1779. In 1873, the local landowner, the Duke of Devonshire, had the figure outlined in yellow bricks to preserve the shape. The Long Man is so-called because of the elongation of the figure, presumably done to counteract the effects of perspective.

Wilmington Priory and church

W

The Long Man is best viewed from the gates of
Wilmington Priory (Church Buildings). The impressive
remains of this priory include most of the outer walls of the
twelfth century building. Founded as a Benedictine priory for
monks from Normandy, it stands next to the parish church,
once part of the priory and also dating from the Norman
period, though restored in the late nineteenth century. A small
museum, housed in an adjacent Tudor house, contains a
unique collection of old hand tools as well as displays on local
village and agricultural life. In the pleasant gardens of the
priory stands a huge yew tree believed to be 1000 years old.

Winchelsea Map 4 Bb

The 'Ancient Town) of Winchelsea was a member of the
Cinque Ports in the thirteenth century. By then it was an
established sea port. By the end of the thirteenth century the
old town had been destroyed by savage storms and a new
settlement was underway. The new town was built by Edward
I after he acquired the manor of Iham in about 1280. It was
carefully planned as a small, orderly trading port for importing
wine from Gascony. There are large vaults, reached from the
road, under some of the buildings and these could date from
that period. Winchelsea's future did not remain secure and by
1601, Sir Walter Raleigh spoke of it as 'gone to decay'. Most of
the destruction was caused by French raids during the
fourteenth and fifteenth centuries. At the same time the
harbour was slowly silting up and by the end of the sixteenth
century it was no longer a port. Yet Winchelsea survived.
Huguenot refugees from France had settled there during
Elizabethan times and it remained a small, peaceful village.

There are many historic buildings in the village. Three
ancient gates still stand, originating from Edward I's defences
for his new town. Strand Gate is early fourteenth century but
Pipewell gate was rebuilt about a century later. The remains of
the third, New Gate, are some distance from the village since
the original town was planned to be far larger than it is today.
The same is true of the parish church of St Thomas. It was
designed to be on the scale of a cathedral but was never fully

completed and it suffered severe damage during French raids.

The remains of a Franciscan friary founded in the early twelfth century stand in the gardens of Greyfriars. This house was built in 1901 and was once the haunt of two notorious local highwaymen, George and Joseph Weston. They lived here under false names; one of them became entrenched sufficiently in the community to become a church warden. The two were finally captured after taking the Bristol Mail. Their story is the basis of William Thackeray's novel *Denis Duval*. Many of the other buildings in the village are nineteenth century, often skilful copies of older styles.

The oldest building in Winchelsea is the town's Court Hall which now houses **Court Hall Museum**. The ancient building dates from the fourteenth century, was extended in the fifteenth and then restored in the nineteenth century. The exhibits depict the period when the town was a Cinque Port with a busy harbour, and also later history. There are paintings and maps, ancient seals and coins, and weights, measures and finds from local archeological digs.

Withyam Map 3 Aa

One of England's most colourful families, the Sackvilles, have their family chapel, monuments and tombs in the village church of St Michael. After being struck by lightning in 1663 it was rebuilt immediately and the new church was completed in 1672. The Sackville Chapel was built in 1680, incorporating parts of the original fourteenth century church. In 1675, 13-year-old Thomas Sackville died and the chapel was built in his memory. The elaborate altar-tomb in which he lies has effigies of his parents, Richard, Earl of Dorset and his wife, kneeling either side in grief. The skull he holds indicates that he died before them. The tomb was carved in grey marble by C.G. Gibber in a style which was then a new departure in England.

Vita Sackville-West, the writer who died in 1962, is remembered by a slate plaque. She grew up at Knole in Sevenoaks and later, with her husband Harold Nicolson, created the magnificent gardens at their home, Sissinghurst

Castle. The church also has fourteenth- and fifteenth-century Italian paintings, bought by William Young Ottley and originally hung in the chapel of Buckhurst, a large Victorian manor nearby. They consist of an altarpiece and painted panels, showing the final stages in the life of Christ.

Worthing Map 2 Ac

Until the late eighteenth century, this large residential resort was a small, but long established, fishing port. In the area, evidence has been found of bronze- and iron-age settlements and of Roman occupation. In Saxon times a village was established and excavations of the Saxon burial ground, on Highdown Hill, have produced many ancient items including weapons and jewellery. After the Norman Conquest, the area was presided over by Robert le Sauvage whose manor was built where the High Street now stands. The oldest section of the town is Tarring, once a separate village. A palace was built here in the thirteenth century for the Archbishops of Canterbury. One stone building of the old palace complex, much restored over the centuries, still exists as part of a school in the lovely Tarring High Street. There are many other old and attractive buildings along the street, including **Parsonage Row** (Museums), a delightful group of late-fifteenth-century cottages. They now contain a museum of Sussex folklore, providing insight to the ancient customs and traditional beliefs of the area.

The invigorating qualities of the south coast were 'discovered' in the mid-eighteenth century when visitors began to frequent the sleepy little fishing village which had stood here for centuries. As with most of the major resorts, royal patronage set the seal for Worthing's success and development. King George III bought his ailing daughter, Princess Amelia, here in 1798. Inspired by the success of Brighton, developers soon started to build fine terraces and squares, such as Montague Place and Bedford Row. In 1829, the ambitious Park Crescent was built, and development continued through the Victorian era. By the late nineteenth century the railway had arrived and so had large numbers of holiday-makers. The long pier was first opened in 1862. It is 960 feet long and was rebuilt in 1914 soon after a severe storm had partially destroyed it.

Worthing Museum and Art Gallery contains over 16,000 items of historic interest from the area, including the finds from the Saxon burial ground at Highdown Hill and other archeological digs. There are paintings and pottery, costumes and toys and lively displays explaining the history of the town.

Worthing is well known for its entertainments. The Connaught Hall was converted to a theatre in 1931 and presents plays and musicals. And at the end of the pier is the Pavilion which has been recently renovated for its big summer spectaculars. The Assembly Hall presents classical concerts during the winter months, featuring Worthing Philharmonic Orchestra and, in summer, as well as regular ballroom dancing, there is the annual BBC Light Music Festival.

Sporting activities are equally important. Bowls is extremely popular here, especially since the world championships were held in Worthing in the 1970s, and there are several lovely greens.

Nearby is some superb Sussex countryside, dotted with delightful villages. Findon is just north of Worthing and has managed to retain its rural charm. It has a fine Norman church with a fifteenth-century timber roof. Close by is **Cissbury Ring**, an Iron Age hill fort. Much earlier, in Neolithic times, the area was mined for flint; traces of the ancient mines can be seen here and on a hill to the west of Findon. Cissbury Ring offers expansive views, stretching from the Isle of Wight to Beachy Head. Sompting, now virtually a suburb of Worthing, has one of the most important churches in Sussex. Its Saxon tower, with a shingled cap, is unique in England, being the only surviving example of Saxon architecture of this kind in the 'Rhenish' style. It is believed to have been built about 1000. Most of the rest of the church is Norman and it contains a chapel of the Knights Templars who took the church in the late thirteenth century.

Sussex Route Map

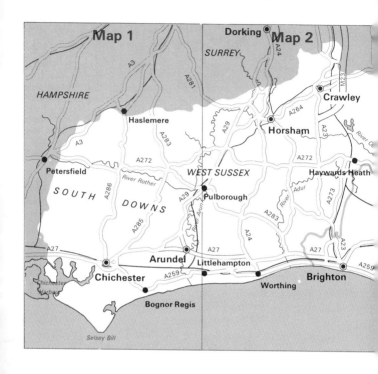

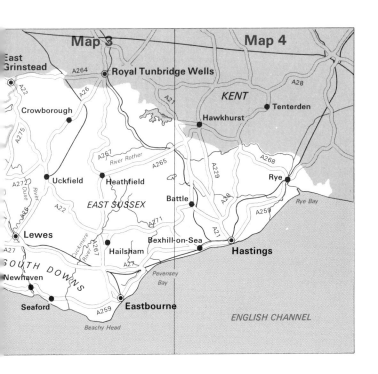

Map 1

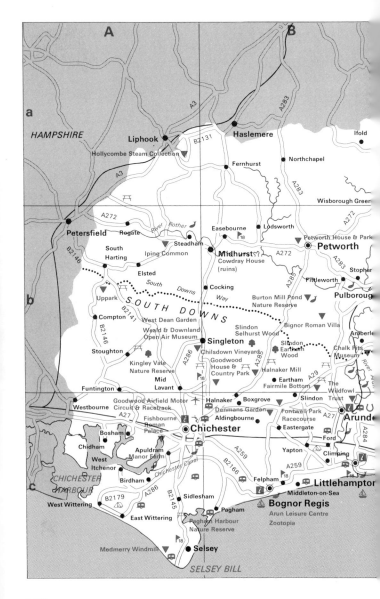

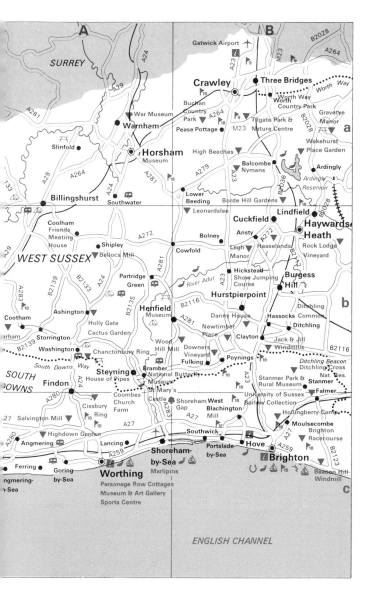

Map 2

107

Map 3

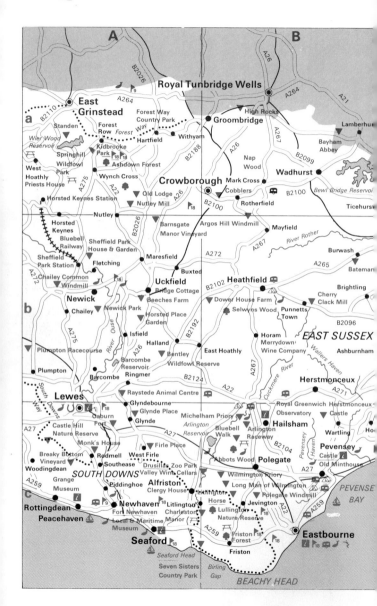

Map 4

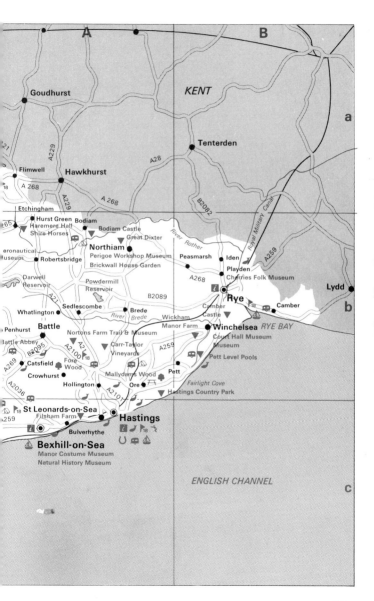

Goudhurst

KENT

A229

Flimwell

Hawkhurst

A 268

Tenterden

A28

A229

A 268

B2082

Etchingham

Hurst Green
Haremere Hall
Shire Horses

Bodiam

Bodiam Castle

Great Dixter

River Rother

Iden

Playden

Cherries Folk Museum

Royal Military Canal

A259

Lydd

eronautical
useum

Northiam

Perigoe Workshop Museum

Brickwall House Garden

Peasmarsh

Robertsbridge

A268

Rye

Darwell
Reservoir

Powdermill
Reservoir

B2089

Whatlington

Sedlescombe

Brede

River Brede

Camber
Castle

Camber

A21

b

Wickham

RYE BAY

Penhurst

Battle

Nortons Farm Trail & Museum

Manor Farm

Winchelsea

Court Hall Museum
Museum

attle Abbey

B2095

A2100

Carr-Taylor
Vineyards

A259

A21

Pett Level Pools

A269

Catsfield

Fore
Wood

Mallydams Wood

Pett

A2036

Crowhurst

Hollington

Ore

A2101

Fairlight Cove

Hastings Country Park

St Leonards-on-Sea

Filsham Farm

A259

Hastings

Bulverhythe

Bexhill-on-Sea

Manor Costume Museum

Natural History Museum

ENGLISH CHANNEL

c

Town Directory

Arundel

Map 1 Bc

U ⊞ ℹ

Bird Reserve: The Wildfowl Trust
Castle: Arundel Castle
Church Building: Arundel Cathedral
Museum: Toy & Military Museum
Museum of Curiosity

Brighton

Map 2 Bc

⚓ ♞ U ⌗ ℹ ⚓

Aquariums: Brighton Aquarium &
Dolphinarium
Horseracing: Brighton Racecourse
Marina: Brighton Marina
Museums: Booth Museum of Natural
History, Brighton Art Gallery &
Museum, National Museum of Penny
Slot Machines, Grange Museum & Art
Gallery
Railways: Volks Electric Railway
Sports Centre: Portslade Community
College
Nearby:
Archaeological Site: Hollingbury
Camp
Mill: Beacon Hill Windmill
Museums: The Barlow Collection,
Stanmer Park Rural Museum

Brighton

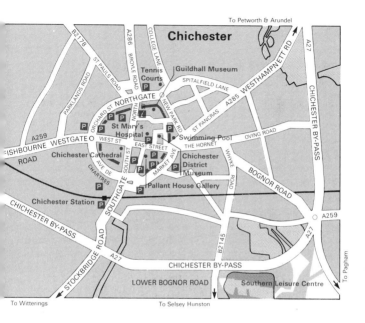

Chichester

Map 1 Ac

➤ ⌨ ℹ️

Art Gallery: Pallant House Gallery
Church Building: Chichester Cathedral
Museums: Chichester District Museum, Guildhall Museum
Other Historic Building: St Mary's Hospital
Nearby:
Bird Park/Nature Reserve: Pagham Harbour
Country Park: Goodwood
Farm: Apuldram Farm
Historic Home: Goodwood House
Motor Racing: Goodwood Motor Circuit
Nature Reserve: Kingley Vale
Roman Site: Fishbourne Palace

Eastbourne

Map 3 Bc

➤ ⌨ ⌨ ⚓ ⚓

Art Gallery: Towner Art Gallery
Museums: Home of Sussex Combined Services Museum, Invasion Coastal Defence Museum
Unusual Outings: Butterfly Centre
Nearby:
Bird Park: Arlington Reservoir
Castle: Pevensey Castle
Country Park: Seven Sisters Country Park
Nature Reserve: Beachy Head
Woodland: Friston Forest

East Grinstead

Map 3 Aa

Historic Homes: Sackville College, Standen, Gravetye Manor
Museum: East Grinstead Town Museum
Sports Centre: King George's Hall
 Nearby:
Bird Park: Springhill Wildfowl Park
Country Parks: Forest Way, Worth Way
Garden: Kidbrooke Park

Hastings

Map 4 Ac

Bird Reserve: Powdermill Reservoir
Castle: Hastings Castle
Country Park: Hastings Country Park
Leisure Centre: Hastings YMCA
Other Historic Buildings: Shovells
Railways: East & West Cliff Railways
Sports Centre: Summerfield Sports Centre
Unusual Outings: Hastings Embroidery, Hastings Model Village, St Clement's Caves
 Nearby:
Woodland: Mallydams Wood

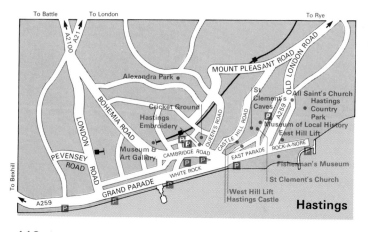

Hove

Map 2 Bc

♪ *i* ⅃ ⸙ Ⅰ₁₈

Museum: Brighton Engineerium, Hove Museum of Art
Mill: West Blachington Windmill
Greyhound Racing: Brighton Stadium

Lewes

Map 3 Ac

Ⅰ₁₈ ∪ ♪ *i*

Archaeological Site: The Caburn
Castle: Lewes Castle
Church Buildings: Priory St Pancras
Museum: Museum of Sussex Archaeology
Other Historic Buildings: Bull House
Nearby:
Historic Homes: Glynde Place, Monks House
Nature Reserves: Castle Hill, Chailey Common

Rye

Map 4 Bb

Ⅰ₁₈ ▭ *i*

Art Galleries: Rye Art Gallery, Easton Rooms
Historic Home: Lamb's House
Museum: Ypres Tower
Nature Reserve: Rye Harbour
Unusual Outings: Rye Town Model & Light Show
Nearby:
Museum: Cherries Folk Museum

Leisure A-Z

Details given have been carefully checked but are subject to change. Last admission can be half an hour before stated closing time.

Symbols: See p 5

Abbreviations: ch children
ch 16 children to age 16
OAP old age pensioners
m   mile
N   north
S   south
E   east
W   west
NCC   Nature Conservation Council
RSNC   Royal Society for Nature Conservation
NGS   National Garden Scheme
SAS   Sussex Archaeological Society
STNC   Sussex Trust for Nature Conservation
RSPB   Royal Society for the Protection of Birds
NT   National Trust
FC   Forestry Commission

Air Sports & Pleasure Flights

Flying Lessons

AIR SOUTH FLYING SCHOOL
Map 2 Ac
Shoreham-by-Sea (07917) 62874
Shoreham Airport off A27
Open: summer, daily 8.00-20.00; winter, daily 8.00-18.00
Charge: flying lessons £35 hour

GOODWOOD FLYING SCHOOL
Map 1 Ac/p 37
Chichester (0243) 774656
Goodwood Airfield, 3m NE Chichester off A286
Charge: flying lessons £44.85 hour (2 seater Tomahawk)

MERCURY FLYING SCHOOL
Map 2 Ac
Shoreham-by-Sea (07917) 62277
Shoreham Airport off A27
Open: daily
Charge: flying training & touring aircraft £36 basic
Instructor rating & instructor renewal courses available, also radio telephone licence training

SOUTHERN AERO FLYING CLUB
Map 2 Ac
Shoreham-by-Sea (07917) 62457
Shoreham Airport off A27
Flying lessons & charter flights; fixed wing & helicopter, details on application

Gliding

080 EAST SUSSEX GLIDING CLUB
Broyle, Ringmer 2m NE Lewes off B2192
Open: w/end & Wed, pupils should arrive at 8.00 for ballot
Membership: £63 per year, £25 entrance fee
Fees: winch & launch £1.40 (members), £4 (non members); aero tow to 2,000ft £6.50 (members), £10 (non members); glider hire 30p for 5 min
Small club 150 members, 2 dual gliders, 3 single seater solos, piper super cub for tugging, open day usually May

SOUTHDOWN GLIDING CLUB
Storrington (09066) 2137
Parham Airfield, Cootham, Pulborough,
1m W Storrington on A283
Open: Wed, Sat, Sun & BHs
Membership: £70 per year, entrance
fee £36 (ch £18)
Fees: winch & launch £1.20; aero
tow to 2,000ft £6.50; flying charge
10p per min; air experience fees, aero
tow launch £10, winch launch £3.50
(including 15 min flying time)
200 members, operates 2 two seat
training gliders, 3 single seat gliders

Pleasure Flights

GOODWOOD AIRFIELD
Map 1 Ac
Chichester (0243) 774656
3m NE Chichester
Goodwood Flying School
Charge: £1.50 hour, £27 half hour,
£18 20 mins (3 passengers)

SHOREHAM AIRPORT
Map 2 Ac
Air South Flying School
Shoreham-by-Sea (07917) 62874
Telephone for details

Southern Aero Flying Club
Shoreham-by-Sea (07917) 62457
Charge: £28 ¼ hour (3 passengers);
helicopter flights (telephone
for details)

Airport

GATWICK AIRPORT
Map 2 Ba/p 38
London (01) 668 4211
Spectator's Gallery, 4th floor,
International Arrivals
Open: May-Sep, daily 8.00-19.15;
Oct-April, daily 8.00-dusk
Charge: 30p (ch & OAPs 15p)
🅿 ♿ ☕

Angling

Organisations

NATIONAL FEDERATION OF ANGLERS
Derby (0332) 362000
Halliday House, 2 Wilson St, Derby
DE1 1PG
The governing body of coarse angling
in Britain. Membership is through
clubs & associations. 420 such
organisations are affiliated,
representing some 450,000 coarse
anglers.

NATIONAL FEDERATION OF SEA ANGLERS
Uckfield (0825) 3589
General Secretary: R.W. Page
26 Downsview Crescent, Uckfield,
East Sussex TN22 1UB
Governing body for sea angling in
Britain. 800 clubs are affiliated & the
federation represents the interests of
nearly 2 million sea anglers

SALMON & TROUT ASSOCIATION
01-283 5838
Fishmongers Hall, London Bridge,
London EC4R 9EL
National body for game fishing, has
over 70 branches in Britain & over
200,000 members

NATIONAL ANGLERS' COUNCIL
Peterborough (0733) 54084
11 Cowgate, Peterborough PE1 1LZ
Governing body for angling (all types)
in England. Runs National Angling
Coaching scheme & a Proficiency
Awards scheme, designed to improve
the proficiency of anglers, with special
emphasis on ecology & protection of
the water environment

CENTRAL ASSOCIATION OF LONDON & PROVINCIAL ANGLING CLUBS
01-686 3199
9 Kemble Rd, Croydon, Surrey
Members & affiliated clubs can use
the waters which the association
either owns or rents. They also provide
an Anglers' Guide to these waters

Rod Licences

SOUTHERN WATER AUTHORITY
Worthing (0903) 205252
Guildbourne House, Worthing, Sussex
The rivers & inland waters of Sussex
are controlled by the Southern Water
Authority. Anglers using these waters
must first obtain an official rod licence.
Even on stretches of water where
there is free fishing, that is where it is
not necessary to obtain a permit from
an angling club or landowner, it is still
essential to have a rod licence in order
to fish. In Sussex rod licences are
available from the secretaries of most
angling clubs (**see** Angling Clubs);
from many fishing tackle shops; or
from the local office of the water
authority:
Sussex Fisheries Officer
Southern Water Authority,
Brighton (0273) 606766
Falmer, Brighton, Sussex

Permits

Almost all rivers & stillwaters are
owned, or leased, by private
individuals, angling clubs or local
authorities.
Although access is sometimes
restricted, often to members of a
particular angling club, many private
waters offer fishing by permit.
These permits are for a day, week
or season & are usually available
from the angling clubs which
control the waters, from bailiffs on
the banks or from local tackle
shops.
In the following section, **Where
to Fish**, the angling clubs, or
others, who control particular
waters, are listed below each entry.
**For the addresses & telephone
numbers of club secretaries &
details of waters controlled by
clubs see** Angling Clubs.
If permits can be obtained
elsewhere, this information is also
given

Where to Fish

Some of the following information
is taken from **The Fishing
Handbook** (1983 edition), a
comprehensive, annual guide to all
angling organisations & locations in
Britain & Ireland. It includes a guide
to day permit fishing & to sea
fishing, a list of angling clubs & a
directory of suppliers. Three smaller
publications separate information
for Coarse Fishing, Game Fishing &
Sea Fishing.
For further details contact:
Beacon Publishing
Northampton (0604) 407288
Jubilee House, Billing Brook Rd,
Weston Favell, Northampton

Coarse Fishing: Rivers

RIVER ADUR

The Adur rises near Haywards Heath & flows into the Channel from its estuary at Shoreham-by-Sea.
Fine coarse fishing including perch, chub, bream & roach
Free Fishing: Wineham, short stretch in village, SW Haywards Heath
Permits: Pulborough, Steyning & District A.S., day permits for tidal stretch at Bramber from
The Newsagency, Bramber Bridge, for Steyning area from local tackle shops; Sussex County A.A.; Shermanbury Place Fishery (0306 883621), N Henfield, day permits on site; Worthing & District Piscatorial S., day permits also from Dunmans Tackle, Worthing; Central Association of London & Provincial A.Cs.

RIVER ARUN

This abundant coarse fishing river rises north of the Sussex border in Surrey & flows south from below Dorking to its estuary at Littlehampton. In its lower reaches sea trout can be caught during the warmer months. Also to be found are bream, chub, dace & pike
Free Fishing: Arundel, right bank between Arundel & Ford railway bridge
Permits: Central Association of London & Provincial A.Cs., Pulborough area permits also from Swan Corner Shop, Pulborough; Sussex County A.A., day permits for stretch from Stoke to Arundel from Black Rabbit (pub), Arundel & George & Dragon (pub), Burpham & G.& A. Shepherd, 10 High St, Arundel; Petersfield & District A.A. (Hants), day permits also from Petersfield tackle shop; Portsmouth & District A.A. (Hants); Worthing & District Piscatorial S., day permits for west bank stretch from Houghton Ridge to Timberley Wood from Dunmans Tackle, Worthing

RIVER CUCKMERE

Well preserved river which rises above Hailsham & flows into the Channel between Seaford & the Seven Sisters
Free Fishing: 2½m stretch from Alfriston Lock to sea
Permits: Compleat Angler., day permits also from Compleat Angler Tackle Shop, Eastbourne; Hailsham A.A.

RIVER OUSE

The Ouse rises to the SE of Horsham & flows through East Sussex via Lewes to reach the sea at the port of Newhaven. It is tidal to a point about 2m N Lewes & sea trout can be caught in its lower reaches as well as coarse fish.
Free Fishing: Lewes town centre
Permits: Old Mill Farm, Barcombe (Brown's Boatyard), permits from bailiff at farm; Haywards Heath & District A.A., no day tickets, holiday permits only

RIVER ROTHER

The river runs through East Sussex & Kent. It rises north of Heathfield and flows east until it drops south to its estuary at Rye.
Free Fishing: between Iden Bridge & Scots Float (1½m N Rye), from roadside (west) bank
Permits: Bodiam A.C., permits from bailiff on bank; Clive Vale A.C.; Rother Fishing A. (club bookings only); Rye & District A.A., day & week permits from the cottage at Iden lock & The Globe, Military Rd, Rye & Ashdowns, Peasmarsh near Rye & Marnies Ltd, High St, New Romney (Kent) & Post Office, Old Romney (Kent) & The Stone Ferry, Stone-in-Oxney (Kent)

(WESTERN) RIVER ROTHER
Rising in Surrey & flowing into the Arun at Pulborough, this is a completely separate river to the Rother which flows through East Sussex & Kent.
Permits: Chichester & District A.S.; Rother A.C., temporary membership from Rice Bros. tackle shop, West St, Midhurst & Burchnalls, North St, Midhurst; Petersfield & District A.C. day permits from tackle shop, Petersfield; Petworth A.C., permits from Howards Tackle & The Red Lion (pub), Petworth; Portsmouth & District A.C. (Hants); Southern Anglers (Hants)

Coarse Fishing: Stillwaters

ABBOTS LAKE
Abbots Wood, Arlington
Permits: Hailsham A.A.

ARDINGLY COLLEGE
N Haywards Heath
Permits: Rev. Waters, 3 Stangrove Cottages, Ardingly

BALCOMBE LAKE
N Haywards Heath
Permits: Haywards Heath & District A.C. (weekly holidays tickets only)

BARRATTS PARK FARM
Heathfield
Permits: from farm

BENNET PARK FARM
Heathfield
Permits: from farm

BUCKSHOLE RESERVOIR
Alexander Park, Hastings Rd, Hastings
Permits: park bailiff (T.Barton), 51 St Helens Park Rd, Hastings (0424 421422); Hastings, Bexhill & District A.A.

BURTON MILL POND
Near Petworth
Permits: bailiff,390a High Hoes, Shopham, Petworth (0798 42647)

CLIVE VALE RESERVOIR
E Hastings
Permits: Clive Vale A.C.; sweetshop in Harold Rd, Hastings

ECCLESBOURNE RESERVOIR
Hastings
Permits: Clive Vale A.C.

FARTHINGS LAKE
Battle
Permits: bailiff (B.Buss), 23 Manley Rise, Battle; Roys Newsagents, Battle; Reenies Tackle Shop, Bexhill; Tony's Tackle Shop, Eastbourne (0323 1388); Hastings Angling Centre, Hastings

MICHELHAM PRIORY
W Hailsham
Permits: on site

PILTDOWN POND
Piltdown, W Uckfield
Free Fishing

PIDDINGHOE POND
Piddinghoe, N Newhaven
Permits: Seaford A.C.

QUARRY (LONG or WHYKE) LAKE
Chichester
Permits: Russel Hillson Ltd, Chichester (02437 83811) (weekly permits only)

SCARLETS LAKE
Cowden, near East Grinstead
Permits: bailiff (J. Jackson), Scarlets Farm, Furnace Lane, Cowden (0 4286 414)

SHERMANBURY PLACE
N Henfield
Permits: Mr Rowles (0306 883621)

SOUTHERN LEISURE CENTRE
Chichester (0243) 787715
6 lake coarse fishery, SE Chichester

VALE BRIDGE MILL POND
Burgess Hill
Permits: Haywards Heath & District
A.A. (weekly holiday permits only)

WEIR WOOD RESERVOIR
East Grinstead
Permits: Recreation Officer (034282)
2731 or (0444) 892453

WISHINGTREE RESERVOIR
Hastings
Permits: park bailiff (T.Barton),
51 St Helens Park Rd, Hastings
(0424 421317)

Coarse Fishing: Land Drains

PEVENSEY HAVEN
One of the Pevensey Levels land
drains E of Hailsham which offers
good coarse fishing with all facilities
Permits: Compleat Angler; Compleat
Angler tackle shop, Eastbourne;
Hailsham A.A.; Tony's Tackle Shop,
Eastbourne; Sussex Armoury, Hailsham

WALLERS HAVEN
The other Pevensey Level land drain
which offers good coarse fishing
Permits: Compleat Angler; Compleat
Angler tackle shop, Eastbourne;
Hailsham A.A. Tony's Tackle Shop,
Eastbourne; Sussex Armoury,
Hailsham; Seaford A.C.; Star Inn (pub),
Pevensey (during opening hours)

Coarse Fishing: Canals

CHICHESTER CANAL
4m canal linking Chichester town with
its harbour. Good for coarse fishing
with most species found
Permits: tackle shops in Bognor Regis
& Chichester; Bognor Regis A.A.;
Chichester Canal A.A.; Petworth A.C.;
Petersfield & District A.C. (Hants);
Portsmouth & District A.C. (Hants)

Game Fishing: Rivers

RIVER ARUN
See Coarse Fishing: Rivers: River
Arun (same information applies for
game fishing)

RIVER OUSE
See Coarse Fishing: Rivers: River
Ouse (same information applies)

RIVER ROTHER
**See description for Coarse Fishing:
Rivers:** River Rother
Free Fishing: between Iden Bridge to
Scots Float, roadside (west) bank
Permits: Bodiam F.C., also from bailiff
on bank; Clive Vale A.C.; Rother
Fishing Association (club bookings
only); Rye & District A.A., permits
from the cottage at Iden lock &
William the Conqueror (pub), Iden

(WESTERN) RIVER ROTHER
See Coarse Fishing: Rivers:
(Western) River Rother (same
information applies)

Game Fishing: Stillwaters

ARDINGLY RESERVOIR
Off College Rd, Ardingly, N Haywards
Heath
Permits: bailiff on bank
(0444 892549) & Southern Water
Authority (034 2822731)

ARLINGTON RESERVOIR
Arlington, NW Eastbourne
Permits: Eastbourne Water Co.
(0323 21371) & bailiff
(0323 870815), advance booking
advised

BALCOMBE LAKE
Near Ardingly, N Haywards Heath
Permits: Haywards Heath & District
A.S. (weekly holiday permits only)

BORINGWHEEL FISHERY
Nutley, W Crowborough
Permits: on site

DARWELL LAKE
Battle
Permits: Hastings Flyfishers Club Ltd

FEN PLACE MILL ESTATE
Off B2110, SW East Grinstead
Permits: T.J. Nelson (0444 52871 or 0342 715466), by arrangement only

NEWELLS LAKE
Lower Beeding, SE Horsham
Permits: T. Cotton, Bodiams, Two Mile Ash, Christs Hospital, Horsham, by arrangement only

PECKHAMS COPSE
See Southern Leisure Centre

POWDERMILL LAKE
Near Sedlescombe, N Hastings
Permits: Hastings Flyfishers Club

SOUTHERN LEISURE CENTRE
Chichester (0243) 787715
Peckhams Copse, SW Chichester
Permits: bailiff on site

WATTLEHURST LAKE
Near Horsham
Permits: G. Nye (030 679341), six rods only allowed, advance booking advised

YEW TREE TROUT FISHERY
E Rotherfield off A267
Permits: J. Schumacher, Yew Tree Farm, Yew Tree Lane, Rotherfield, near Crowborough (0892 852529)

Sea Fishing

BEACHY HEAD
This location, beneath the famous chalk outcrop, can be dangerous because of strong tides but is famous for its bass & tope catches. Bass is best caught from Beachy Head Ledge, between May & July when the weather is calm. Tope can be found to the west of Beachy Head Ledge during the summer. black bream can also be caught here then. Plaice & sole are best caught from a mark called Goldmine which is west of Sugar Loaf Rock at Hollywell & best results come after high tide. The Head & surrounding area offers fine, year round fishing from the rocks & other species found here include huss, pout, skate & even whiting & cod in winter

BEXHILL
There is no pier here but beach fishing offers quite good results. Cod can be found in winter & is joined by bass, rockling, pout, whiting & dabs during the warmer months. Bass is best from May to July

BOGNOR REGIS
Boat fishing is excellent here for dogfish, skate, conger & bull huss with bream in the summer. Cod & whiting are also caught in winter. Beach fishing produced good catches of bass, whiting & flatties in winter. The bass is particularly good in summer

BRIGHTON
The Blue Lagoon beaches offer excellent flounder & bass fishing particularly after dark. Black Rock & the surrounding area, at the east of town, is a good boat fishing mark where conger, skate, whiting (in winter) & bream (in summer) are found. Rock Taw offers fine tope (over 40lbs) during summer & autumn as well as other species

Boat charter:
Brighton Sea Angling Services
(0273) 685713 or 689528
Wreck & general fishing
'Compass Rose'
Skipper: Peter Hayles
0273 689528
'Royal Eagle'
Skipper: Peter Blacklock
04446 3876
'Nimrod'
Skipper: Jim Hollingsworth
07917 4793
'Skintus II'
Skipper: Fred Cox
01647 8414
'Sea Jay'
Skipper: Robert Whitehead
07917 3374
'May Archer'
Skipper: R.A.May
0273 592251
'Riptide'
Skipper: Derek Dalmon
0903 36759
'Cee Heather'
Skipper: Eric Collins
0323 896793
'Sea Break'
Skipper: Brian
0273 556601

EASTBOURNE
Anglers enjoy good fishing here from
the shore, pier or from boats. Species
to expect include pouting, plaice,
bream, conger & dab

HASTINGS
Hastings pier offers fine summer
fishing for mackerel, garfish, dabs,
sole, bass & mullet. In winter silver
whiting, cod, flounder & sometimes
plaice are caught. Extensive areas of
rocks near the old town offer the best
shore fishing and the most popular
baits are lugworm, white rag &
peeler crab.

Offshore wreck fishing can produce
good results with conger, cod, pollack
& ling to be found. Further inshore
flatties are abundant & in winter cod
can be caught. The best inshore bait is
lugworm & in winter squid or herring
Boat charter:
'Helping Hand'
0424 433923
36ft, 10 rods

HOVE
Beach fishing here yields good flatties
& bass while boat fishing offers
catches of plaice, skate, dab &
mackerel in summer, whiting in winter

LITTLEHAMPTON
Littlehampton has a well earned
reputation as one of West Sussex's
best fishing locations & is particularly
famous for its black bream. This
species is abundant at Kingsmere
Rocks, about 5½m south of town & at
the Ditches nearby. Another good
mark for black bream is Winter Knoll,
about 1½m out. The season lasts
from April to June. Other species
found in the area include bull huss,
mackerel, tope & conger
Boat charter:
'Best of All'
Skipper: R.E.Hughes
0903 44375
Wreck & mark fishing day or night
'Charlotte Newman'
Skipper: Brian Barret
0243 551666
'Patricia A'
Skipper: Alan Walker
09064 33437
'Starbreaker'
0256 61758
32ft, 10 rods
'Lisamarie of Arun'
Skipper: Michael Driscol
0243 821655
'Tarka'
Skipper: Ross Fisher
0243 694863
'Jung Frau'
Skipper: Ian Warren
09063 3976

'Ariel'
Skipper: Mike Pratt
0798 42370
'Our Gay'
Skipper: Brian Ferris
09064 4927
'Tobermory'
Skipper: Peter Hill
09064 5763
'Margaret Elaine'
Skipper: Tony Steel
09064 3870

NEWHAVEN

The main catch from Newhaven's two piers is cod & other species include bass, flounder, conger, dab & pout. Good catches of bass can be expected from the beach between May & October.

Mile out from the breakwater lies the Red Shrave where excellent catches of whiting, codling, plaice, dab & pout can be found. A mile further out is the Dredger Dumping Ground which is an excellent mark for catching plaice, dab, sole & whiting

Some of the best wrecks in the area lie about four miles out between Newhaven & Peacehaven. Good catches of conger, pollack, black bream & pout can be found here

RYE

Pett Level beach offers plenty of bass & flatties, flounder & dab. Rye Bay's main catches are cod & whiting inshore but the variety of species widens the further out you go. Deep water wrecking means fishing in the English Channel so beware of shipping traffic. In a suitable safe place the fishing can be exellent with large conger & big tope common catches. Spurdog, black bream, mackerel, bull huss, pout & dogfish can also be found at varying times of year

ST LEONARDS-ON-SEA

Good all year fishing here from both beach & boat. The many species to be caught include bass, mackerel, whiting, cod, bull huss, turbot & flatties

SEAFORD

A fine area for beach fishing. One of the good marks is Tide Mills, on the west end of Seaford's long promenade. From March to April excellent plaice & flounder can be caught here. Another important mark is the Buckle, on the eastern side of the promenade. It is a rough beach which produces fine catches of conger in the summer.

The whole length of the promenade offers fine bass & flatties in the warmer months & the main winter catches are codling, whiting, pout & dab, & at night excellent conger.

Boat fishing is also good at Seaford. About 300yds out from Tide Mills fine hauls of sole & flounder can be found. At the other end of town, opposite the Martello Tower & Splash Point, about 500yds from the shore lies Town Rock. This mark yields good catches of bass in summer & cod & whiting in winter. Another good mark is the Martello Tower itself. About a mile out there are dogfish, huss, conger, skate & pout to be caught. Between Seaford & Cuckmere Haven is the Birling Gap which offers fine bass fishing

SELSEY BILL

The rocks off Selsey produce fine catches of many species. Strong tides help create the excellent fishing but also make both beach & boat fishing somewhat treacherous. Beach fishing offers bass & bream in summer, whiting & cod in winter. Offshore in summer black bream, conger, ray & tope are frequently caught

SHOREHAM-BY-SEA
See Worthing

WORTHING

Beach fishing in the area is good for black bream, bass & mullet in summer & sole is a common catch during autumn & winter. Flatfish are found in abundance in the area, especially plaice, which can be caught in good numbers from the beach.

Worthing pier offers fine catches of flounder, whiting & sole in winter & black bream & mullet during spring & summer

Boat Charter:
From Shoreham Harbour
'John LL'
Skipper: John Landale
0273 594930
'Cecilia Rose'
Skipper: Ken Voice
0273 592461
'Buci'
Skipper: Ron Saunders
0273 417485

Angling Clubs
Abbreviations:
A. Angling
A.A. Angling Association
C. Club
F. Fishing
P. Preservation
S. Society

East Sussex Coarse Clubs

CLIVE VALE A.C.
Secretary: D. Swain
Hastings (0424) 713240
81 Amherst Rd, Hastings
Membership: restricted to those living within 20m radius
Formed: 1912
Members: 700
Facilities: Clive Vale & Ecclesbourne reservoirs; River Rother; day permits available

COMPLEAT ANGLER
Secretary: V.W. Honeyball
Eastbourne (0323) 54598
The Cottage, Parkland School, Eastbourne
Membership: unrestricted
Formed: 1926
Members: 800
Facilities: 20m land drains on Pevensey Marshes (Pevensey Have & Wallers Haven); 6m River Cuckmere; various other marsh drains & ponds

COPTHORNE & DISTRICT A.S.
Secretary: FE.E Munro
East Grinstead (0342) 715933
9 Medway Estate, Turner's Hill
Membership: restricted
Formed: 1928
Members: 450
Facilities: Rowfant Millpond; Horse Pasture Lake; Worth; Little Rowfant Lakes; Claypit; Godstone; River Eden; Haxted Mead; Cernes Farm; Prinkham Mead; River Arun; Bucks Green; River Mole

CROWBOROUGH & DISTRICT A.A.
Secretary: K.J.B. Wilson
Crowborough (08926) 4722
'Elysium' 35 Southridge Rd, Crowborough
Membership: restricted, junior membership available
Members: 150
Facilities: local lakes, streams & rivers within a 15m radius of Crowborough Cross

HASTINGS, BEXHILL & DISTRICT FRESHWATER A.A.
Secretary: G. Gutsell
Hastings (0424) 421422
14 Jameson Crescent, St Leonards-on-Sea
Membership: restricted to those living within a 20m radius
Formed: 1895
Members: c.600

Facilities: local park reservoirs; Alexander Park; marsh & drain waters on Romney Marsh, River Rother (affiliated to Rother Fisheries); lake waters at Catsfield, Battle; Wishingtree Reservoir leased from Southern Water Authority

RYE & DISTRICT A.S.
Secretary: A.V. Curd
Peasmarsh (079721) 427
34 The Maltings, Peasmarsh, Rye
Membership: unrestricted, junior membership available
Formed: 1920
Members: 150
Facilities: Many waters in & around Rye including Rivers Tillingham, Brede & Rother (well known permanently pegged match water); most drains & dykes on Romney Marsh; waters available for closed events, club & league matches

SEAFORD A.C.
Secretary: Mr B.White
Seaford (0273) 38513
62 Eley Drive, Rottingdean, Brighton
Membership: unrestricted
Members: c.200
Facilities: Wallers Haven; Normans Bay; Old River, South Heighton; Piddinghoe Pond, Piddinghoe

SOUTH EAST SPECIMEN GROUP
Secretary: P.Jones
50 Parsons Close, St Leonards-on-Sea

WADHURST A.C.
Secretary: R.Stone
Crowborough (08926) 4779
47 Medway, Crowborough
Membership: restricted
Formed: 1972
Members: 150

West Sussex Coarse Clubs

ASH ANGLING MATCH CLUB
Secretary: P. Carter
83 Longfield Rd, Horsham
Membership: unrestricted
Formed: 1979
Members: 20

HASSOCKS & DISTRICT A.S.
Secretary: J. Piper
Hassocks (07918) 4285
28 Ockendon Way, Hassocks
Membership: unrestricted

HAYWARDS HEATH & DISTRICT A.S.
Secretary: S.F. Whetstone
Lindfield (04477) 3059
2 West View, Lewes Rd, Lindfield
RH16 2LT
Membership: unrestricted
Year formed: 1915
Members: 500
Facilities: River Ouse 12m from Avins Bridge to Gold Bridge, Newick; other waters at Balcombe & Burgess Hill

HENFIELD & DISTRICT A.S.
Secretary: D.W.Newnham
Bolney (044482) 434
Membership: unrestricted
Members: 400
Facilities: River Adur, 6m (tidal & non-tidal); small lake (30 swims); Chichester Canal (member of association); brooks, 2m near Upper Beeding; member of Sussex County A.A.

HORSHAM & DISTRICT A.A.
Secretary: N. Farley
Horsham (0403) 60104
37 Hurst Ave, Horsham
Membership: restricted to district of Horsham
Formed: c.1910
Members: 850

PETWORTH A.C.
Secretary: D.A. Pugh
Petworth (0798) 42866
3 Cherry Tree Walk, Petworth
Membership: unrestricted
Formed: 1957
Members: 200

PULBOROUGH & STEYNING A.S.
Secretary: M.Booth
Bury (079881) 525
5 South Lane, Houghton, Arundel
Membership: unrestricted
Formed: 1919
Members: 400
Facilities: River Arun, 3m (tidal);
River Rother, 1m; River Adur, 3m;
main species bream, roach, chub, dace
& pike main species; several small
lakes

ROTHER A.C.
Secretary: C.Boxhall
Midhurst (073081) 3897
4 Half Moon Cottages, Petersfield Rd,
Midhurst
Membership: unrestricted
Formed: 1953
Members: 300
Facilities: (Western) Rother, 1½m
upstream of North Mill (south bank),
¾m upstream of Woolbeding Bridge
(north bank); 1½ acre pond at Bepton
(1m SW Midhurst); 1½ acre pond on
north bank of (Western) Rother

STEDHAM A.C.
Secretary: P.J.West
25 Park Crescent, Midhurst GU29 9ED
Membership: unrestricted
Formed: 1934
Members: 150
Facilities: (Western) Rother, c.1m;
small picturesque pond

SUSSEX COUNTY A.A.
Secretary: Mrs J.Cranford
Brighton (0273) 492714
5 Myrtle Terrace, Weavers Lane,
Henfield
Membership: restricted

SUSSEX SPECIMEN GROUP
Secretary: G.Jenner
60 Cuckmore Crescent, Goddops
Green, Crawley

VICTORIA A.C.
Secretary: J.Young
3 Sextant Court, North Beaumont
Park, Littlehampton, West Sussex
Membership: unrestricted
Members: 130
Facilities: River Arun; dridge,
Fittleworth to Shoplane

**WORTHING & DISTRICT
PISCATORIAL S.**
Secretary: R.Tunicliffe
79 North Lane, Portslade
Membership: unrestricted
Formed: 1953
Members: 650

Game Clubs

**HAYWARDS HEATH & DISTRICT
A.S.**
Secretary: S.F.Whetstone
Lindfield (04447) 3059
2 West View, Lewes Rd, Lindfield
RH16 2LT

LECONFIELD FLYFISHING CLUB
Secretary: Sir C. Wolseley Bt
Petworth (0798) 42502
Estate Office, Petworth GU28 0DU
Membership: restricted
Formed: 1980
Members: 70 full rods, 30 half
Facilities: 7 stocked trout ponds, 13
acres total, Leconsfield Estate,
Petworth

OUSE ANGLING PRESERVATION
Secretary: Dr J.L.Cotton
Lewes (07916) 4883
Down End, Kingston Rd, Lewes
Membership: unrestricted

PETWORTH A.C.
Secretary: D.A.Pugh
Petworth (0798) 42866
3 Cherry Tree Walk, Petworth
Membership: unrestricted
Formed: 1957
Members: 200

PITSHILL FLYFISHING WATERS
Secretary: R.Etherington
c/o Messrs King & Chasemore
Petworth (0798)42011
Lombard St, Petworth
Membership: restricted
Members: 40
Facilities: c.1½m rain fed river
containing brown & sea trout, also
stocked with brown & rainbow trout

ROTHERBRIDGE FLYFISHING A.
Secretary: R.Etherington
c/o Messrs King & Chasemore
Petworth (0798) 42011
Lombard St, Petworth
Membership: restricted
Formed: 1972
Members: 50
Facilities: c.4½m rain fed river
containing brown & sea trout, also
stocked with brown & rainbow trout

Sea Angling Clubs

BOGNOR REGIS AMATEUR A.S.
Festival Secretary: B Spriggs
Bognor (0243) 864842
8 The Midway, Feltham, Bognor
Membership: unrestricted
Members: 90

CROWBOROUGH & DISTRICT A.A.
Secretary: K J B Wilson
Crowborough (08926) 4722
Elysium 35, Southridge Rd,
Crowborough
Members: 150
Membership: restricted, junior
available

EAST HASTINGS S.A.A.
Secretary: D W Brockington
Hastings (0424) 426644
Club room (0424) 430230
c/o East Hastings SAA, The Stade,
Hastings
Formed: 1908
Membership: unrestricted
Members: 1200 angling, 1400 social

EASTBOURNE A.A.
Secretary: C Parsons
Eastbourne (0323) 23442
Formed: 1905
Membership: unrestricted
Members: 700

HASTINGS & ST LEONARDS A.A.
Secretary: G Wall
Hastings (0424) 431923
Marine Parade, Hastings
Formed: 1895
Membership: unrestricted
Members: 1,762

HOVE DEEP SEA ANGLERS
Secretary: R E L Robinson
Brighton (0273) 43100
Clubhouse, Western Esplanade, Hove
BN4 1WB
Formed: 1908
Membership: unrestricted
Members: 335 men, 160 ladies

PULBOROUGH & HORSHAM D.S.A.
Secretary: C Denyer
(09066) 4739
40 Warren Hamlet, Sullington RH20
3NL
Formed: 1964
Membership: unrestricted
Members: 25

RYE S.A.C.
Secretary: R Coates
10 Battle Crescent,
St Leonards-on-
Sea
Formed: 1977
Membership: unrestricted
Members: 100

ST LEONARDS S.A.A.
Secretary: R J Towner
St Leonards-on-Sea (0424) 51652
Yolinar, Churchwood Road,
St Leonards-on-Sea
Formed: 1901
Membership: unrestricted
Members: 150-200

SELSEY BILL F.C.
Secretary: P W Cooper
Selsey (024361) 4048
2 Ruskin Close, Selsey
Formed: 1965
Membership: restricted
Members: 52

SHOREHAM A.C.
Secretary: K Weaver
Shoreham (0273) 415132
5 Thornhill Way, Mile Oak, Portslade
BN4 2YY
Formed: 1949
Membership: unrestricted
Members: 137

SUSSEX OFFSHORE SEA ANGLERS
Secretary: A McTaggart
Littlehampton (09064) 24385
80 Parkside Ave, Littlehampton
Formed: 1976
Membership: restricted
Members: 10

WORTHING DEEP S.A.C.
Secretary: B J Devitt-Spooner
Worthing (0905) 44456
Formed: 1975
Membership: restricted
Members: 22

Aquarium

BRIGHTON AQUARIUM & DOLPHINARIUM
Map 2 Bc
Brighton (0273) 604233
Marine Parade, Brighton
Open: Easter-late Oct, daily
9.00-17.15; late Oct-Easter, daily
11.00-16.15
Charge: £1.80 (ch, OAP & disabled
visitors 90p)
No dogs
🐾 ♿ 🚻

Archeological Sites

THE CABURN
Map 3 Ac
2m SE Lewes off A27
No restrictions
13 acre, Iron Age, originally circular
hill fort

CHANCTONBURY RING
Map 2 Ab
2.5m W Steyning off A283 near
Washington
No restrictions
Small oval Iron Age fort on ridge of
South Downs, good views, ring of
Beech trees planted 1760, occupied
by Romans in 3rd & 4th centuries,
remains of small Roman temple

CISSBURY RING
Map 2 Ac
2m N Worthing off A24,
1m E Findon
No restrictions
Iron age fort with traces of Neolithic
flint mines, good views
NT

HOLLINGBURY CAMP
Map 2 Bc
Brighton, follow public footpath from
Ditchling Rd across Hollingbury Park
golf course
No restrictions
Rampart & shallow ditch of ancient
settlement, good views over Brighton
and westwards

LONG MAN OF WILMINGTON
See Hill Figures

HIGH ROCKS
Map 3 Ba
1.5m E Groombridge, off A26 &
A264
Ancient fort, extensive ramparts,
430yds across, can be seen in
woodland by public footpath from
High Rocks country park
See Country Parks

Art Galleries

**BRIGHTON ART GALLERY &
MUSEUM**
See Museums

CHICHESTER
See Pallant House Gallery

EASTBOURNE
See Towner Art Gallery

EASTON ROOMS
Map 4 Bb/p 84
Rye (0797) 222433
107 High St, Rye
Extension of Rye Art Gallery
Open: all year, Mon-Sat 10.30-13.00
& 14.15-17.00, Sun 14.30-17.00
Free
Exhibitions of paintings, prints, crafts;
works for sale
🏧

**GRANGE MUSEUM & ART
GALLERY**
See Museums

**HASTINGS MUSEUM & ART
GALLERY**
See Museums

HOVE MUSEUM OF ART
See Museums

PALLANT HOUSE GALLERY
Map 1 Ac/p35
Chichester (0243) 774557
9 North Pallant, Chichester
Open: all year (closed Dec 25 & 26),
Tue-Sat 10.00-17.30
Charge: 50p (ch & OAP 30p), group
rate available (must book)
&

RYE ART GALLERY
Map 4 Bb/p 84
Rye (0797) 223218
Ockmans Lane, East St, Rye
Open: all year, Tue-Sat 10.30-13.00
& 14.15-1700, Sun & BHs 14.30-
17.00
Free
Permanent collection of paintings and
special exhibitions
See also Easton Rooms

TOWNER ART GALLERY
Map 3 Bc/p 41
Eastbourne (0323) 21635
Borough Lane, Eastbourne
Open: all year (closed Good Fri &
Dec 25 & 26), Mon-Sat
10.00-17.00, Sun 14.00-17.00
Free
& 🏧

Bird Parks

ROYAL SOCIETY FOR THE PROTECTION OF BIRDS

The Lodge, Sandy, Beds SG19 2DL
The RSPB is a charity and part of its work involves managing 85 bird reserves in Great Britain. The aim of these reserves is the conservation of birds and their habitat. The RSPB organises many activities connected with birdwatching and bird conservation. There is a special organisation for young people: Young Ornithologists Club (YOC).

If you would like to know more about the RSPB and YOC, if you would like to make a donation or to become a member contact the address above.

The following list includes reserves, parks, reservoirs, marshes and hunting ground for the bird watcher. The reserves are free to members of the RSPB but there is sometimes a charge for the general public. When visiting reserves remember that they are there for the birds so do nothing which would in any way disturb them or harm their environment. Always keep to marked paths. Reserves are closed on Nov 2-5 & Dec 25-26.

ARLINGTON RESERVOIR
See Nature Reserves: Arlington Reservoir

BARCOMBE MILLS
Map 3 Ab
Haywards Heath (0444) 57711
3m N Lewes, 1½m E Barcombe off A26
Small reservoir on E bank of R Ouse attracting wildfowl; breeding birds include garganery, mallard, shoveler, tufted duck, kingfisher & grey wagtail; in winter wigeon, mallard, teal & pochard
Keep to public footpaths; owned by mid Sussex Water Co

BENTLEY WILDFOWL RESERVE
Map 3 Ab/p 13
Halland (082584) 573
Halland, 7m NE Lewes off B2192
Open: April-Oct, daily; Nov, Jan-March, w/ends 11.00-16.30 (closed Dec); March-Oct house only
Charge: £1.60 (ch 80p, OAPs £1.30), 10% reduction for groups (11)
Guided tours for schools by arrangement, vintage & veteran motor museum, play area
No dogs
🅿 🍴 ♿ ▱⛱

DARWELL RESERVOIR
Map 4 Ab
Hastings (0424) 438666
4½m NW Battle off A2100
Reservoir NOT open to public but good views from road on north side & footpath on south side; wildfowl, tufted duck & pochard; owned by Southern Water Authority

FILSHAM FARM
See Nature Reserves: Filsham Farm

FORE WOOD
Map 4 Ab
Shoreham (07917) 63642
3m NW Hastings, W Crowhurst off A2100
Open: all year
Hole-nesting birds, woodpeckers, nuthatchers & tree creepers
Managed by RSPB, keep to marked trails

PAGHAM HARBOUR
Map 1 Ac/p 38
Pagham, 4½m S Chichester off B2145
1,000 acres of tidal mud flats, shingle beach & farmland; contact information centre Sidlesham for species; 1½m nature trail, leaflet available; managed West Sussex County Council
Dogs on leads

PETT LEVEL POOLS
Map 4 Bb
2m S Winchelsea
Pools behind sea-wall attract migrating birds, particularly July-early Sep; no public footpaths but good view from road; owned by Southern Water Authority

SPRING HILL WILDFOWL PARK
Map 3 Aa
Forest Row (034282) 2783
Forest Row, 3m S East Grinstead signposted from village
Open: all year, daily 10.00-18.00 (closed Dec 25 & 26)
Charge: £1 (ch 50p, OAPs 70p)
🅿 🏃 ⊑ ♿

TILGATE PARK NATURE CENTRE
See Country Parks: Tilgate Park

WEIR WOOD RESERVOIR
Map 3 Aa
2m S East Grinstead, 1½m W Forest Row, access from A22 at Wych Cross or B2110
Reserve NOT open to public but good views from road on west side of reservoir; most interesting season winter, many ducks, great crested grebes; owned by Southern Water Authority

PEVENSEY LEVELS
N Pevensey off A259
Privately owned farmland, take care not to trespass, good view from old A259 E of Pevensey village; wet pasture, main interest wintering birds, snipe, golden plover & lapwings

THE WILDFOWL TRUST
Map 1 Bc
Arundel (0903) 883355
Mill Rd, ½m N Arundel
Open: all year, daily 9.30-17.00 (closed 25 & 26 Dec)
Charge: £1.30 (ch 4-16 65p, OAPs £1.10); groups (20) 90p (ch 80p, OAPs 70p) telephone in advance
No dogs
🅿 🏃 ♿ ⊑

Boat Trips

BRIGHTON MARINA
Map 2 Bc
Harbour Tour: June-Sep, Tue-Sun 9.00-18.00 (departing every hour)
Charge: £2 per person half hour
See also: Marinas

CHICHESTER HARBOUR CONSERVANCY
Map 1 Ac/p 38
Birdham (0243) 512301
Itchenor, 4½m SW Chichester off A286
Tour: June-mid Sep, daily at 10.00, 13.00 & 15.30 (subject to tides)
Charge: £1.50 (ch £1) group reductions, capacity 40 seats; contact Southdown Bus Co (0243) 783251 for tickets
Day or evening trips, whole boat private yacht charter
🅿

EASTBOURNE
Map 3 Bc
Allchorn Bros.
Eastbourne (0323) 34701
Tour: departs west side of pier, open boats maximum seating 80 people; 10.30-17.30, 45 min trip from Eastbourne Pier to Beachy Head & lighthouse
10.30, 2 hour trip to Beachy Head, lighthouse, Burling Gap & Pevensey
Charge: £1.20 (ch 70p), £2 (ch £1)
All trips weather permitting

Canoeing

THE BRITISH CANOE UNION
Weybridge (0932) 41341
Flexell House, 45-47 High St,
Addlestone, Weybridge, Surrey
The British Canoe Union is the
governing body for the sport in this
country.

Although it is possible to enjoy
canoeing without belonging to a club,
many inland waterways are not open
to the general public for canoeing but
are open to clubs. It is also safer to
undertake any water sport as part of
an organised group.

For local clubs and secretaries
contact: The British Canoe Union

Caravan & Camping Sites

CARAVANS
Any reference in this section to
caravans is to touring vans, not to
permanent vans. Some of the sites will
have permanent caravans for hire
(perhaps being very large holiday
camp caravan parks) while others are
open only to touring caravans,
dormobiles & tents. If you have a
preference for a particular type of
caravan park always telephone ahead
to check.

There are many other sites which
have only permanent caravans for hire
(usually on a weekly basis). Contact
local tourist information centres for
details.

TENTS
Tents are admitted to the following
camping and caravan sites where
indicated.

CHARGES
Charges given are for one day/night.
Unless otherwise indicated charges
for caravans & tents include a car;
charges for caravans, tents &
dormobiles include two people.
There may be a range of charges for
tents depending on size.

LOCATIONS
The sites are listed under the
nearest town.

Arundel

SHIP & ANCHOR MARINA LTD
Map 1 Bc
Yapton (0243) 551262
Ford, 2m S Arundel off A259
Pitches: 160 (total) caravans, tents,
dormobiles
Charge: £3, extra adults £1 each
(ch 50p), awning £1, £1 for mooring
boats, half normal launching price
Fishing, dogs on leads, good walking
🛥 ⌂ ✕

Battle

BRAKES COPPICE FARM PARK
Map 4 Ab
Crowhurst (042483) 322
Crowhurst, 2m SE Battle off A2100
Pitches: 30 (total) caravans,
motorised vans, tents
Charge: £2 per pitch, 35p per person
(high season); £1.50 per pitch, 25p
per person (low season)
Beautiful setting, working farm, coarse
fishing, farm tours & produce
Dogs on leads

CROWHURST PARK CARAVANS
Battle (04246) 3344
Crowhurst Park, Telham, Battle,
2m S Battle off A2100
Pitches: 40 (total) caravans,
motorised vans
Charge: £3.50 per pitch (2 adults);
extra adults 50p; awning 50p
Adventure playground, fishing pond
🛥 ⌂ ♀

Caravans

TELLIS COPPICE TOURING CARAVAN PARK
Map 4 Ab
Battle (04246) 3969
Catsfield, 1½m SW Battle off B2204
Pitches: 32 (total) caravans, tents, motorised vans
Charge: £1 tents,(all year); £3 caravans, £2.50 motorised vans (high season); £2.50 caravans, £2 motorised vans (low season); awning 50p; extra adults 40p (ch 5-15 25p); dogs 10p
Attractive small site, 15 acres, milk & newspapers

Bexhill-on-Sea

COBBS HILL FARM
Bexhill-on-Sea (0424) 213460
Watermill Lane, Bexhill-on-Sea, 1m N of town off A269
Pitches: 45 (total) caravans, tents, motorised vans
Charge: £2.30 caravans (April-June & Sep), £2.10 motorised vans, £2.10-£2.30 (electrical hookup 75p); awning 40p (April-June & Sep); extra persons 40p (July & Aug 50p)

KLOOFS CARAVAN PARK
Map 4 Ac
Cooden (04243) 2839
Sandhurst Lane, Whydon, 4m W Bexhill-on-Sea off A259
Pitches: 30 (total) caravans, tents, motorised vans
Charge: £2.50; 30p extra persons
Quiet countryside, telephone

Billingshurst

BAT & BALL
Map 2 Aa
Wisborough Green (0403) 700313
New Pound, Wisborough Green, 2m W Billingshurst on B2133
Pitches: 5 caravans, 80 tents
Charge: £2
Fishing, walking

LIMEBURNERS CARAVAN & CAMPING SITE
Map 2 Ab
Billingshurst (040381) 2311
Newbridge, ½m W Billingshurst off A272
Pitches: 42 (total) caravans, tents, motorised vans
Charge: £2.50
Dogs under control

Bodium

TERRACE WOOD CARAVAN/CAMPING SITE
Staplecross (058083) 658
Bodium, 1m S town on A229
Pitches: 40 (total) caravans, tents, motorised vans
Charge: £1 per pitch, £1 per person (ch 50p)
Games room, television lounge

Bognor Regis

CHURCH FARM CARAVANS LTD
Map 1 Bc
Pagham (02432) 2635/6
Church Farm, Pagham, 3m SW Bognor Regis off B2145
Pitches: 50 (total) caravans, motorised vans (no tents)
Charge: £4 ,£25 per week
No dogs, games room

ORCHARD CARAVAN PARK
Map 1 Bc
Bognor (0243) 864063
1½m NW Bognor off A259
Pitches: 100 (total) caravans,
motorised vans (no tents)
Charge: £4
No animals
🛁

Chichester

BELL CARAVAN PARK
Map 1 Ac
Birdham (0243) 512264
Bell Lane, Birdham, 5m SW Chichester
off B2198
Pitches: 13 (total) caravans &
motorised vans (no tents)
Charge: £3, awning 50p

GOODWOOD CARAVAN PARK
Map 1 Bc
Chichester (0243) 774486
2m N Chichester off A286 (next to
Goodwood Racecourse)
Pitches: 80 (total) caravans, tents,
motorised vans (closed race days)
Charge: £3.70 (high season), £2.60
(low season), 60p extra persons (ch
60p for 2)
Dogs on leads, play area

SOUTHERN LEISURE CENTRE
Map 1 Ac
Chichester (0243) 787715
Vinnettow Rd, Chichester
Pitches: 141 caravans only
Charge: £4.80 (high season), £3.80
(low season)
Swimming pool, windsurfing, trout &
coarse fishing
🛁 ⊡ ♀

WEST SANDS CARAVAN PARK
Map 1 Ac
Selsey (0243) 602654
Selsey, 7m S Chichester on B2145
Pitches: 100 (total) caravans, motor
vans
Charge: £7 (includes awning & club
membership 6 people), £47 per week
(high season), £4 per night, £25 per
week (low season)
2 swimming pools, betting shop, play
areas
🛁 ⊡ ✕ ♀

WICKS FARM CARAVAN PARK
Map 1 Ac
West Wittering (024366) 3116
Redlands Lane, West Wittering, 6 m S
Chichester on B2179
Pitches: 40 (total) tents, motorised
vans (no caravans)
Charge: £2.50, includes 5 people
(low season); £3 (high season)
Milk & gas, playground, beach 1m,
dogs under control

Crowborough

RENHURST FARM
Map 3 Ba
Rotherfield (089285) 2897
Mark Cross, 3½m E Crowborough
off B2100
Pitches: 20 caravans, 6 tents
Charge: £1 tents, £1.50 caravans
Dogs on leads

Eastbourne

CASTLE VIEW CARAVAN SITE
Map 3 Bc
Eastbourne (0323) 763038
Eastbourne Rd, Pevensey Bay, off
A259
Pitches: 150 (total) caravans, tents,
motorised vans
Charge: £4 (low season), £5 (high
season), £6 touring caravans
Dogs on leads, play area, fishing,
off licence
🛁 ⊡ ✕ ♀

FAIRFIELD FARM CAMPING/CARAVAN SITE

Eastbourne (0323) 763165
Fairfield Farm, Eastbourne Rd,
Westham, E Eastbourne on B2191
Pitches: 60 (total) caravans, tents,
motorised vans
Charges: £1.30 caravans, £1.30
tent, £1 motorised vans, awning
40p, adults 90p (ch 60p)
Farm site, fishing, pony rides, dogs on
leads
🏕

KINGS HOLIDAY PARK & COUNTRY CLUB
Map 3 Bc

Eastbourne (0323) 21466
Pevensey Bay Rd, 3m E Eastbourne
Pitches: 25 caravans (no tents)
Charge: £5 (high season), £2.50 (low
season); awning £1
Games room, playground, swimming
pool, amusement arcade
🏕 🛏 ✕ ♀

Hailsham

BOSHIP FARM HOTEL
Map 3 Bc

Hailsham (0323) 844826
Lower Dicker Rd, Hailsham on A22
Pitches: 12 (total) caravans, tents
Charge: £2-£3
✕ ♀

GREENVIEW CARAVAN FIELDS
Map 3 Bc

Heathfield (04352) 3531
Broad Oak, 7m N Hailsham, 1m
E Heathfield on A265
Pitches: 10 (total) caravans, tents,
motorised vans
Charge: £3.50 caravans & motorised
vans, £3.50 large tents, £2 small
tents
Club house, no dogs or pets
♀

THE OLD MILL CARAVAN PARK
Map 3 Bb

Chiddingly (082583) 532
Chalvington Rd, Golden Cross, 4½m
NW Hailsham on A22
Pitches: 120 (total) caravans,
motorised vans
Charge: £2.50, extra persons 40p,
awning 30p
Quiet country site, dogs on leads,
shop, pub and P.O. nearby

SANDY BANK CARAVAN PARK
Map 3 Bb

Hailsham (0323) 842488
Magham Down, 2m NW Hailsham
off A271
Pitches: 10 caravans only
Charge: £3.50, 85p each extra
person, awnings 85p
Dogs on leads
🏕

Hastings

BEAUPORT CARAVAN PARK
Map 4 Ab

Hastings (0424) 51246
The Ridge, St Leonards-on-Sea on A21
Pitches: 20 (total) caravans,
motorised vans
Charge: £3 caravans, £2.50
motorised vans
Dogs under control
🏕

OLD COGHURST FARM
Map 4 Ab

Hastings (0424) 753622
Rock Lane, Three Oaks, 3m
N Hastings off A259
Pitches: 60 (total) caravans, tents,
motorised vans
Charge: £2.10 caravans, £2.10 large
tent, £1.70 small tent, £1.90
motorised van, 80p per person
(ch 50p), 50p awning (high season);
£1.70 caravans, £1.70 large tents,
£1.40 small tents, 70p per person (ch
40p), 50p awning (low season);
electrical hookup 60p
Dogs on leads, off licence
🏕

Henfield

SOUTHDOWN CARAVAN SITE
Map 2 Ab
Steyning (0903) 814323
3m S Henfield on A2037
Pitches: 10 caravans
Charge: £3, 50 awning
Dogs on leads

HARWOODS FARM
Map 2 Ab
Henfield (0273) 492820
West End Lane, Henfield 2m W
Henfield off A281
Pitches: 38 (total) tents (no caravans)
Charge: 50p per person (ch 14 25p),
25p per car; £3.25 per person per
week (ch 14 £1.50), 25p per car
Free fishing on R. Adur, walking, dogs
under control

WINCAVES PARK CAMPING SITE
Map 2 Ab
Partridge Green (0403) 710923
Grinders Lane, Dial Post
Pitches: 25 caravans, 25 tents &
motorised vans
Charge: £2.25, extra persons 25p
Dogs on leads, no lavatories (disposal
unit)
🅿

Horsham

RAYLANDS PARK
Map 2 Aa
Southwater (0403) 730218
Jackrells Lane, Southwater, 3½m S
Horsham, 1m NE town off A24
Pitches: 25 caravans, 5 tents, 5
motorised vans
Charge: £3
Children's play area, club house
♀

Lamberhurst

CEDAR GABLES CAMPING SITE
Map 3 Ba
Lamberhurst (0892) 890566
Lamberhurst, 8½m SE Tunbridge
Wells on A21 between Lamberhurst
& Flimwell
Pitches: 5 caravans, 30 tents
Charge: £2 per pitch, extra persons
50p
Small farm site, fresh dairy produce,
nature walks

Littlehampton

WICK FARM CAMPING SITE
Map 1 Bc
Littlehampton (09014) 4707
Clun Rd, 2m NW of town
Pitches: 310 tents only
Charge: £2.70, extra persons 70p
Children's play area
🅿 ♀

Middleton-on-Sea

LANE END FARM
Map 1 Bc
Middleton-on-Sea (024 369) 2498
Middleton-on-Sea off B2132
Pitches: 20 caravans
Charge: £3
Quiet site

Newhaven

DOWNLAND CARAVAN SITE
Map 3 Ac
Newhaven (07912) 4351
Court Farm Rd, Newhaven
Pitches: 6 caravans (no awnings)
Charge: £3.50
Quiet site, dogs on leads
🅿

RUSHY HILL CARAVAN SITE
Map 3 Ac
E Peacehaven off A259
Pitches: 30 (total) caravans
Charges: £3, £18 per week (high season); £2, £12 per week (low season)
Under development to improve facilities

Rye

FRENCHMANS BEACH CARAVAN PARK
Map 4 Bb
Rye (0797) 223011
Rye Harbour, Rye
Pitches: 12 caravans, motorised vans
Charge: £7 June, July & Sep (includes awning & club membership), £42 per week; £8 July & Aug, £48 per week; £5 mid Sept-early Oct, £30 per week
Swimming pool, play area, club house
🛒 ⌂

RYE BAY CARAVAN PARK
Map 4 Bb
Rye (0797) 226340
Rye, 3 m S of town on Pett Level Rd
Pitches: 90 (total) caravans, motorised vans
Charge: £4.50 per pitch, 50p awning
Club House, play area
🅿 🛒 ⌂

Worthing

THE TOWERS
Map 2 Ab
Ashington (0903) 892869
Washington, 2 m N Worthing on roundabout off A24/A283
Pitches: 12 caravans, 20 tents, 12 motorised vans
Charge: £3.50 caravans, £22.20 per week; £2.50 tents & motorised vans, £15 per week; £1.20 one person plus bicycle & tent (ch 65p); £1.40 one person plus motorbike & tent; £1.20 Down walkers (ch 12 65p); extra adults 80p (ch 65p); dogs on leads 25p
Quiet site
🛒 ✕ ♀

ONSLOW CARAVAN PARK
Map 2 Ac
Worthing (0903) 43170
Onslow Drive, Ferring-by-Sea, W Worthing off A259
Pitches: 4 (total) caravans, motorised vans
Charge: £3
No awnings

NORTHBROOK FARM CARAVAN CLUB SITE
Map 2 Ac
Worthing (0903) 502962
Titnore Rd, West Worthing off A2032
Pitches: 120 (total) caravans, motorised vans
Charge: £3.15 members, £4 non members (high season); £2.50, £4 (low season); extra persons £1.15 (ch 65p)
Electrical hookup, milk & gas

Castles

ARUNDEL CASTLE
Map 1 Bc/p 11
Arundel (0903) 883136/882173
Arundel, 4 m N Littlehampton on A27
Open: April-Oct, Sun-Fri
13.00-17.00, June-Aug & BHs
2.00-13.00, last admission 16.00
Charge: £2 (ch15 £1.20)
No dogs
Arundel festival (Aug)
🅿 🚾 ♿ ☕

BODIAM CASTLE
Map 4 Ab
Bodiam, 3 m S Hawkhurst off A229
Open: April-Oct, daily 10.00-19.00;
Nov-Mar, Mon-Sat 10.00-sunset
(closed Dec 25, 26); last admission
half hour before closing
Charge: 85p (ch 40p); groups (15)
Mon-Fri, 65p (ch 35p) must book
NT 🅿 🚾 ♿ ☕ ♀

BRAMBER CASTLE
Map 2 Ab/p 21
Bramber, 4 m N Shoreham-by-Sea
off A283
Ruins only
No restrictions
NT

CAMBER CASTLE
Map 4 Bb/p 85
Not open at present but castle, built
1539, due to open to public in future
DoE

EASTBOURNE REDOUBT
FORTRESS
See Museums: Combined Services
Museum

HASTINGS CASTLE
Map 4 Ac/p 49
Hastings (0424) 424242
Castle Hill Rd, West Hill, Hastings
Open: late March-late Sep, daily
10.00-12.30 & 13.30-17.00
Charge: 50p (ch 25p), groups (20)
35p (ch 20p)
🚾 ☕

HERSTMONCEUX CASTLE
Map 3 Bc
Herstmonceux, 1 m S village
Exhibition rooms & exterior only can
be viewed at convenience of Royal
Observatory
See Unusual Outings: Royal
Greenwich Observatory
DofE

LEWES CASTLE
Map 3 Ac/p 59
Lewes (07916) 4379
High St, Lewes
Open: all year, Mon-Sat 10.00-17.00,
April-Oct also Sun 14.00-17.00
Charge: 65p (ch 35p), groups (20)
45p (ch 25p); these charges also
provide admission to Barbican House
Museum
SAS
🅿

PEVENSEY CASTLE
Map 3 Bc/p 75
Pevensey, 4 m NE Eastbourne on
A259
Open: standard DofE, see p 5, also
open from 9.30 Sun April-Oct
Charge: 40p (ch & OAP 20p); group
discounts (11)
Dogs on leads
🚾 ♿ ⛱

Church Buildings

ARUNDEL CATHEDRAL
Map 1 Bc/p 12
Arundel (0903) 882297
London Rd, Arundel
Open: all year, daily 9.00-dusk
Free

BATTLE ABBEY
Map 4 Ab/p 13
Battle
Open: standard DofE, see p5, also
opens 9.30 Sun April-Oct
Charge: summer £1 (ch & OAP 50p),
winter 50p (ch & OAP 25p); group
discounts (11)
Dogs on leads
DofE ▣ ☶

BAYHAM ABBEY
Map 3 Ba
Tunbridge Wells (0892) 41835
Lamberhurst, 2 m W village
Open: standard DoE, see p5, also
opens 9.30 Sun April-Oct
Charge: 40p (ch 16 & OAP 20p)
DoE ▣

CHICHESTER CATHEDRAL
Map 1 Ac/p 33
Chichester (0243) 782595
The Royal Chantry, Cathedral Cloisters,
Chichester
Open: guided tours only, must be
booked in advance through the
cathedral office; treasury all year,
Mon-Fri 8.30-16.00
Charge: 50p (ch 10p), treasury 20p
Guided tour lasts 1 hour
No dogs
▣ ☶ ᗉ ⌸

LAMBERHURST
See Bayham Abbey

LEWES
See Priory of St Pancras

MICHELHAM PRIORY
Map 3 Bc/p 65
Hailsham (0323) 844244
Upper Dicker, nr Hailsham, 7 m N
Eastbourne off A22
Open: April-mid Oct, daily
11.00-17.30 (closed 13.00-14.00)
Charge: £1 (ch 50p)
Groups (20), schools, disabled
reductions by arrangement; £1.20
crafts exhibition (first week Aug)
No dogs
▣ ☶ ᗉ ⌸ ⌇

PRIORY OF ST PANCRAS
Map 3 Ac
Lewes (07916) 6151
Priory St, Lewes
Open: any reasonable time
Free
Ruins only

WILMINGTON PRIORY
Map 3 Bc/p 100
Alfriston (0323) 870537
Wilmington, 9m E Lewes, 2m W
Polegate on A27
Open: mid March-mid Oct, Mon &
Wed-Sat 11.00-17.00, Sun
14.00-17.00
Charge: 55p (ch 25p), reductions for
groups (must book), disabled visitors
free (main museum reached via 13
steps)
Maximum 30 visitors at a time, no
lavatories
▣

Country Parks

Unless otherwise stated parks are open all year, daily and are free. There is sometimes a small charge for car parks

BEWL BRIDGE RESERVOIR
Map 3 Ba
Lamberhurst (0892) 890661
W Wadhurst, access via B2100 & B2099
Largest inland water in south east (770 acres) with wide range of recreational activities: walking, riding, fishing, sailing, rowing, canoeing, diving, windsurfing
Most of these activities are organised by private clubs. Contact Activities Centre for details.
Marked trails (2 m), footpaths, adventure playground, visitor centre
🅿 ⛐♿ 🚻

BUCHAN COUNTRY PARK
Map 2 Ba
SW Crawley off A264
Public footpaths & informal walks
🅿

FOREST WAY COUNTRY PARK
Map 3 Aa
Disused railway line from East Grinstead to Groombridge
Most of route is wooded. Links up with Worth Way, another section of the line
Leaflet from East Sussex County Council, County Planning Dept, Southover House, Southover Road, Lewes, East Sussex
Lewes (07916) 5400
See also Worth Way

GOODWOOD COUNTRY PARK
Map 1 Bb/p 37
Chichester (0243) 789660
4m N Chichester, between A286 & A285 near Goodwood Racecourse
Area of wood & downland with views, playgrounds, nature trail
Information centre
Part of the Goodwood House complex with wide range of activities
See also Historic Homes, Golf, Air Sports & Pleasure Flights, Riding, Caravan Parks, Grass Ski Slope

HASTINGS COUNTRY PARK
Map 4 Ab/p 53
Fairlight Rd, 1 m E Hastings off A259
520 acres of natural coastal countryside including cliff tops walks, glens, nature trails, good views across English Channel, naturists' beach
Interpretive centre (open summer only), leaflets available
Lavatories
🅿 🚻

HIGH ROCKS
Tunbridge Wells (0892) 26074
High Rocks Lane, 3m W Tunbridge Wells
Area of high (70 ft) rock outcrops, rustic bridges between canyons
Open: all year, daily 9.00-sunset
Charge: 20p (ch 10p, climbers 50p)
Rock climbing, gardens
🅿 ⛐✗ 🍸

PETWORTH PARK
Map 1 Bb
5.5m E Midhurst on A283
Open: all year, daily 9.00-sunset
700 acre deer park, landscaped by Capability Brown, several pedestrian access points, dogs must be kept under control
See also Historic Homes: Petworth House
🅿

SEVEN SISTERS COUNTRY PARK
Map 3 Ac
3m E Seaford off A259
692 acres of down & marshland
including bridleways, angling,
canoeing, nature trails
Visitor centre (open Easter-Oct, w/ends
11.00-17.00), leaflets available
🅿 🏖 ♿ 🚏

SHOREHAM GAP
Map 2 Bc/p 91
2m NE Shoreham
596 acres of farm & downland.
Contains remains of part of an
extensive Iron Age & Roman Briton
field system
Areas at Southwick Hill & Whitelot
Bottom have free access to public;
some restrictions in other areas
NT

STANMER PARK
Map 2 Bb/p 30
Stanmer, 4m NE Brighton off A27
near University of Sussex
200 acres woodland & parkland, grey
squirrels & badgers can be seen in
wood, circular nature trail, guide
available from Brighton Parks Dept or
General Stores in Stanmer
Visitor & Interpretive Centre housed in
Stanmer House
Lavatories
🅿 🍴

TILGATE PARK
Map 2 Ba/p 38
½m S Crawley off M23
No restrictions
400 acres of woodland, lawns, lakes
& ornamental gardens. The park
includes a nature centre (see Nature
Reserves); 3 lakes used by fishermen
and canoeists (contact: Tilgate Nature
Association Secretary, Mr Phillips,
Crawley 0293-23722); 18 hole golf
course (see Golf Clubs)
Dogs on leads, lavatories
See also Zoos & Bird Parks
🅿 ♿ 🚏

WICKHAM MANOR FARM
Public footpaths across 392 acres of
farmland
See Farms: Wickham Manor Farm

WORTH WAY
Map 2 Ba
Disused railway line from Three
Bridges to East Grinstead
6m path for walking, cycling
riding
Wood & farm land
Fifteenth century house, Gulledge
Farm, accessible from path
Leaflet available from West Sussex
County Council, County Hall,
Chichester
See also Walking, Worth Way
🅿

Crafts

SOUTH EAST ARTS
Tunbridge Wells (0892) 41666
9-10 Crescent Rd, Tunbridge Wells,
TN1 2LU
The Regional Arts Association for East
Sussex, Surrey & Kent
The opening times of the craft centres
listed below may vary, so it is advisable
to contact them in advance

Brighton

BARCLAYCRAFT
Brighton (0273) 21694
The Brighton Craft Gallery, 7 East St
Open: Mon-Sat 10.15-17.30,
Thur 10.15-13.00
Work of contemporary British artist
craftsmen including pottery, weaving,
jewellery, ceramics, glass and wood

Ditchling

THE CRAFTSMAN
Hassocks (079 18) 5246
18 The High St, Ditchling
Open: Mon-Sat 10.00-13.00 &
14.00-17.00, Wed 10.00-13.00
Small craft shop and gallery selling
pottery, weaving, wood, engraving,
metalwork and copperware

Eastbourne

FOUR WORLDS
Vincents Yard, Susans Rd
Open: Mon-Sat 10.00-15.00
New craft shop specialising in paintings,
reproduction and modern furniture,
pottery, medieval musical instruments
and armour

OPUS
Susans Rd
Open: Mon-Sat 10.00-17.00 (closed
Wed afternoon)
Small local crafts selling pottery, small
wall hangings, knitwear, stuffed toys

TOWNER GALLERY
Eastbourne (0323) 21635/25112
Towner Art Gallery, Manor Gardens,
Borough Lane, Old Town, Eastbourne
Primarily a gallery for painting and
sculpture with some craft exhibitions
See also: Art Galleries

Lewes

TALENTS
Lewes (079 16) 5176
3 St Martins Lane
Open: summer, Mon-Sat 10.00-13.30
& 14.15-17.30, winter closed Wed;
Feb & March Fri & Sat only
Mainly patchworks, clothes and
cushions with some small imported toys
and jewellery

Lindfield

WHYTCHCRAFTS
53a High St
Open: Mon-Sat 9.30-17.30
Local craft shop selling pottery, peg
dolls, soft toys, candles, jewellery,
copper and pewterware, glass
engraving, corn dollies, leather and
wood work, basketry, oil paintings and
watercolour

Rye

COUNTRYCRAFT
Rye (079 73) 3407
Open: Mon-Sat 9.30-13.00 &
14.15-15.15, Sun 14.30-17.30
Retailers for the Rural Industries
specialising in crafts using wood, wool,
and iron, Scottish mohair, Welsh
tapestry

EASTON ROOMS
Rye (079 73) 2433
Rye Art Gallery, 107 High St
Open: Mon-Sat 10.30-17.00,
Sun 14.30-17.00
Non-commercial organisation
exhibiting work of South East artists and
craftsmen; prints, jewellery, ceramics
and variety of crafts
See also: Art Galleries

IDEN POTTERY
Rye (079 73) 3413
The Strand (Showroom, Conduit Hill)
Open: Mon-Sat 9.00-12.00 &
13.00-17.00, Sun afternoon
Showroom and retail outlet for work of
Iden Pottery; hand-made coffee sets, tea
sets, lamp bases, studio vases,
ovenware

KURREIN GALLERY
Rye (079 73) 3833
7 Lion St
Open: summer, daily 9.30-17.00;
winter daily 10.00-17.00
(Tue 9.30-13.00)
Small gallery exhibition paintings, prints
and old maps, also selection of ceramics,
glass and jewellery

RYE POTTERY
Rye (079 73) 3218
Ferry Rd
Open: Mon-Fri 8.30-12.30 &
13.30-17.30, Sat 9.30-12.30 &
14.30-17.00 (closed Sun)
Earthenware and stoneware made and
decorated by hand

RYE CERAMIC CONSULTANTS LTD
Rye (079 73) 3038
The Old Brewery, Wishward
Open: daily 9.30-17.00,
Sat 11.00-17.00
Outlet for hand-printed and
hand-painted tiles

THE TOWER FORGE
Rye (079 73) 2280
Cottage Industry Centre, Hilders Cliff
Open: daily 9.30-17.00
Wide range of crafts, patchwork,
pottery, wood, knitwear, weaving,
jewellery, soft toys, hessian sculpture

Seaford

HOME CRAFTS
18 Clifford Place
Open: 9.30-17.00 (closed Wed)
Variety of craftwork, domestic pottery,
corn dollies, stuffed toys, knitting
& crochet

St Leonards

PHOTOGALLERY
Hastings (0424) 440140
The Foresters Arms, Shepherd St
Open: summer, Wed-Sun; winter
Thur-Sun
Gallery exhibiting the best photography
available

Upper Hartfield

THE FOREST CRAFT CENTRE
Forest Row (034 282) 2686
Upper Hartfield
Open: Tue-Sat 10.00-18.00,
Sun 11.00-18.00 (closed
Mon mornings)
Centre providing studio workshops for
craftsmen including potters, silversmith,
rush and cane weaver

Upper Dicker

THE DOVECOTE
Michelham Priory
Open: April-Oct, daily 11.00-13.00 &
14.00-17.30
Small craft shop in grounds of 13th
century priory selling traditional Sussex
crafts, including pottery, ironwork, trugs
and corn dollies

Cricket

Since the 18th century when this
national summer sport evolved, cricket
continues to be enjoyed in Sussex by
spectators and players alike. Grounds
with particularly pleasant surroundings
include Hove County Cricket Ground
(home of Sussex County C.C.),
Henfield Common, Horsham, Lindfield
Common (200 yrs old), Haywards
Heath and Ringmer with its typical
village green. The season stretches
from mid March-early Sep and the
following organisations can provide
details of fixtures and membership.

SUSSEX CRICKET ASSOCIATION
This governing body for Amateur Club Cricket in Sussex can provide information on all aspects of the game. The following clubs are affiliated to the Association and able to direct players
Secretary: Mr A C Austin
Wivelsfield Green (044484) 252
Sunny Wood, Wivelsfield Green, Haywards Heath

Local Cricket

ARUN-CHICHESTER & DISTRICT C.A.
New district association covering area west of River Arun to Hampshire border; those individuals or clubs interested should contact: Malcolm Griffin, Rustington (09062) 4522

BRIGHTON CRICKET LEAGUE
Secretary: J Taylor
Brighton (0273) 501562

BRIGHTON & HOVE D.C.C.A.
Secretary: P Banfield
Brighton (0273) 28854
30 Clifton Hill, Brighton

EASTBOURNE, LEWES, NEWHAVEN D.C.A.
Secretary: P R Bell
Uckfield (0825) 3277
Forest View, 2 Claremont Rise, Uckfield

EAST SUSSEX CRICKET LEAGUE
Secretary: B R Martin
Lewes (07916) 4092
21 South Way, Lewes

HASTINGS & DISTRICT C.A.
Secretary: Mrs S Nice
Hastings (0424) 421237
134 St Helens Rd, Brighton

WORTHING & DISTRICT C.A.
Secretary: A Overington
Worthing (0903) 61511

HARTFIELD KNOCK-OUT TOURNAMENT
Hartfield Town Croft
An annual tournament played between 8 village clubs: Hartfield, Groombridge, Ashurst, Coleman's Hatch, Ashurst Wood, Fordcombe, Hammerwood & Cowden
Fixture: annually, Sun nearest to summer solstice (10.00-24.00 approx)
Facilities: public address system, beer tent & afternoon teas

Women's Cricket

SUSSEX WOMEN'S CRICKET ASSOCIATION
Secretary: Miss J C Johnson
Hastings (0424) 424877
9 Holmesdale Court, Holmesdale Gardens, Hastings
Club Grounds: Hampden Park, Eastbourne
Central Cricket Ground, Hastings
Players & umpires always needed, spectators welcome
County Ground: Mountfield Rd, Lewes

County Cricket

SUSSEX COUNTY CRICKET CLUB
Secretary: B E Simmonds
Brighton (0273) 732161
County Ground, Eaton Rd, Hove
Fixtures: scores & prospects of play contact: Brighton (0273) 772766
Membership: application forms & information contact: The Welfare Office, (0273) 732161 ext 4 (9.30-16.30, Mon-Fri; Sat 9.30-12.00)
Library: open to members during lunch, intervals & most Sats (10.00-12.00)
Contains books, collectors' items & records

Youth Cricket

Fify-five Sussex cricket clubs run
youth sections with competitions
for 11-16 year olds. For details of
clubs and information contact:
A C Austin
Wivelsfield (044484) 252
Sunny Wood, Wivelsfield Green,
Haywards Heath

Disabled

This section highlights those places
and organisations in Sussex which
offer special facilities for disabled
people. There are many other places
which are accessible to disabled
visitors and these will be found in the
various sections and are marked with
the symbol: ♿

Crafts

CHAILEY HERITAGE CRAFT SCHOOL
Contact: The Headmaster
Newick (082572) 2122
North Chailey, Lewes

Museum

LIFEBOAT HOUSE
This museum welcomes disabled
visitors
See Museums: Lifeboat House

Picnic Site

WILMINGTON-ABBOTS WOOD PICNIC PLACE
This woodland site has a walk suitable
for disabled visitors
See Picnic Sites: Wilmington-Abbots
Wood Picnic Place

Sports

BRITISH SPORTS ASSOCIATION FOR THE DISABLED
Hon Development Officer (SE region):
Mr P Jamieson
'Fairholme', Mark Beach, Edenbridge
TN8 5NR
Specialist advice and encouragement
organisation which coordinates
activities, facilities and clubs for
disabled people who want to take part
in sports. The following clubs are
affiliated to the Association.

ARUN SPORTS ASSOCIATION FOR THE DISABLED
Contact: S Riddell, 4 Stalham Way,
Felpham, Bognor Regis

BRIGHTON & HOVE SPORTS ASSOCIATION FOR THE DISABLED
Contact: Mrs A Antonio
(0273) 770013
40 Tisbury Rd, Hove

CHASELEY SPORTS & GAMES CLUB
Secretary: Mrs M Seiffert
(0323) 21865
Chaseley, South Cliff, Eastbourne

SUSSEX WHEELCHAIR BASKET BALL CLUB
Contact: Mr C Grace
(0903) 208336
68 Tristram Close, Sompting, Sussex

WORTHING SPORTS ASSOCIATION FOR THE DISABLED
Contact: Mrs A Terry
(0903) 202338
25 Westcourt Rd, Worthing

Sports Centres

KING GEORGES HALL
East Grinstead (0342) 21096
Moat Rd, East Grinstead
Disabled swimming club (Thurs morn)

WHEEL RECREATION CENTRE
Billingshurst
Under construction for autumn 1983
Further information contact:
Mr Bridges (0403) 64191 ext 278
Horsham District Council

Events

Annual events are listed under the
month in which they normally occur
but for exact dates and further details
of events contact local Tourist
Information Centres

February

GOODWOOD
The Spring South East Counties
Antique Dealers' Fair

March

BRIGHTON
Historic Motor Cycle Rally
Southern Garden Show
British Coach Rally

HICKSTEAD
Showjumping: Kerrygold International

April

EASTBOURNE
International Folk Festival
Spring Flower Show
Hove Easter Carnival

May

BRIGHTON
Historic Commercial Vehicles Rally
Festival
Boat Show
Old Ship Royal Escape Yacht Race
Torchlight Procession & Fireworks

HASTINGS
Rogationtide Blessing of the Sea

UCKFIELD
Bluebell Railway Parade Weekend

June

ARDLINGLY
South of England Agricultural Show

ARUNDEL
Carpet of Flowers & Feast of
Corpus Christi

BEXHILL-ON-SEA
Rowing Regatta

BOGNOR REGIS
International Birdman Rally

BRIGHTON
Motor Rally & Concours d'Elegance
National Squib Championship
Harlem Globetrotters
Regency Exhibition (Royal Pavilion)

EASTBOURNE
BMW Women's International Tennis
Tournament

GOODWOOD
Inchcape International Dressage
Championship CDI
The Summer South East Counties
Antique Dealers' Fair

July

BATTLE
Festival

Events

BEXHILL
Carnival
Sea Week

BRIGHTON
Peter Stuyvesant Offshore Trophy
'Old Gaffers Sailing Boat Reunion'

CHICHESTER
908 Festivities

EASTBOURNE
Prudential County Cup Tennis
Carnival
Longest off-shore Dinghy Race in
the World

GOODWOOD
Glorious Goodwood

HASTINGS
Carnival

HICKSTEAD
Benson & Hedges European
Championships

August

ALFRISTON
Cider Fayre

ARUNDEL
Festival

EASTBOURNE
Eastbourne Show
Maritime Regatta
Cricket Week

HAILSAM
Sussex Rural Crafts & Small Industries
Exhibition

HASTINGS
National Town Criers Championships
Old Town Carnival & Regatta
Festival

HICKSTEAD
The Hambro Life Derby Showjumping
International

RYE
Carnival

SELSEY
Annual Crabbers Race

September

ALFRISTON
Festival of English Vineyard Wine

UCKFIELD
Bluebell Railway Vintage Weekend

October

BRIGHTON
International Tennis

EASTBOURNE
Autumn Flower Show

GOODWOOD
Horse Trials

HASTINGS
Hastings Day

November

BRIGHTON
London-Brighton RAC Veteran Car
Run

EASTBOURNE
Antiques Fair

LEWES
Lewes Bonfire Celebrations

Farms

When visiting a farm wear protective footwear and keep to marked paths.

APULDRAM MANOR FARM
Map 1 Ac
Chichester (0243) 782522
Apuldram, 1 m SW Chichester off
A286
Open: to view display of roses, June,
July & Aug, daily at any reasonable
time
Farm tours: by arrangement only,
groups (30) only (1 hour tour)
Charge: to view roses free, tour £1
(ch 50p)
Lunches & teas by arrangement, roses
for sale at garden centre
🅿 🍴 🚻

BATES GREEN FARM
Bluebell Walk & Farm Trail
See Woodland: Bluebell Walk

COOMBES CHURCH FARM
Map 2 AC
Shoreham (07917) 2028
Coombes, 1½m N Shoreham off
A283
Open: April-Oct, daily by arrangement
only
Charge: £1.20 (ch 60p, OAP &
students £1)
Groups welcome
No dogs
🍴 ♿ 🚻🪑

DOWER HOUSE FARM TRAIL
Map 3 Bb
Heathfield (04352) 2016
Blackboys, 3m E Uckfield off B2102
Open: all year, daily 8.00-dusk
Free: donations to Sussex Farming
and Wildlife Advisory Group
Groups by arrangement
Dogs on leads, leaflet available
🅿 🪑

NORTONS FARM MUSEUM &
FARM TRAIL
See Museums: Nortons Farm
Museum

WICKHAM MANOR FARM
Map 4 Bb
Winchelsea, SW of village on road to
Pett
Free access to public footpaths across
farmland
392 acres include large sections of
village of Winchelsea and 1½m
section of Royal Military Canal
Restored 15th century farmhouse
not open
NT

Gardens

Sussex has many beautiful gardens
which are open to the public. Many of
them are owned by the National Trust
or are attached to Historic Homes or
Castles. Others are privately owned.

NATIONAL GARDENS SCHEME
01-730 0359
57 Lower Belgrave St, London
SW1W OLR
This charitable trust receives its funds
from many gardens throughout
England and Wales. Most of them are
small, private gardens which open
only a few times a year. Some larger
gardens also contribute their takings
on particular days. Money raised helps
many causes, but particularly district
nurses in need, either because of old
age or illness or because of the stress
and pressure of their work.
   Those gardens which support the
scheme are indicated by the
initials NGS.

Gardens

It is not possible to list here all the gardens in Sussex which support the scheme since many of them are open only once a year. Included here are a selection of those open more often. The NGS publishes a booklet describing all the gardens in Sussex which support the scheme, as well as a booklet giving a complete list of all NGS gardens in England and Wales. To obtain copies of these booklets and for further information contact the address above.

ALFRISTON CLERGY HOUSE
See Historic Homes: Clergy House

APULDRAM MANOR FARM
See Farms: Apuldram Manor Farm

BATEMAN'S
Large peaceful garden containing restored watermill
See Historic Homes: Bateman's

BEECHES FARM
Map 3 Ab
Uckfield (08525) 2391
Uckfield, 1½ m W Uckfield on B2102
Open: all year, daily 10.00-17.00;
16th century farmhouse open by arrangement only
Charge: gdn 20p (ch 12 10p), guided tour of farmhouse 75p
Garden centre
□ ⚑ ⅄

BORDE HILL GARDEN
Map 2 Ba/p 54
Haywards Heath (0444) 450326
Balcombe, 1½m N Haywards Heath on B2036
Open: March & Oct, Sat & Sun; April-Sep, Wed, Thur, Sat, Sun & BHs 10.00-18.00
Charge: £1.00 (ch 30p), groups (20) 60p (must book)
Plants for sale
Dogs on leads
□ ⚑ ⅄ ✕ ⍽ ⅄

BRICKWALL HOUSE GARDEN
Map 4 Ab/p 70
Northiam (07974) 2494
Northiam, 12m N Hastings on A28
Open: late April-early July, most Weds & Sats 14.00-16.00, telephone curator for details, other times by arrangement
Charge: 50p (ch 25p)
No dogs

CHARLESTON MANOR GARDENS
Map 3 Ac/p 62
Alfriston (0323) 870267
Charleston, 1m S Alfriston
Open: May-Sep, Mon-Fri 11.00-17.00
(closed BHs & w/nds)
Charge: 75p (ch & OAP 50p)
No dogs
□

COBBLERS
Map 3 Ba
Crowborough (08926) 5969
Crowborough, 7½ m SW Tunbridge Wells, off B2100
Open: May-Aug, selected w/ends 14.30-18.00, telephone for details
Groups by arrangement
Charge: 70p (ch 40p)
No dogs
□ ⅄ ⍽

DENMANS
Map 1 Bc
Eastergate (024368) 2808
Denmans Lane, Fontwell, on A27
Open: late Feb-late Oct, Sat & Sun 14.00-18.00, other times by arrangement
Charge: 50p, group tours weekdays by arrangement £1
Plants for sale, teas for groups by arrangement
No lavatories
NGS □ ⅄ ⍽

FISHBOURNE ROMAN PALACE
Map 1 Ac/p 35
Formal garden replanted to original
1st century plan using plants of the
period
See Roman: Fishbourne Roman
Palace

GRAVETYE MANOR
Map 2 Ba/p 45
East Grinstead (0342) 810367
3m SW East Grinstead, off B2028
Open: all year, Tues & Fri
10.00-17.00
Free
Gardens surround Elizabethan manor
house, now a private hotel, limited
access by arrangement
🅿 ⌒✕ 𝖄

GREAT DIXTER
Garden containing variety of unusual
plants, notably herbaceous long border
See Historic Homes: Great Dixter

HEASELANDS
Map 2 Bb/p 55
Haywards Heath (0444) 454053
1m S Haywards Heath on A273
Open: May, selected Suns & Weds,
July selected Suns 14.00-18.30,
telephone for details
Charge: 75p (ch 25P)
Groups by arrangement in Oct only
(must book)
No dogs
NGS 🅿 🐾 ♿ ⌒

HIGH BEECHES
Map 2 Ba
Handcross (0444) 400589
1m E Handcross on B2110
Open: Spring BH Mons
10.30-18.00, Oct selected Sun
10.30-17.00 (telephone for details),
groups of 20 at other times by
arrangement
Charge: £1.20
Guided tour for groups
No dogs or picnics
🅿 🐾

HIGHDOWN
Map 2 Ac
Worthing (0903) 39999 x255
Highdown, 3m W Worthing off A259
Open: April-Sep, Mon-Sun;
Oct-March, Mon-Fri 8.00-16.30
Free: donations accepted
No dogs
NGS 🅿 ♿ ⌒

HOLLY GATE CACTUS GARDEN
Map 2 Ab
Ashington (0903) 892930
Billinghurst Lane, Ashington, 10m N
Worthing off A24
Open: all year, daily (closed Dec 25 &
26) 9.00-17.00
Charge: 40p (ch 25p)
Plants for sale
No dogs
NGS 🐾 ⌒

HORSTED PLACE GARDENS
Map 3 Ab
Isfield (082575) 315
1½m S Uckfield, 6m NE Lewes on
A26
Open: May-Sep, Wed, Thur, Sun &
BH 14.00-18.00
Charge: 70p (ch 35p)
No dogs
🅿 ♿ 🎪

KIDBROOKE PARK
Map 3 Aa/p 45
Forest Row (034282) 2275
Forest Row, 3m S East Grinstead on
A22
Open: Aug, daily 9.00-dusk
Charge: 30p
🅿 ♿

LAMB HOUSE
See Historic Homes: Lamb House

LEGH MANOR
Attractive garden good views
See Historic Homes: Legh Manor

LEONARDSLEE GARDENS
Map 2 Bb/p 55
Lower Beeding (040376) 212
Lower Beeding, ½m S of village, 4m
SE Horsham on A281
Open: late April-mid June, Wed, Thur,
Sat & Sun 10.00-18.00; May & Oct
w/ends & BHs 10.00-17.00
Charge: £1.50 (ch 50p); groups (20)
£1.20 (must book, no groups Suns,
May)
No dogs
NGS 🅿 🍴 🛒

NEWICK PARK
Map 3 Ab
Newick, 1m S village, 6m N Lewes
off A272
Open: end April-end Oct, Sat, Sun &
Mon 14.00-17.30
Charge: 75p (ch 25p)

NYMANS
Map 2 Ba/p 54
Handcross, S of village, 4½m
S Crawley off M23/A23
Open: April-Oct, Tues, Wed, Thurs,
Sat 14.00-1900; Sun & BHs 11.00-
19.00
Charge: £1 (ch 50p)
Groups by arrangement, 80p each
Dogs on lead
🅿 🍴 ♿ 🛒

PARHAM GARDENS
Map 2 Ab/p 72
Storrington (09066) 2866
1m W Storrington, 3m S Pulborough
off A283
Open: April-Oct, Wed, Thurs, Sat, Sun
& BHs 13.00-18.00
Charges: 75p (ch & OAP 60p)
No dogs
Elizabethan manor house with display
of rare needlework, antiques, paintings
Open by arrangement
See also Historic Homes: Parham
House
🅿 🍴 ♿ 🎪

PETWORTH HOUSE
700 acre deer park
See Historic Homes: Petworth
House

SHEFFIELD PARK GARDEN
Map 3 Ab/p 46
5m E Haywards Heath, 10m N Lewes
off A275
Open: April-mid Nov,
Tues-Sat 11.00-18.00, Sun & BHs
14.00-18.00 dusk if earlier (closed
Good Friday, BH Mon, Tues)
Charge: £1.60 (ch 80p) groups
£1.20 each (no reductions Sat, Sun,
BHs)
No dogs or picnics
NT 🅿 🍴 ♿ 🛒

STANDEN
Hillside garden with fine views
See Historic Homes: Standen

WAKEHURST PLACE GARDENS
Map 2 Ba/p 96
Ardingly (0444) 892701
1 m N Ardingly on B2028
Open: Nov, Dec (closed 25 Dec), Jan
10.00-16.00, Feb 10.00-17.00,
March 10.00-18.00, April-Sep
10.00-19.00, Oct 10.00-17.00
Charge: £1.25 (ch 60p) Group rate
except Sat, Sun, BHs (must book)
Ch under 10 must be accompanied
No dogs
NT 🅿 🍴 ♿ ⌂🎍

WEST DEAN GARDENS
Map 1 Ab/p 92
Singleton (024363) 301
6 m N Chichester on A286
Open: April-Sep, daily 13.00-18.00
Charge: 75p (ch 40p, OAP 65p)
Group rates (12 must book)
🅿 🍴 ♿ ⌂🎍

Golf Clubs

BEAUPORT PARK PUBLIC GOLF
COURSE
Map 4 Ab
Hastings (0424) 52977
The Ridge West, Hastings
18 Holes/undulating parkland/6282
yds
Par 71/SSS 71/pro
Visitors: anytime (public course)
Charge: w/days £3.25 (OAPs £2)
per round, w/ends & BHs £4
(OAPs £3) per round, weekly season
ticket £15
🅿 🍴 ⌂ ♀

BOGNOR REGIS GOLF CLUB
Map 1 Bc
Bognor Regis (0243) 865867
Downview Rd, Felpham, 1 m NE
Bognor Regis off A259
18 holes/parkland/6219 yds
Par 70/SSS 70/pro
Visitors: April-Sep must be with
member, other times must have
handicap certificate
Charge: w/days £6.50 per round,
w/ends £8 per round
🅿 🍴 ⌂ ♀

BRIGHTON & HOVE GOLF CLUB
Map 2 Bc
Brighton (0273) 556482
Dyke Rd, ½m NW Brighton
9 holes/downland/5722 yds
Par 68/SSS 68/no pro
Visitors: anytime (except Sun before
12.00, match days, etc), telephone
in advance
Charge: w/days 18 holes £5,
9 holes £3.50, £6 per day (under 18
£2.50, £1.25 & £3); Sat, Sun & BHs
18 holes £6, 9 holes £4 (under 18
£3, £1.50 & £3.50)
Practice ground 50p, trolley & club
hire
⌂ ♀

COODEN BEACH GOLF CLUB
Map 4 Ac
Cooden (04243) 2040
Cooden Beach, 1½m W Bexhill off
A259
18 holes/downland/6411 yds
Par 72/SSS 71/pro
Visitors: telephone in advance, must
have club membership &
handicap certificate
Charge: w/days £7.50,
w/ends £8.50
🅿 🍴 ⌂ ♀ ✗

COTTESMORE GOLF CLUB
Map2 Ba
Crawley (0293) 28256
Buchan Hill, Pease Pottage, ½m S
Crawley at junction M23 & A23
18 (18) holes/woodland/6097
(5321) yds
Par 71 (68)/SSS 70 (66)/pro
Visitors: anytime, telephone
in advance
Charges: w/days £6, w/ends £9;
members' guests w/days £3, w/ends
£4.50
🅿 ♀ ✗

COWDRAY PARK GOLF CLUB
Map 1 Bb
Midhurst (073081) 3599
1m NE Midhurst on A272
18 holes/parkland/6200yds
Par 70/SSS 70/pro
Visitors: anytime, telephone
in advance
Charge: w/days £6, w/ends £8;
members' guests w/days £3, w/ends
£4 (under 18 members £1)
🅿 🐾 ⌁ ♀ ✗

CROWBOROUGH BEACON GOLF CLUB
Map 3 Aa
Crowborough (08926) 4016
Beacon Road, 7m SW Tunbridge
Wells on A26
18 holes/heathland/6304 yds
Par 71/SSS 70/pro
Visitors: after 12.30, w/ends
Telephone in advance, must have
recognised handicap certificate
Charge: w/days £10 per day, £7 per
round, w/ends £7 per round
🅿 🐾 ♀

DALE HILL GOLF CLUB
Map 4 Aa
Ticehurst (0580) 200112
Ticehurst, 4m E Wadhurst on B2087
18 holes/6062 yds
Par 69/SSS 70/pro
Visitors: telephone in advance
Charge: w/days £7 per day, BHs &
w/ends £8 per day
🅿 🐾 ♀

DYKE GOLF CLUB
Map 2 Bc
Poynings (079156) 296
Dyke Rd, 4½ m NW Brighton
18 holes/downland/6519 yds
Par 72/SSS 71/pro
Visitors: restricted, telephone in
advance, must have handicap
certificate
Charge: w/days £7, w/ends £10
🅿 🐾 ⌁ ♀ ✗

EAST BRIGHTON GOLF CLUB
Brighton (0273) 603989
Roedean Rd, E Brighton off A27
18 holes/downland/6291 yds
Par 72/SSS 70/pro
Visitors: w/days, w/ends not before
11.30, must telephone in advance,
own clubs & neat dress required
Charge: w/days £6 per day, BHs &
w/ends £7.50
🅿 🐾 ⌁ ♀

EASTBOURNE DOWNS GOLF CLUB
Map3 Bc
Eastbourne (0323) 20827
East Dean Rd, ½m W of town on
A259
18 holes/seaside downland/6629
yds
Visitors: anytime (Sun after 11.00,
BHs after 9.30)
Charge: w/days £5 per day, w/ends
& BHs £6.75 per round
🅿 🐾 ⌁ ♀ ✗

EFFINGHAM PARK GOLF CLUB
Map 2 Ba
Copthorne (0342) 716528
Copthorne, 4m NE Crawley off A264
9 holes/parkland/1725 yds
Par 30/pro
Visitors: anytime
Charge: w/days 9 holes £2.50,
18 holes £3.50; w/ends 9 holes
£3.50, 18 holes £4.50 (under 18s
half price)
🅿 🐾 ⌁

FAIRWAY GOLF DRIVING RANGE
Map 2 Ba
Crawley (0293) 33000
Horsham Rd, Pease Pottage, 1½m S
Crawley off A23
Open: all year, daily 9.00-22.30
Membership: £10 per year
Charge: £1.10 or £2.20 depending
on number of balls (members 80p or
£1.60)
12 hole course, floodlit
🅿 🛅 ⛽ ⛾

GATWICK MANOR
Map 2 Ba
Crawley (0293) 24470
Lowfield Heath, 1m S Gatwick Airport
on A23
9 holes/parkland/1109yds
Par 3/SSS 27/pro
Visitors: anytime
Charge: w/days 75p, w/ends & BHs
£1
Suitable for beginners
🅿 🛅 ⛽ ⛾

GOODWOOD GOLF CLUB
Map 1 Ab
Chichester (0243) 774968
Goodwood, 5m N Chichester off
A286
18 holes/downland-parkland/6370
yds
Par 72/SSS 70/pro
Visitors: anytime, telephone
in advance
Charge: w/days £6, w/ends &
BHs £9
🅿 🛅 ⛽ ⛾

HAM MANOR GOLF CLUB
Map 2 Ac
Rustington (0935) 3288
Angmering, 4m W Worthing
off A280
18 holes/parkland/6216 yds
Par 70/SSS 70/pro
Visitors: anytime
Charge: w/days £8, w/ends £12
Special package for 4 people
comprising 2 rounds of golf, coffee,
lunch & tea £11 (by arrangement)
🅿 🛅 ⛽ ⛾

HASTINGS PUBLIC GOLF COURSE
Map 4 Ac
Hastings (0424) 52977/52981
Beauport Park, St Leonards-on-Sea,
2½m N Hastings on A2100
18 holes/undulating parkland/
607 yds
Par 70/SSS 70/pro
Visitors: anytime (public course)
Charge: w/days £3.25, w/ends £4
(under 18s £2, 2.50); 9 holes
£2.25 (after 3.00)
🅿 🛅 ⛽ ⛾ ✕

HAYWARDS HEATH GOLF CLUB
Map 2 Bb
Haywards Heath (0444) 414457
High Beech Lane, 2m N Haywards
Heath off B2028
18 holes/parkland/6202 yds
Par 71/SSS 70/pro
Visitors: telephone in advance
Charge: w/days £7.50, w/ends &
BHs £9
🅿 🛅 ⛽ ⛾ ✕

HIGHWOODS GOLF CLUB
Map 4 Ac
Bexhill-on-Sea (0424) 212625
Ellerslie Lane, 1m NW Bexhill-on-Sea
off A259
18 holes/parkland/6218 yds
Par 70/SSS 70/pro
Visitors: telephone in advance, must
have membership of other club &
handicap certificate
Charge: w/days £7.50 per round or
per day, w/ends £8 (members' guests
half price)
🅿 🛅 ⛽ ⛾ ✕

HILL BARN PUBLIC GOLF COURSE
Map 2 Ac
Worthing (0903) 37301
Hill Barn Lane, 1m N Worthing
off A27
18 holes/downland/6224 yds
Par 70/SSS 69/pro
Visitors: anytime (public course)
Charge: w/days £3.80, w/ends
£4.90
🅿 🛅 ⛽ ⛾ ✕

HOLLINGBURY PARK GOLF CLUB
Map 2 Bc
Brighton (0273) 552010
Ditchling Rd, ¾m N Brighton centre
18 holes/links/6415 yds
Par 69/SSS 71/pro
Visitors: anytime, telephone
in advance
Charge: w/days £3.70 per round,
£4.60 per day; w/ends £4.60 per
round, £2.80 after 4.00 (under 18s &
OAPs w/days only £1.90); reductions
for the unemployed
🅿 🏌 ☕ ♀ ✕

HOLTYE COMMON GOLF CLUB
Map 3 Aa
Cowden (034286) 635
Cowden, 4m E East Grinstead
off A264
9 holes/heathland/5265 yds
Par 66/SSS 66/pro
Visitors: w/days, w/ends (telephone
in advance)
Charge: w/days £4.25, w/ends
£6.50
🅿 🏌 ♀ (weekends only)

IFIELD GOLF CLUB
Map 2 Ba
Crawley (0293) 20222
Rusper Rd, Ifield, ½m W Crawley
off A23
18 holes/parkland/6265 yds
Par 70/SSS 70/pro
Visitors: w/days telephone in
advance, w/ends with member only,
must have other club membership
Charge: w/days £5.50 per round,
£7.50 per day (with member £3, £6);
w/ends £6
Squash courts & snooker
🅿 🏌 ♀ ✕

LITTLEHAMPTON GOLF CLUB
Map 1 Bc
Littlehampton (09064) 7170
Riverside West, 1m W Littlehampton
off A259
18 holes/links/6145 yds
Par 70/SSS 69/Pro
Visitors: telephone in advance
Charge: w/days £7, w/ends £8
🅿 🏌 ☕ ♀ ✕

MANNINGS HEATH GOLF CLUB
Map 2 Aa
Horsham (0403) 66217
Goldings Lane, Mannings Heath, 3m
SE Horsham on A281
18 holes/undulating heathland/
402 yds
Par 73/SSS 71/pro
Visitors: Oct-March, w/days only;
w/ends April-Sep telephone in
advance, must have handicap
certificate
Charge: w/days £7 per day, w/ends
& BHs £9
🅿 🏌 ☕♀ ✕

LEWES GOLF CLUB
Map 3 Ac
Lewes (07916) 3074
Chapel Hill, ½ E Lewes off A27
18 holes/downland/5800 yds
Par 71/SSS 68/pro
Visitors: w/days & w/ends (not before 10.30)
Charge: w/days £5, w/ends £7
🅿 🖳 ♟

PEACEHAVEN GOLF CLUB
Newhaven (07912) 4049
Brighton Rd, W Newhaven on A259
18 (9) holes/downland/5473 yds
Par 67/SSS 66/no pro
Visitors: w/days anytime, w/ends not before 12.00
Charge: w/days £3, w/ends £4.50
🅿 🖳 ⛌ ♟ ✕

PILTDOWN GOLF CLUB
Map 3 Ab
Newick (082572) 2033
Uckfield, 1 m SW Maresfield off A272
18 holes/heathland/6045 yds
Par 68/SSS 69/pro
Visitors: w/ends & BHs (telephone or write in advance)
Charge: £7.50 per day or round
🅿 🖳 ⛌ ♟ ✕

PYECOMBE GOLF CLUB
Map 2 Bb
Hassocks (07918) 4176
Clayton Hill, Pyecombe, 4m
N Brighton on A273, ½m N junction
A23 & A273
18 holes/downland/6207 yds
Par 71/SSS 70/pro
Visitors: w/days after 9.15, Sat after 10.00, Sun & BHs after 11.00
Charge: w/days £6, w/ends & BHs £8
🅿 🖳 ⛌ ♟ ✕

ROYAL ASHDOWN FOREST GOLF CLUB
Map 3 Aa
Forest Row (034282) 2018
½m S Forest Row off A22
18 (18) holes/5161 (6168) yds
Par 69 (72)/SSS 67 (71)/pro
Visitors: w/days except Tues, w/ends telephone in advance, must have handicap certificate & letter of introduction
Charge: w/days £9.50, w/ends £10.50
🅿 🖳 ♟ ✕

ROYAL EASTBOURNE GOLF CLUB
Map 3 Bc
Eastbourne (0323) 30412
Paradise Drive, Eastbourne, ½m W of town off A 259
18 (9) holes/undulating downland/6084 (2147 x2) yds
Par 70 (64)/SSS 69 (61)/pro
Visitors: anytime, telephone in advance, must have handicap certificate
Charge: w/days £7.50, w/end & BHs £8 (9 holes £5.50); reduced rates after 4.30
🅿 🖳 ♟ ✕

RYE GOLF CLUB
Map 4 Bb
Rye (0797) 225241
1 m SE Rye
18 holes/links/6301 yds
Par 68/SSS 71/pro
Visitors: introduction by member only
Charge: £8.50 per round, £11.50 per day
🅿 🖳 ⛌ ♟ ✕

SEAFORD GOLF CLUB
Map 3 Ac
Seaford (0323) 892597
Firle Rd, Blatchington, 1¼m
N Seaford off A 259
18 holes/downland/6330 yds
Par 69/SSS 72/pro
Visitors: anytime (not before 13.00 w/ends), telephone in advance
Charge: £8
🅿 🖳 ♟ ✕

SEAFORD HEAD GOLF COURSE
Seaford (0323) 890139
Southdown Rd, Seaford, E of town
off A259
18 holes/undulating downland/
5812 yds
Par 70/SSS 68/pro
Visitors: anytime, handicap certificate
useful
Charge: £4 per round w/days, £5
w/ends & BHs
🅿 🎦 ♀ ✕

SELSEY GOLF CLUB
Map 1 Ac
8m S Chichester on B2145
Selsey (0243) 602203
9 holes/flat seaside/5730 yds
Visitors: anytime (except Mon
mornings)
Charge: w/days £5 per round, £7
per day, w/ends £6 per round, £8
per day
🅿 🎦 ☕ ♀ ✕

TILGATE FOREST GOLF COURSE
Map 2 Ba
Crawley (0293) 30103
Tilgate, ½m S Crawley on M23
9 holes/wooded heathland/6278 yds
Par 72/SSS 70/pro
Visitors: anytime, telephone
in advance
Charges: w/days £3.50 per round,
£5 per day (£1.50 after 18.00),
w/ends £5 per round
🅿 🎦 ☕ ♀ ✕

WATERHALL GOLF COURSE
Map 2 Bc
Brighton (0273) 508658
Devils Dyke Rd, ½m NW Brighton off
B2038
18 holes/hilly downland/5626 yds
Par 68/SSS 67/pro
Visitors: anytime (Sun mornings
telephone in advance)
Charge: w/days £3.75 per round,
£4.60 per day, w/ends £4.60
🅿 🎦 ♀ ✕

WEST HOVE GOLF CLUB
Map 2 Bc
Brighton (0273) 413494
369 Old Shoreham Rd, Brighton on
A27
18 holes/downland/6130 yds
Par 69/SSS 69/pro
Visitors: w/days anytime, w/ends
must have handicap certificate
Charge: w/days £6, w/ends £8
(under 18s £2.50, members' guests
£2.50)
🅿 🎦 ♀ ✕

WEST SUSSEX GOLF CLUB
Map 2 Ab
Pulborough (07982) 2563
Pulborough, 2m SE Pulborough off
A283
18 holes/heathland/6131 yds
Par 67/SSS 70/pro
Visitors: telephone in advance
Charge: w/days £10, w/ends & BHs
£12
🅿 🎦 ♀ ✕

WILLINGDON GOLF CLUB
Map 3 Bc
Eastbourne (0323) 638728
Southdown Rd, Eastbourne, ½m N of
town on A22
18 holes/downland/6049 yds
Par 69/SSS 69/pro
Visitors: with member only, w/ends
must have letter of introduction or
handicap certificate
Charge: w/days £7.25, w/ends &
BHs £8
🅿 🎦 ☕ ♀ ✕

WORTHING GOLF CLUB
Map 2 Ac
Worthing (0903) 60801
Links Rd, Worthing, N of town on
A24
18 (18) holes/downland/6470
(5700) yds
Par 71 (64)/SSS 71 (66)/pro
Visitors: telephone in advance
Charge: w/days £8, after 16.00 £6
(with member £4, £3); w/ends £12,
after 16.00 £6 (with member £6, £3)
🅿 🎦 ☕ ♀ ✕

Grass Skiing

BRIGHTON GRASS SKI CENTRE
Brighton (0273) 552476
Waterhall Park, Brighton
200 metre slope at Moulsecombe,
Brighton on A27
Open: April-Oct, Sun 12.00-dusk
Charge: Grillson skis (beginners)
80p per hr, Rollka skis £1.60 per hr,
boots 40p per hr, lift (150 metres)
50p per hr
Informal instruction if needed
Old clothes & thick socks advised

BRIGHTON GRASS SKI CLUB
Secretary: Ms Bartlett
Brighton (0273) 605507

Greyhound Racing

BRIGHTON STADIUM
Map 2 Bc/p 29
Neville Park House, Brighton
Meetings: all year, Thurs & Sat
19.45
Charge: £2.40 (restaurant enclosure);
£1.50 (main enclosure); £1 (popular
enclosure)
🅿 ⛀ ♀ ✗

Gymnastics

**AMATEUR GYMNASTICS
ASSOCIATION**
c/o The Sports Council, Greater
London & SE Region
01-580 9092/7
160 Great Portland St, London W1
5TB
This is the governing body for the
sport in Britain.

BEVENDEAN G.C.
Secretary: Mrs B Howell
Brighton (0273) 682886
94 The Highway, Moulsecomb,
Brighton

BOGNOR G.C.
Secretary: Mrs S Moore
Pagham (02432) 4584
20, Anson Rd, Rose Green, Bognor

**BRIGHTON SCHOOL OF
GYMNASTICS**
Secretary: Mr P Niblett
Brighton (0273) 602315
79 The Avenue, Moulsecomb,
Brighton BN2 4GG

CRAWLEY BOYS GYMNASTICS
Secretary: Mrs G Monk
Smallfield (034284) 2174
Homestead Farm, Redehall Rd,
Smallfield, Surrey

DURRINGTON G.C.
Secretary: Mrs S Clarke
Rustington (09062) 3049
Overdale, Lansdowne Close,
Angmering

HENFIELD G.C.
Secretary: Mrs P Edwards
Henfield (0273) 492920
16, Lower Faircox, Henfield

HOLLINGTON G.C.
Secretary: Mr M Haslin
Hastings (0424) 52371
1 Wishing Tree Close,
St Leonards-on-Sea

LANCING G.C.
Secretary: Mrs P Ryan
Worthing (0903) 60005
28 Salvington Gardens, Worthing

LANCING MANOR G.C.
Secretary: Mr G Jones
Worthing (0903) 30773
37 Church Walk, Worthing

PORTSLADE
Secretary: Mrs C Robinson
Brighton (0273) 414936
2 Meads Avenue, Hove

LITTLEHAMPTON G.C.
Secretary: Mrs J Mason
Middleton-on-Sea (024369) 4905
7 Alfriston Close, Middleton-on-Sea,
Bognor

SOUTHDOWN OLYMPIC G.C.
Secretary: Mrs M Hopewell
Middleton-on-Sea (024369) 5409
Bardo Hopa, 15 Flansham Lane,
Bognor Regis

SUMMERFIELDS G.C.
Secretary: Mrs I Poole
Hastings (0424) 431967
c/o Hastings Sports Centre
Bohemia Rd, Hastings

CRAWLEY GIRLS
Secretary: Mrs M Harrold
Crawley (0923) 514777
2 Gales Drive, Three Bridges, Crawley

CHELSEA G.C.
Secretary: Miss F Smith
Eastbourne (0323) 21400
Chelsea School of Human Movement,
Brighton Polytechnic, Denton Rd,
Eastbourne

Hill Figures

Cut into the chalky soil of the Wessex landscape, the origins of these mysterious and spectacular hill figures remain obscure. They have been linked to pagan rites, battles and even the unexplained 'ley lines' which cross the country. Take care not to walk on the edge of the figures as this causes erosion

DITCHLING CROSS
Map 2 Bb/p 40
Ditchling Cross, 5m W Lewes, S Ditchling off B2116
Visible from the north, the cross spans one hundred feet and is probably connected to the defeat of Henry III by Simon de Montfort at the Battle of Lewes, 1264

LITLINGTON HORSE
Map 3 Bc
Windover Hill, Litlington E Alfriston off B2108
Cut in 1920s to replace the 1838 horse which is believed to have been cut in celebration of Queen Victoria's coronation; visible from Beachy Head

LONG MAN OF WILMINGTON
Map 3 Bc/p 99
Windover Hill, nr Eastbourne, 1½m W Polegate off A27
The origin of this slim figure clutching a staff on each side remains unknown, though local legend speaks of the giant of Windover Hill who was killed by the Firle Beacon giant and lies where he fell

Historic Homes

ANNE OF CLEVES HOUSE
See Museums: Anne of Cleves House

BATEMANS
Map 3 Bb/p 32
Burwash, ½m SW town on A265
Open: Oct, March-May, Sat-Thur
14.00-18.00 (last admission 17.30);
June-Sep, Mon-Thur 11.00-18.00,
Sat-Sun 14.00-18.00
Charge: house, mill & gdn £1.40
(ch 70p), groups £1.10 each, must
book
Indoor photography with
permission, restored mill in working
order, grain on sale
No dogs or picnics
NT ⓟ ⓔ ⓖ ⌷

BRICKWALL HOUSE
See Gardens: Brickwall House

BRIDGE COTTAGE
Map 3 Ab
Nutley (082571) 2632
High St, Uckfield, on A22
Open: all year, Sat 10.00-16.00;
groups by arrangement at other
times
Free: donations accepted
No dogs
ⓟ ⓔ

BRIGHTON ROYAL PAVILION
Map 2 Bc/p 24
Brighton (0273) 603005
Open: all year, daily 10.00-17.30;
early June-late Sep 10.00-19.30
(closed 25 & 26 Dec, 1 Jan)
Charge: £1.35 (ch 60p, OAPs 95p),
reduction for groups
Guided tours
No dogs
ⓟ ⓔ ⓖ ⌷

CHARLESTON MANOR
See Gardens: Charleston Manor
Gardens

CLERGY HOUSE
Map 3 Ac/p 7
Alfriston (0323) 870001
Alfriston, 4m NE Seaford,
off B2108
Open: early April-late Oct, daily
11.00-18.00 (dusk if earlier)
Charge: 50p (ch 25p), groups must
book (20 people in house at any
time)
No dogs, parking in village
NT ⓔ

COURT HALL
See Museums: Court Hall

COWDRAY HOUSE (RUINS)
Map 1 Bb/p 67
Midhurst (073081) 2215
Open: April-Oct, Fri-Tues
10.30-17.00 (telephone in advance)
Charge: 40p (ch 25p)
Museum

DANNY HOUSE
Map 2 Bb/p 58
Hurstpierpoint (0273) 833000
Hurstpierpoint off B2116
Open: May-Sep, Wed & Thur
14.00-17.00
Charge: 50p (ch 25p)
ⓟ ⓔ

FIRLE PLACE
Map3 Ac/p 98
Glynde (079159) 335
Firle, 5m SE Lewes on A27
Open: June-Sep, Mon & Wed,
Easter, spring & summer BHs
14.00-17.00
Charge: £1.50 (ch 70p),
Connoisseurs' Day £1.60; groups
(25) £1 each
Guided tours, Connoisseurs' Day
first Wed in every month
ⓟ ⓔ ⓖ ⌷

GLYNDE PLACE
Map 3 Ac/p 47
Lewes (07916) 71743
Glynde, 2 m SE Lewes off A27
Open: late May-late Oct, Easter
Sun & Mon, May 1, spring &
autumn BHs (telephone in
advance) 14.15-17.30, last
admission 17.00
Charge: £1.30 (ch 65p);
Connoisseurs' Day £1.30; groups
(20) 95p each
Connoisseurs' Day last Wed
in month
No dogs
🅿 🐾 ⊑🎋

GOODWOOD HOUSE
Map 1 Bb/p 36
Chichester (0243) 774107
Goodwood, 3½m NE Chichester off
A286
Open: mid May-July,Oct, Sun &
Mon; Aug, Tues-Thurs; BHs (closed
selected days Sep) 14.00-17.00
Charge: £1.50 (ch 90p, disabled
90p); groups (20) £1.15 by
arrangement (write: Goodwood
House, Goodwood, West Sussex)
Open for special event
No dogs
🅿 ⊑

GRAVETYE MANOR
See Gardens: Gravetye Manor

GREAT DIXTER
Map 4 Ab/p 71
Northiam (07974) 3160
Northiam, 8m NW Rye, ½m N
Northiam off A28
Open: April-mid Oct, Tue-Sun &
BHs, selected days late Oct
14.00-17.00
Charge: house & gdn £1.30
(ch 40p); groups (20) 95p by
arrangement; gdn 65p (ch 20p);
OAPs & NT members 95p (Fri only)
Guided tours, plants for sale
No dogs
🅿 🐾🎋

HAREMERE HALL
Map 4 Ab/p 45
Etchingham (058081) 245/275
½m N Etchingham on A265
Open: BH Suns & Mons
12.30-17.30, other times by
arrangement for groups (20)
Charge: £1.25 (ch 12 65p)
Facilities: teas for groups by
arrangement, no dogs
See also Unusual Outings: The
Sussex Shire Horses
🅿

KIDBROOKE PARK
See Gardens: Kidbrooke Park

LAMB HOUSE
Map 4 Bb/p 83
West Street, Rye
Open: April-Oct, Wed & Sat
14.00-18.00 last admission 17.30
(closed Good Friday)
Charge: house & gdn 70p
No lavatories
NT

LEGH MANOR
Map 2 Bb/p 54
Lewes (07916) 4379
Ansty (nr Cuckfield), 2 m W
Haywards Heath off B2036
Open: April-Oct selected Wed &
Sat 14.30-17.30 (telephone for
details)
Charge: 40p (ch 20p)
No dogs
SAS

MONKS HOUSE
Map 3 Ac
**Rodmell, 2½m S Lewes off C7 in
Rodmell village**
Open: April-end Oct, Wed & Sat
14.00-18.00 (last admissions
17.30)
Charge: 90p
15 people in house at any time
No lavatories
NT

NEWTIMBER PLACE
Map 2 Bb/p 79
Hurstpierpoint (0273) 833104
Newtimber, 4m N Brighton off A23
Open: May-Aug, Thur 14.00-17.00
(other times by arrangement)
Charge: 80p, reduction for groups
(15)
🅿

OLD MINT HOUSE
Map 3 Bc
Eastbourne (0323) 762337
High St, Pevensey
Open: all year, Mon-Sat 9.00-17.00
(closed Sun, BHs, 25 & 26 Dec, 1
Jan)
Charge: 30p (ch 10p)
🅿 🍴

PARHAM
See Gardens: Parham

PETWORTH HOUSE
Map 1 Bb/p 72
Petworth, 5½m E Midhurst
off A283
Open: April-end Oct, Sat, Sun,
Tue-Thur & BH 14.00-18.00
Charge: £1.60 (ch 65p),
Connoisseurs' Day £2 (ch £1);
group reductions Wed, Thur & Sat
by arrangement
Connoisseurs' Day Tues (extra
rooms)
No dogs, prams or pushchairs
NT 🅿 🍴 ♿ 🛍🍴

PRESTON MANOR
Map 2 Bc/p 26
Brighton (0273) 603005/552101
Preston Park, N Brighton off A 23
Open: all year (closed 25 & 26
December, 1 Jan & Good Fri),
Wed-Sat 10.00-17.00, Sun
14.00-17.00
Charge: 75p (ch 45p, OAP 60p),
groups (20) 70p
No dogs
🅿 🍴

PRIESTS HOUSE
Map 3 Aa/p 98
Sharpthorne (0342) 810479
West Hoathly, 4m NE Haywards
Heath off B2028
Open: April-Sep, Mon-Thur & Sat
11.00-17.00, Sun 14.00-17.00
Charge: 50p (ch25p),groups by
arrangement
No lavatories
SAS

ST MARYS & THE NATIONAL BUTTERFLY MUSEUM
Map 2 Ab/p 21
Steyning (0903) 813158
Bramber, 3m N Shoreham-by-Sea
on A283
Open: early April-late Oct, daily
11.00-18.00; early Nov-late March,
Sat & Sun 11.00-17.00 (closed 25
& 26 Dec)
Charge: £1.15 (ch 65p, OAPs 75p);
groups (25) 75p (ch 65p),
telephone in advance
🅿 🍴 🖥

SACKVILLE COLLEGE
Map 3 Aa/p 44
East Grinstead (0342) 21639
High Street, East Grinstead
Open: early May-late Sep, Mon-Fri
& Sun 14.00-17.00
Charge: 50p (ch 25p), groups by
written arrangement
Guided tours of common room,
dining hall & chapel
No dogs
🅿 ♿

SHEFFIELD PARK
Map 3 Ab/p 46
Danehill (0825) 790531
5m E Haywards Heath off A275
Open: early May-late Oct, Wed,
Thur, Sun, BHs, Easter Sun & Mon
14.00-17.00
Charge: £1, groups (30) 75p by
arrangement
🅿 🍴

STANDEN
Map 3 Aa/p 44
East Grinstead, 1½m S town
off B2110
Open: April-Oct, Wed, Thur & Sat
14.00-17.30 (closed BHs & Good
Fri)
Charge: £1.20, gdn only 60p
No dogs in house
NT 🏠

UPPARK
Map 1 Ab/p 94
South Harting, 5m SE Petersfield,
1m S village on B2146
Open: April-Sep, Wed, Thur, Sun &
BH Mons (closed Good Fri)
14.00-18.00 (last admission 17.00)
Charge: £1.40, group reductions
by arrangement in writing with the
administration
Guided tour for all visitors Wed
NT 🏠 ☕

FONTWELL PARK
RACECOURSE
Map 1 Bc
Haywards Heath
(0444) 50989/51597
2m E Chichester off A27
Meetings: 15 per year
Charge: £2 enclosure, £4 tattersall
stand, £6 club (ch 16 free, not
tattersall)
National Hunt racing
🅿 ☕ 🍷 ✕

GOODWOOD RACECOURSE
Map 1 Ac/p 37
Chichester (0243) 774107
Goodwood, N Chichester off A286
Meetings: May-Sep, first race 14.00
Charge: July meetings, £7.50
grandstand & paddock, £2.50
paddock enclosure, £1 trundle
enclosure; other meetings £5.50,
£2, members badge £8.50; groups
reductions by arrangement
🅿 ☕ 🍷 ✕

PLUMPTON RACECOURSE
Map 3 Ab/p 78
Haywards Heath (0444) 450989
N Brighton on A2116
Meetings: Jan-Dec, 17 per year
Charge: £2 enclosure, £4 tattersall
stand, £6 club (ch 16 free, not
tattersall)
National Hunt Racing
🅿 ☕ 🍷 ✕

Horseracing

BRIGHTON RACECOURSE
Map 2 Bc/p 29
Brighton (0273) 682912/603580
Elm Grove, East Brighton
Meetings: April-Oct, 17 per year
Charge: £6 (£2) club enclosure, £4
tattersall stand, £2.50 grandstand,
£2 car park; group reductions (20)
Membership: £50 per year,
includes admission to Fontwell,
Goodwood & Plumpton
🅿 ☕ 🍷 ✕

Lifeboats

ROYAL NATIONAL LIFEBOAT INSTITUTE
SE Regional Office
Uckfield (0825) 61466
River House, Bell Lane, Uckfield,
Sussex
The RNLI was founded in the
1820s in order to provide a rescue
service for Britain's coastal waters.
Since then over 90,000 lives have
been saved as a result of this
charity.

When the local coastguard calls
out a lifeboat, a crew of mainly
volunteers could be risking their
lives to save others. Yet there is
never any shortage of local sailors
to crew the lifeboats and many
volunteers follow a family tradition
of service.

There are 200 lifeboat stations
on Britain's coast and they cost the
RNLI £17 million a year to run. This
vast sum of money comes entirely
from contributions given by the
public. Volunteers are always
needed to help raise these funds. If
you would like to help raise money,
or if you wish to make a donation,
or if you want to know more about
the RNLI contact the address
above.

Sussex has eight lifeboats most
of which can be seen at selected
times.

BRIGHTON
'Lions International' Atlantic 21
lifeboat moored inside Brighton
Marina

EASTBOURNE
Founded in 1822 this is the oldest
station housing the 'Duke of Kent'
not open to the public but
Eastbourne does have the first
permanent lifeboat museum in Old
Lifeboat House, Wish Tower in
memory of the actor William Ferris
See also Museums: Lifeboat
Museum

HASTINGS
Lifeboat house containing the
'Fairlight' beyond fish market on
beach by the Old Town
See also Museums: The Lifeboat
Museum

LITTLEHAMPTON
Inflatable craft bought by Blue
Peter is named 'Blue Peter 1' an
Atlantic 21
Open: occasionally

NEWHAVEN
Moored on river, the 'Louis
Marchesi of Round Table' can be
viewed at any time. The station
itself established in 1803 is one of
the oldest but not open

RYE HARBOUR
Small inflatable, open at times

SELSEY
Original lifeboat house built in
1861, due to erosion of coastline a
new one erected 1960. 'Charles
Henry'
Open: Sat 10.00-12.00 &
14.00-16.30

SHOREHAM HARBOUR
Located on Kingston beach off
A259 between Shoreham &
Southwick, opposite harbour
entrance. 'The Davys Family'
lifeboat
Open: Whitsun-mid Sep, Sat & Sun
14.15-17.30

Marinas

BRIGHTON MARINA
Map 2 Bc/p 29
Brighton (0273) 693636
Off Madeira Drive, Brighton, 1 m E
Palace Pier
Open: all year, daily 9.00-dusk
Charge: entrance 50p (ch & OAP
25p); group rate (20) 40p (ch & OAP
20p); educational groups 20p; guided
tours for groups from £9 (for group);
car parking fee 75p per hour, £1.50
per day, coach parking £6 per day
(10-seater), £12 per day (20-seater)
Water sports, fish farm, boat yard,
charter fishing boats, historic boats,
exhibition moorings, yacht brokerage
Events held here include Brighton
Marina Boat Show (May); National
Squib Championship (last week June);
Brighton Marina Powerboat Race
(July); Old Gaffers Rally & Races
(August); Brighton Marina, Yacht Club
Regatta (August)
See also: Water Skiing, Windsurfing,
Boat Trips, Sailing
🅿 🐾 ⚒ 🛏 ✕ ⚲

Markets

Markets are an important aspect of
rural life and Sussex offers a wide
variety. It is possible to buy fresh fruit
and vegetables from the farms;
antique markets and flea markets are
plentiful as are more general markets
selling an enormously wide range of
goods from street stalls.

Go early if you want to buy fresh
produce or catch a real bargain.

Markets which are labelled General,
WI or Livestock are explained below,
other descriptions, such as Antiques,
are self-explanatory.

GENERAL
General markets offer a wide range of
inexpensive new goods from clothing
and bedding to jewellery and china; in
addition many of these markets also
sell fresh food including meat and
vegetables and have stalls selling such
things as sweets and cosmetics.

WI
Women's Institute markets are run by
members of the institute and usually
sell home-made foods such as jams
and cakes, pot plants and other home
produced products.

LIVESTOCK
These are the markets to which
farmers bring their sheep, cattle and
other animals for selling and to buy
livestock through auctions.

ARUNDEL
Antiques Market: daily 9.00-17.00,
Sat 9.30-17.00
River Road

BATTLE
General: Fri 10.00-16.00; Sat
9.30-15.00, car park rear of
56 High St
WI: Fri 9.45-11.30, Langton
Memorial Hall

BEEDING & BAMBER
WI: Fri (summer only) 15.00-16.30,
Village Hall, High St

BEXHILL
General: Tue 9.00-16.00, Marina,
Wilton Rd

BOSHAM
WI: Fri 9.30-10.30 (summer
9.30-11.00)

BRIGHTON
General: Mon 8.00-12.00, Tue-Sat
8.00-17.00, London Rd; Sat
8.00-13.00, Upper Gardner St;
BH Mons 10.00-17.00, Racecourse
Paintings: daily (May-Sep)
10.00-dusk

BURGESS HILL
General: Wed & Sat 9.30-16.30,
adjoining Martlets shopping precinct

BURWASH
WI: Tue 10.30-11.00, Village Hall

CHICHESTER
General/Livestock: Wed
9.00-12.00, Cattle Market, Eastgate;
Mon-Sat 8.00-15.30,
Thur 8.30-13.00, Butter Market,
North St
WI: Tue-Sat 8.00-15.00
(half day Thur), Butter Market,
North St

CRAWLEY
General: Fri & Sat 9.00-17.00,
Orchard St
WI: Thur 9.30-11.00, St John's
Ambulance Hut, Orchard St
Street: Sat 9.00-16.30, High St

CROWBOROUGH
WI: Fri 7.30-12.00, Community
Assoc. Hall, The Broadway

DURRINGTON
WI: Thur 10.30-11.30, Church Hall,
New Rd

EAST GRINSTEAD
Street: Sat 9.00-16.00,
Cantelupe Rd

FELPHAM
WI: Fri 10.00-11.30, Memorial
Village Hall, Vicarage Lane

FERRING
WI: Wed 10.00-11.30, Village Hall,
Ferring St

HAILSHAM
General/Livestock: Wed
8.00-13.00, Market St
WI: Fri 9.30-11.30, St Wilfred's
Church Hall, South Rd

HASTINGS
General: Mon-Sat 9.00-17.00,
Wed 9.00-13.00, George St
WI: Fri 10.00-11.30, All Saints
Church Hall, All Saints St

HAYWARDS HEATH
Livestock: Tue 9.00-16.30, Market
Place
General: Sun 10.00-14.00, Market
Place

HEATHFIELD
General: Tue 9.30-13.00, Sat 10.00-
13.00 by Crown Inn

HENFIELD
WI: Sat (summer only) 9.30-11.30,
Village Hall

HORSHAM
WI: Fri 8.15-14.00, Piries Place,
Carfax
General: Sat 8.00-17.00, Central
Market, Carfax

LANCING
WI: Fri 9.30-11.00, R.C. Church Hall,
North Rd

LEWES
Livestock/General: Mon
10.00-14.00, Garden St
WI: Tue 7.30-12.30, Market Tower

LINDFIELD
WI: Thur 10.00-11.30, King Edward
Hall, High St

LITTLEHAMPTON
General: Fri & Sat 9.00-17.00,
Surrey St

MIDHURST
WI: Fri 9.00-11.30, PO Car Park,
Grange Rd

NEWICK
WI: Fri 10.00-11.00, Village Hall,
Western Rd

NINFIELD & HOOE
WI: Fri 10.00-11.30, Reading Room,
Church Lane

NYETIMBER
WI: Pagham Cricket Pavilion,
Nyetimber Lane, Thur 10.00-11.00

PETWORTH
WI: Fri 10.00-12.00,
Leconfield Hall, The Square

PEVENSEY BAY
WI: Fri 10.30-11.30 (May-Dec),
St Wilfred's Church Hall

ROTTINGDEAN
WI: Fri 10.00-11.30, Whiteway
Centre, Whiteway Lane

RUSTINGTON
WI: Thur 10.00-11.00, Leconfield
Hall, The Square

RYE
General: Thur 9.00-16.00, Rope Walk
Livestock: Wed 8.00-14.00, Rope
Walk
WI: Fri 10.00-10.30 (March-Dec),
Community Centre, Conduit Hill
Antiques: daily 10.00-17.30, Pocket
Full of Rye, Strand Warehouses; Wed,
Thur, Sat (daily in summer)
9.30-16.30, Old Dairy Market, Cinque
Ports St

SELSEY
WI: Tue (summer only) 10.00-11.30,
barn behind Fire Station

SOUTHWICK
WI: Fri 10.00-11.30, Craft Room,
Community Centre

STAPLECROSS
WI: Fri 10.00-11.00, Village Hall,
Northern Rd

STEYNING
WI: Fri (summer only) 9.30-12.00,
Penfold Church Hall, Church St

STORRINGTON
WI: Fri 9.00-12.00, Village Hall,
West St

WICK
WI: Fri 10.00-11.00, Small Church
Hall, Wick St

WINCHELSEA
WI: Fri 9.30-11.00 (summer only),
Castle St

WORTHING
General: Sat 9.00-16.30, Surrey St

Mills

ARGOS HILL WINDMILL
Map 3 Ba
1 m N Mayfield, on high ground close
to junction of A267 & B2101
View from outside only; built 1835,
post mill restored to near working
condition with fantail, roundhouse &
collection of tools

BATEMANS
See Historic Homes: Batemans

BEACON HILL WINDMILL
Map 2 Bc
3 m E Brighton at junction of A259
& B2123
View from outside only; late 18th
century smock mill, large wagon roof
cap, retains bare sail frames

BELLOCS MILL (KINGS MILL)
Map 2 Ab/p 90
Shipley, 5m S Horsham off B2224
Open: May-Oct, last w/end in month,
Easter Mon & Aug BH 14.30-17.30
Groups at other times by arrangement
(write: Mr P J Crowther, 13 Church
Close, Shipley)
Charge: 50p (ch16 20p)
Built 1879, largest & only working
smock mill in West Sussex, double
shuttered sails, octagonal cap & three
pairs of stones; home of Hilaire Belloc
containing museum of his life &
writing
See also Museums: Bellocs Mill
Museum

BURTON MILL
Map 1 Bb/p 74
2½m S Petworth off A285 (in nature
reserve)
Open: all year, Fri-Wed 14.00-16.00,
Sun 10.00-13.00 & 14.00-16.30
Free
18th century water mill in working
order, flour on sale; fishing permits
available for Burton Pond, nature trail
See also Nature Reserves: Burton
Pond

CHERRY CLACK MILL
Map 3 Bb
Punnett's Town, 3m E Heathfield off
B2096
Open: visible from road only
Restored & removed from Kent in
1956, surrounded by cherry orchards
& referred to as 'Cherry Black Mill' in
Rudyard Kipling's Sussex Stories;
under restoration having been recently
struck by lightning

CHAILEY WINDMILL
Map 3 Ab
4m SE Haywards Heath off A272
& A275
Open: view from outside only
Well restored timber building, not
working

HALNAKER WINDMILL
Map 1 Bb
Halnaker, 4m NE Chichester off A285
on Halnaker Hill, accessible by 3¼m
footpath from road
Open: anytime
Built 1740, earliest Sussex tower mill
of brick & unusual tile hanging,
restored 1934 (no machinery)

JACK & JILL WINDMILLS
Map 2 Bb/p 79
Hassocks (07918) 3297
Clayton, 1½m S Hassocks off A273
Open: both mills visible from adjacent
car park anytime; selected Suns &
BHs access to Jill windmill by
arrangement (telephone Mr S Potter
as above)
Black tower mill (Jack) built 1866;
post mill (Jill) built 1821 &
transported from Brighton, restored &
working

KINGS MILL
See Belloc's Mill

LURGASHALL MILL
See Museums: Weald & Downland
Open Air Museum

MEDMERRY WINDMILL
Map 1 Ac/p 89
West Sands Leisure Centre, Selsey,
7m S Chichester, 1m off B2145 at
entrance to caravan park
Open: anytime (exterior), mid May-
mid Sep (interior)
Build c. 1750, circular brick tower
mill, domed cap, 4 complete sails; toy
shop inside

MICHELHAM PRIORY MILL
Restored 14th century watermill,
medieval machinery, flour on sale
See Historic Buildings: Michelham
Priory

NUTLEY MILL
Uckfield (0825) 2969
Nutley, 3½m N Maresfield, ½m from
village (signposted from Nutley to
Duddleswell Rd)
Open: May-Sep, last Sun in month,
BH Mons & Easter (weather
permitting) 14.30-17.30; school
groups at other times by arrangement
Charge: 30p (ch 15p)
No lavatories

POLEGATE WINDMILL
Map 3 Bc/p 44
Polegate (03212) 4763
Polegate, 4m N Eastbourne W of A22
Open: Easter-Oct, Sun & BH Mons
14.30-17.30; groups at other times
by arrangement
(write: Mr C E Waite, 48a Wannock
Lane, Lower Willingdon)
Charge: 30p (ch 10p)
Built 1817, red brick with domed cap;
restored, internal machinery intact,
museum
See also Museums: Polegate
Windmill Museum

SALVINGTON MILL
Map 2 Ac
2m N Worthing, ½m N of A27
Open: visible from road anytime; open
one day in year
Built 1710, restored post mill
Charge: 30p (open day)

WEST BLATCHINGTON WINDMILL
Map 2 Ba/p 29
Brighton (0273) 775400
N Hove on A2038
Open: May-Sep, Suns & BHs 14.30-
17.30; school groups (15) by
arrangement at other times
Charge: 20p (ch 10p)
No lavatories
See also Museums: West
Blatchington Windmill Museum

WOODS MILL
Map 2 Ac/p 55
Haywards Heath (0444) 413678
Henfield, 1½m S Henfield on A2037
Open: early April-late Sep, Tue-Thur &
Sat 14.00-18.00, Sun & BH 11.00-
18.00
Charge: 75p (ch 50p), reduced rates
for groups by arrangement
Headquarters for STNC Nature
Reserve
No dogs
See also Nature Reserves: Woods
Mill

Motor Sports

ARLINGTON RACEWAY
Map 3 Bc
Hailsahm (0323) 841642
S Hailsham off A22
Speedway & stock cars
Open: speedway, Suns 15.30; stock cars, BH Mons 14.30, June-Sep, Wed 20.00
Charge: Speedway £2.50 & £1.50; stock cars £2.50 & £1; 20p car park
P ⌨ ♟

GOODWOOD MOTOR CIRCUIT
Map 1 Ac/p 37
Goodwood, 4m N Chichester off A286
Not open to public; formerly famous grand prix circuit still serving motor sport; 2.4m circuit used by motor sport clubs for members meetings & competitive events also by British & European car manufacturers for demonstrations, endurance and fuel economy runs

Museums

ANNE OF CLEVES HOUSE
Map 3 Ac/p 62
Lewes (07916) 4610
Southover High St, Lewes
Open: mid Feb-mid Nov, Mon-Sat 10.00-17.00; April-Oct daily (Sun 14.00-17.00)
Charge: 60p (ch 30p), groups (20) 50p (ch 20p) by arrangement
No parking
SAS ♟

ARUNDEL MUSEUM & HERITAGE CENTRE
Map 1 Bc/p 12
Arundel (0903) 882726
61 High Street, Arundel
Open: Easter-Oct, Tues-Sat 10.30-12.30 & 14.00-17.00, Sun 14.00-17.00
Charge: 25p (ch 10p); school groups welcome (ch 10p, adults free); evening guided tours by arrangement (50p,with coffee 75p)
♟ ♿

ARUNDEL TOY AND MILITARY MUSEUM
Map 1 Bc/p 13
Arundel (0903) 883101/882908
23 High Street, Arundel
Open: Oct-May, w/ends & BHs; June-Sep, daily; other times by arrangement
Charge: 50p (ch15 & OAPs 25p); reductions for groups
♿ ♟

BARBICAN HOUSE MUSEUM
Map 3 Ac/p 61
Lewes (07916) 4379
169 High Street, Lewes
Open: all year, Mon-Sat 10.00-17.00, Sun 14.00-17.00
Charge: 65p (ch 35p); groups 45p (ch 25p) by arrangement; tickets valid also for Lewes Castle

THE BARLOW COLLECTION
Map 2 Bc/p 30
Brighton (0273) 606755
University of Sussex, Falmer on A27
Open: University term, Thur & Tue 11.30-14.30
Free

**BATTLE HISTORICAL SOCIETY
MUSEUM**
Map 4 Ab/p 15
Langton House, Abbey Green, Battle
Open: Easter-end Sep, Mon-Sat
10.00-13.00 & 14.00-17.00, Sun
14.30-17.30
Charge: 20p (ch 10p)
No dogs
🅿️ 🐾

**BEACHY HEAD NATURAL
HISTORY CENTRE**
See Nature Reserves: Beachy Head

BELLOCS MILL MUSEUM
See Mills: Bellocs Mill

**BEXHILL-ON-SEA NATURAL
HISTORY MUSEUM**
Map 4 Ac/p 17
Bexhill-on-Sea (0424) 211769
Egerton Park, Bexhill-on-Sea
Open: April-Oct, Mon-Thur & Sat
10.00-13.00 & 14.30-16.30 (July-
Sep, Sun 14.30-16.30); Nov-March,
Mon, Wed & Sat 10.00-13.00 &
14.30-16.30
Charge: 20p (ch 10p)
No lavatories

**BEXHILL MANOR COSTUME
MUSEUM**
Map 4 Ac/p 17
Bexhill-on-Sea (0424) 215361
Manor Gardens, Bexhill-on-Sea
Open: Easter-Sep, Tue-Fri & BHs
10.30-13.00 & 14.30-17.30; Sat &
Sun 14.30-17.30
Charge: 50p (ch25p, OAPs 40p)
🅿️ 🐾 ♿ ☕

**BOOTH MUSEUM OF NATURAL
HISTORY**
Map 2 Bc/p 28
Brighton (0273) 552586
194 Dyke Rd, Brighton
Open: all year, Fri-Wed 10.00-17.00,
Sun 14.00-17.00 (closed 25 & 26
December, 1 Jan & Good Fri)
Free
No dogs
🐾 ♿

**BRIGHTON ART GALLERY &
MUSEUM**
Map 2 Bc/p 27
Brighton (0273) 603005
Open: all year, Tue-Sat 10.00-17.45,
Sun 14.00-17.00
Free (except festival exhibitions in
May & June)
No dogs
♿ ☕ 🐾

BRITISH ENGINEERIUM
Map 2 Bc/p 28
Brighton (0273) 559583
Hove, off Nevill Rd
Open: daily 10.00-17.00 (closed
23 & 25 Dec, 'in steam' Suns & BHs)
Charge: £1 (ch & OAPs 60p)
Snacks when 'in steam'
No dogs
🖼 ⟨ 🚻

CHALK PITS MUSEUM
Map 1 Bb/p 9
Bury (079881) 370
Amberley, 4m N Arundel off B2139
Open: April-Oct, Wed-Sun & BHs
11.00-17.00
Charge: £1.20 (ch 60p, OAPs 90p);
group reductions by arrangement in
writing
🅿 🖼 ⟨ 🚻

CHERRIES FOLK MUSEUM
Map 4 Bb/p 85
Rye (0797) 223224
Playden, 1 m N Rye on A268
Open: daily, by arrangement with
Dr & Mrs W H Townsend
Free (donations gratefully accepted)
🅿 ⟨

CHICHESTER DISTRICT MUSEUM
Map 2 Bb/p 35
Chichester (0243) 784683
29 Little London, Chichester
Open: all year, Tue-Sat 10.00-17.30
Free
No dogs 🖼 ⟨

COURT HALL MUSEUM
Map 4 Bb/p 101
Rye (0797) 226257
Court Hall, Winchelsea, 1 m SW Rye
on A259
Open: first three weeks May, w/ends;
late May-late Sep, Mon-Fri 10.30-
12.30 & 14.30-17.00; Sun 14.30-
17.30
Charge: 35p (ch15p)
Guides, old maps of Winchelsea &
copies of seal available

COWDRAY RUINS
See Historic Homes: Cowdray
House

**EAST GRINSTEAD TOWN
MUSEUM**
Map 3 Aa/p 45
East Court, East Grinstead
Open: all year, Wed 14.00-16.00, Sat
14.00-17.00, groups at other times
by arrangement (telephone Mr
Leppard, Sackville School (0342)
25005)
Free
Publications on sale
🅿

**FISHBOURNE ROMAN PALACE &
MUSEUM**
See Roman Sites: Fishbourne
Roman Palace & Museum

FISHERMANS MUSEUM
Map 4 Ac/p 51
Hastings (0424) 424787
Rock-a-Nore Rd, Hastings
Open: all year, Sat-Thur 10.00-12.00
& 14.00-17.00; school groups by
arrangement (write: J Burron, 11
Harold Rd, Hastings)
Free (donations gratefully accepted)
⟨

FORT NEWHAVEN MUSEUM
See Unusual Outings: The Fort

**GRANGE MUSEUM & ART
GALLERY**
Map 3 Ac/p 31
Brighton (0273) 31004
The Green, Rottingdean, 4m E
Brighton on A259
Open: all year, Thur-Tue 10.00-
17.00, Sun 14.00-17.00 (closed
Good Fri, 25 & 26 Dec)
Free
No dogs
🖼

GUILDHALL MUSEUM
Map 1 Ac/p 35
Chichester (0243) 784683
Priory Park, Chichester
Open :June-Sept, Tue-Sat 13.00-
17.00
Free
No dogs
P ♿ ♿

HAILSHAM MUSEUM
Map 3 Bc
Hailsham (0323) 840947
The Library, Western Road, Hailsham
Open: early April, Spring BH-early
Sep, Wed 10.30-13.00; groups at
other times by arrangement
Free (donations gratefully accepted)
P

**HASTINGS MUSEUM OF LOCAL
HISTORY**
Map 4 Ac/p 52
Hastings (0424) 425855
The Old Town Hall, High St, Hastings
Open: Easter-Sep, Mon-Sat 10.00-
12.30 & 14.00-17.00; Oct-Easter,
Sun 15.00-17.00 (closed Good Fri)
Charge: 10p; school groups by
arrangement
No dogs
P ♿

**HASTINGS MUSEUM & ART
GALLERY**
Hastings (0424) 435952
Open: all year, Mon-Sat 10.00-13.00
& 14.00-17.00; Sun & BHs 15.00-
17.00 (closed Good Fri, 25 & 26
Dec); school groups by arrangement
Free
No dogs
P ♿ ♿

HENFIELD MUSEUM
Map 2 Ab/p 56
No telephone
New Village Hall, Henfield, 8m N
Shoreham-by-Sea
Open: all year, Tue, Thur & Sat
10.00-12.00, Wed 14.30-16.30
Free

HOLLYCOMBE MUSEUM
See Unusual Outings: Hollycombe
Steam Collection

HORSHAM MUSEUM
Map 2 Aa/p 57
Horsham (0403) 4959
The Causeway, Horsham
Open: all year, Tue-Fri 13.00-17.00,
Sat 10.00-17.00 (closed BH)
Free
No dogs
♿ ♿

HOUSE OF PIPES
Map 2 Ab/p 21
Steyning (0903) 812122
Bramber, 3½m N Shoreham on A283
Open: all year, daily 9.00-19.00
(closed 25 Dec)
Charge: 35p (10p ch 14); groups
(25) 25p
Guided tours (also evenings); catering
in Calabash Room for groups by
arrangement
P ♿ ♿

HOVE MUSEUM OF ART
Map 2 Bc/28
Brighton (0273) 779410
19 New Church Rd, Hove
Open: all year, Tues-Fri 10.00-13.00
& 14.00-17.00, Sat 10.00-13.00 &
14.00-16.30 (closed BHs)
Free
P ♿ ♿

LIFEBOAT HOUSE
Map 4 Ac/p 53
Hastings (0424) 425502
The Stade, Old Town, Hastings
Open: any reasonable time, school
groups by arrangement (write: Mr J
Martin, Coxswain, c/o The Lifeboat
Museum, The Stade, Hastings)
Free
Disabled groups welcome
♿ ♿

LIFEBOAT MUSEUM
Map 3 Bc/p 42
Eastbourne (0323) 301717
Wish Tower, Green Parade,
Eastbourne
Open: all year, (winter) Mon-Sat 9.30-
17.30 & 18.30-21.00
Free
P ↟ & ⌂

LITTLEHAMPTON MUSEUM
Map 1 Bc/p 64
Littlehampton (09064) 5149
Littlehampton, 12A River Rd, on
A259
Open: April-Sep, Tue-Sat 10.30-
13.00 & 14.00-16.00; Oct-March,
Thur-Sat 10.30-13.00 & 14.00-
16.00; groups by arrangement
Free
↟

MARLIPINS MUSEUM
Map 2 Ac/p 91
Shoreham-by-Sea (07917) 62994
High St, Shoreham-by-Sea
Open: May-Sep, Mon-Sat 10.00-
12.30 & 14.00-17.00; Sun 14.00-
17.00
Free (donations gratefully accepted)
No lavatories
SAS P

MILITARY HERITAGE MUSEUM
Map 3 Ac/p 62
Lewes (07916) 3139
Regency House, Albion St, Lewes
Open: early April-Sep, Mon-Fri 10.00-
13.00 & 14.00-17.00
Charge: 65p (ch 20p, OAPs 40p);
group reductions by arrangement
Guided tours for adults & OAPs
↟

MUSEUM OF CURIOSITY
Map 1 Bc/p 13
Arundel (0903) 882420
6 High Street, Arundel
Open: April-Sep, Mon-Fri 10.30-
13.00 & 14.15-17.30; w/ends
11.00-13.00 & 14.15-17.30; Oct-
Nov, daily 14.15-17.00 (or dusk)
Charge: 50p (ch 25p, OAPs 35p)
↟

NATIONAL MUSEUM OF PENNY SLOT MACHINES
Map 2 Bc/p 27
Brighton (0273) 608620
Pier Pavillion, Palace Pier, Brighton
Open: Easter-Oct, daily; Nov-March,
Sun 11.00-18.00 (may be closed due
to bad weather)
Charge: 30p (accompanied ch free,
OAPs 15p)
No unaccompanied children
P ↟

NATIONAL BUTTERFLY MUSEUM
See Historic Homes: St Marys &
National Butterfly Museum

NORTONS FARM MUSEUM
Map 4 Ab
Sedlescombe (042487) 471
Sedlescombe, 4½m NW Hastings on
A21
Open: late June-Sep, daily 9.00-
17.00; groups by arrangement
Free
Charge for guided tours
P ⌂⌖↟

OLD MINTHOUSE
See Historic Homes: Old Minthouse

PARSONAGE ROW MUSEUM OF SUSSEX FOLKLORE
Map 2 Ac
Worthing (0903) 36385
Parsonage Row, W. Tarring, Worthing
Open: March-mid Dec, Tue-Sat
14.15-17.00 (other times by
arrangement with custodian)
Charge: 20p (ch 10p)
Not suitable for groups
No dogs

POLEGATE WINDMILL MUSEUM
See Mills: Polegate Windmill
Museum

**NEWHAVEN & SEAFORD
HISTORICAL SOCIETY**
Newhaven (07912) 4760
Open: April-end Oct, Sat, Sun & BHs
14.30-18.00; groups by arrangement
at other times
Charge: 10p (accompanied ch free),
£2 per group (w/days)
🅿 ♿

PERIGOE WORKSHOP MUSEUM
Map 4 Ab/p 72
Northiam (07974) 3203
Northiam, 9½m N Hastings on A28
Open: April-Sep, Tue-Sun 14.00-
17.00, other times by arrangement
Charge: 50p
🅿

PRIEST HOUSE MUSEUM
See Church Buildings: Priest House

REDOUBT FORTRESS
Map 3 Bc/p 43
Eastbourne (0323) 33952
Royal Parade, Eastbourne
Open: April-Nov, daily 10.00-17.00
Charge: 50p (ch, OAPs 25p)
No dogs
🍽

**ROBERTSBRIDGE AERONAUTICAL
MUSEUM**
Map 4 Ab/p 80
Lamberhurst (0892) 890386 or
Robertsbridge (0580) 880499
Bush Barn, Robertsbridge, 1m N of
town off A21
Open: last Sun in month (except Dec)
14.30-17.30; April-Sep, Tue evenings
from 19.30; other times by
arrangement
Free (donations gratefully accepted)
No coaches
🅿 🍽 ♿ 🚃

RURAL CIDER MUSEUM
See Vineyards: Valley Wine Cellars

SEAFORD MARTELLO TOWER
Map 3 Ac/p 87
Seaford (0323) 892132
The Esplanade, Seaford
Open: April-Sep, Wed, Sat, Sun &
BHs
Charge: 15p (accompanied ch free)
🅿 🍽

**SHEFFIELD PARK RAILWAY
STATION MUSEUM**
See Railways: Bluebell Railway

**STANMER VILLAGE RURAL
MUSEUM**
Map 2 Bb/p 30
Brighton (0273) 556529
Stanmer, 4m N Brighton off A27
Open: Easter-Oct, Thur 14.30-17.00
& Sun 14.00-17.00
Free
🅿 ♿

WARNHAM WAR MUSEUM
Map 2 Aa
Horsham (0403) 65607/65179
Warnham, 2½m N Horsham on A24
Open: April-Sep, daily 10.00-18.00;
Oct-March, daily 10.00-1600
Charge: 80p (ch 14, OAPs 40p);
group reductions (12) by arrangement
🅿 🍽 ♿ 🚃🍴

**WEALD & DOWNLAND OPEN AIR
MUSEUM**
Map 1 Ab/p 92
Singleton (024363) 348
Singleton, 6m N Chichester on A286
Open: early April-Oct, Tue-Sun 11.00-
17.00; June-Aug, daily & BHs 11.00-
17.00; Nov-March, Sun & Wed
11.00-16.00
Charge: £1.30 (ch & OAP 80p);
group reductions during winter by
arrangement
Restored 17th century Lurgashall mill
🅿 🍽 🚃🍴

**WEST BLATCHINGTON MILLING
MUSEUM**
See Mills: West Blachington
Windmill

WILMINGTON PRIORY
See Church Buildings: Wilmington
Priory

WISH TOWER 73
Eastbourne (0323) 35809
King Edwards Parade, Eastbourne
Open: April-Oct, daily 10.00-17.00
Charge: 30p (ch & OAPs 15p,
school); school groups (12p each)
No dogs
🏛 ⌂

**WORTHING MUSEUM & ART
GALLERY**
Worthing (0903) 39999 ext 121
Chapel Rd, Worthing, West Sussex
Open: April-Sep, Mon-Sat 10.00-
18.00; Oct-March 10.00-17.00
Free
No dogs
🅿 🏛 ♿

YPRES TOWER MUSEUM
Map 4 Bb/p 81
Rye (0797) 223254
Gun Garden, Rye
Open: Easter-mid Oct, Mon-Sat
10.30-13.00 & 14.15-17.13; Sun
11.30-13.00 & 14.15-17.30
Charge: 50p (ch 15p, OAP 25p);
school groups (20) by arrangement
(ch 10p, adults 30p); adult groups
(10) 30p
No dogs
🏛

Nature Reserves

ARDINGLY RESERVOIR
Map 2 Ba
3m N Haywards Heath off B2028
Small picturesque reservoir adjoining
valley of R. Ouse, footpaths skirt parts
of lakeside
Trout fishing mid April-late Oct
(permits: Manager Bewl Bridge
Reservoir)
Lavatories
🅿 🚻

ARLINGTON RESERVOIR
Map 3 Bc
Eastbourne (0323) 2137
3m SW Hailsham off A27
150 acre reservoir, an increasingly
important site for wildfowl; Oct-Feb,
wintering populations of Canada
geese, mallard, wigeon, pochard,
tufted duck & shoveler; July-Sep
unusual waders (spotted redshank)
have been seen
Public permitted to use footpath
around reservoir only; owned by
Eastbourne Waterworks
Lavatories
🅿 🚻

BARCOMBE MILLS
See Bird Parks: Barcombe Mills

BEACHY HEAD
Map 3 Bc/p 43
4½m SW Eastbourne
Open: all year; April-Sep, w/ends &
BHs nature trail & natural history
centre
Dramatic headland with high south-
facing chalk cliffs, excellent for
watching migrant birds
Leaflet available
🅿

BEWL BRIDGE RESERVOIR
See Country Parks: Bewl Bridge
Reservoir

BURTON POND
Map 1 Bb
2½m S Petworth off A285
30 acres of woodland & common, 12 acres of water; access by public footpaths only, nature trail, leaflet available; owned by WSCC & STNC
See also Mills: Burton Mill
🅿

CAMBER DUNES
Map 4 Bb
Camber, 4m E Rye, SW of village off A259
Only sand dunes in E Sussex, interesting variety of animals & plants; keep to footpaths from Camber through the dunes
🅿

CASTLE HILL
Map 3 Ac
Lewes (07916) 6595
2m W Lewes, 1m NE Woodingdean, access from footpath off B2123
470 acres of downland, chalk grassland & rich flowering plants; keep to footpaths; permits from NCC necessary to visit other parts of reserve

CHAILEY COMMON
Map 3 Ab
8m N Lewes at junction of A275 & A272
Open: all year
290 acres of heathland, boggy in parts, thin soil; July-Sep heather in flower; in summer look out for grasshoppers; privately owned & managed by Chailey Common Nature Reserve

DITCHLING BEACON
Map 2 Bb/p 39
6m N Brighton, 2m S Ditchling off B2116
Open: all year
50 acres of chalk grassland, scrub & ashwood on downland scarp; chalk-loving wild flowers & insects; owned by Ditchling Common, Tenantry Down Ltd & NT, managed by Sussex Trust for Nature Conservation, Henfield (0273) 2630
🅿

DITCHLING COMMON
Map 2 Bb/p 39
2½m N Ditchling on B2112
185 acres scrub covered common land; 1½m nature trail, leaflet available
Lavatories, ranger service
🅿

FILSHAM FARM
Map 4 Ac
1½m W Hastings on B2092, public footpath from Bulverhythe
Reed bed, water meadows and drainage ditches at lower end of Coombe Haven Valley; wildfowl, water & marsh plants; good views
Managed by Sussex Trust for Nature Conservation
🅿

IPING COMMON
Map 1 Ab
2m W Midhurst off A272
Forms part of open heathland on a low ridge of sandstone hills; varied insect life & birds
Access by public footpath
🅿

KINGLEY VALE
Map 1 Ab
Wye (0233) 812525
3m NW Chichester, access at West
Stoke village car park off B2178
Open: all year, daily 24 hrs; Easter-
Oct, w/ends 11.00-17.00 field
museum
One of the finest yew forests in
Europe; variety of plants & animals;
information centre & nature trail;
leaflet 10p
No lavatories, dogs on lead
NCC

LULLINGTON HEATH
Map 3 Bc
Lewes (07916) 6595
2m SW Polegate, 1m E Jevington off
A22, access from paths at both ends
National nature reserve, 155 acres of
chalk heath; keep to paths along
northern boundary & through middle
of reserve; permits from NCC
necessary for entry to reserve itself

OLD LODGE
5m W Crowborough off B2026
Open: all year, daily
250 acres; newly opened to conserve
heathland; circular trail planned for
future
P

PAGHAM HARBOUR
Map 1 Ac
2m NE Selsey Bill, 5½m S Chichester
Public footpaths round harbour &
across farmland; keep to footpaths,
tides in harbour treacherous, do not
stray to mud flats (access to part of
shingle beach prohibited from April-
July); restrictions & country code
must be respected; managed by
WSCC
Nature trail, information centre, leaflet
available
Dogs on lead
See also Bird Parks: Pagham
Harbour
P

RYE HARBOUR
Map 4 Bb
Rye (07973) 3862
585 acres shingle beach, wet gravel
pits & farmland; noted for shorebirds,
colonies of common & little terns
(May-July), plants & wader roosts
(winter)
Open: all year
Keep to footpaths; information centre,
displays, leaflets; owned by Southern
Water Authority
P

SEAFORD HEAD
Map 3 Ac
1½m SE Seaford off A259
Open: all year
275 acres downland, cliffs, foreshore
& farmland; refuge for migrating
birds; leaflet available from Lewes
District Council & Country Park Centre
P

WOODS MILL
Map 3 Ac
Henfield (0273) 492630
1½m S Henfield on A2037
Open: Easter-end Sep, Tue-Sat
14.00-18.00; Sun & BHs 11.00-
18.00 (may be closed in wet weather)
Charge: telephone for details, group
rates by arrangement
Headquarters of STNC, information
centre, exhibition, nature trails; variety
of aquatic plants & animals, nature
trails
See also Mills: Woods Mill
STNC P

Other Historic Buildings

BULL HOUSE
Map 3 Ac/p 60
Lewes (07916) 3936
High Street, Lewes
Open: by appointment with tenant,
property being let as restaurant
Late medieval inn
SAS

FRIENDS MEETING HOUSE
Map 2 Ab/p 90
Coolham, nr Horsham, 1 m N Coolham
on A276
Open: all year, daily 9.00-dusk
Free
Guest house with Quaker meeting
house attached; cream teas on BHs
for groups by arrangement; camping
facilities in grounds £2 per night

PARSONAGE ROW COTTAGES
See Museum: Parsonage Row
Cottages

ST MARYS HOSPITAL
Map 1 Ac/p 34
Chichester (0243) 78337
Nr St Martin's Square, Chichester
Open: April-Oct, Tue-Sat 11.00-17.00
(closed 12.00-14.00); Oct-March
11.00-16.00 (closed 12.00-14.00)
Free
Donations gratefully received
No dogs, no lavatories

SHOVELLS
Hastings (0424) 420241
All Saints Street, Old Town Hastings
Open: by arrangement with tenant
Two small timber framed buildings,
said to be home Admiral Sir
Cloudesley Shovell's mother
SAS

Picnic Sites

The following sites have been specially
created for picnics and usually have
picnic tables. They have car parks, are
open at all times and are free unless
otherwise stated.

BUTCHERSOLE PICNIC PLACE
Map 3 Bc
3m W Eastbourne off A259,
N Friston
Small secluded place in woodland,
pleasant walks through forest
& downland
FC

CHANCTONBURY RING
Map 2 Ab
½m S A283, 3m W Steyning, picnic
site below ring

FAIRLIGHT GLEN PICNIC SITE
Map 4 Ab
Fairlight, Fairlight Rd, NE Hastings off
A259
Fairlight glen, deep sandstone ravine,
ferns butterflies, nesting sites for
summer migrant birds; nature trail
starts here, leaflet available, Hastings
Country Park Interpretive Centre

FAIRMILE BOTTOM
Map 1 Bb
2m N Slindon on A29
126 acres of chalk downland, beech
woods & open grassland; 1½m nature
trail starts here, leaflet available,
owned by WSCC
Lavatories
⌕

FINCHFIELD
Map 3 Aa
West Hoathly, 5½m S East Grinstead
off A275
Picnic site, car park in village

FOOTLAND WOOD PICNIC PLACE
8m N Hastings on A21 off B2089
On high escarpment bordered by
young pine forest; 1m forest walk
starts here, leaflet available
FC

GRAVETYE PICNIC PLACE
Map 2 Ba
West Hoathly, 3m SW East Grinstead
off B2110
Small open grassy area fringed by ash,
red oak, norway spruce & grand fir
trees; Gravetye forest walk (1½m),
leaflet available
FC

HALNAKER WINDMILL
Map 1 Bb
1m NE Halnaker off A285, picnic site
at windmill

HARTING HILL
Map 1 Ab
1m SE South Harting on B2141
Picnic site & car park

KIDDERS LANE
Map 2 Ab
2m N Henfield on A281

MARDEN-STOUGHTON DOWN
PICNIC PLACE
Map 1 Ab
1m NE Stoughton, 8m
NW Chichester off B2141
Secluded picnic place in heart of
South Downs, picnic tables in beech
woodland; Marden-Stoughton Down
forest walk starts here (1½m)
FC

ROGATE TULLCOMBE
PICNIC PLACE
Map 1 Aa
N Rogate, 5m W Midhurst off A272,
east at first crossroads
Set in pine & sweet chestnut woods,
fine views over Warting Combe valley;
½m forest walk starts here
FC

SIDLESHAM
Map 1 Ac
3m S Chichester, ½m S Sidlesham on
B2145
Picnic site, nature trail, leaflet available
& information centre

SLINDON EARTHAM WOOD
PICNIC PLACE
Map 1 Bb
6m NE Chichester, 1m N Eartham off
A285
Woodland setting with picnic tables
set among beech trees; 2m forest
walk starts here (including Roman Rd,
Stane St)
FC

SLINDON SELHURST PARK
Map 1 Bb
7m NE Chichester, ¾ W A285 at
Benges Corner
Open grassy picnic area set among
150 year old beech trees, overlooks
Chichester to Isle of Wight; Slindon
Selhurst Park forest walk (1m) starts
here
FC

SLINFOLD
Map 1 Bb
Slinfold, 3½m N Billingshurst/ ½m E
Slinfold off A29 adjoining caravan club
site
Nature trail, leaflet available

THE TRUNDLE
Map 1 Ab
1½m S Singleton off A286

WILMINGTON-ABBOTS WOOD
PICNIC PLACE
Map 3 Bc
7m N Eastbourne on A22, turn left
along Arlington for 2m
¼m inside a young woodland of
beech, Douglas Fir, pine; 1¾m forest
walk starts here, leaflet available;
Plackett Walk suitable for wheelchairs
(400 yds)
FC

WEST DEAN PICNIC PLACE
Map 3 Ac
2m E Seaford on A259, turn N at
Exceat Farm
Roadside picnic place flanked by
beech & sycamore woodland; pleasant
views across the river valley to the
Downs; 2¾m forest walk, leaflet
available
Lavatories
FC

WHITEWAYS LODGE
Map 1 Bb
2m NW Arundel, on roundabout at
junction of A29, A284 & B2139
Lavatories

Railways

BLUEBELL RAILWAY
Map 3 Ab/p 46
Newick (082572) 2370
Sheffield Park Station, 4½m
E Haywards Heath off A275
Open: May & Oct, Wed, Sat & Sun;
March, April & Nov w/ends; Dec-Feb,
Sun only; June-Sep, Easter week &
BHs, daily
Museum & locomotive sheds open all
year, daily
Charge: £1.80 (ch90p) includes
return fare & admission to museum;
groups (15) £1.40 (ch70p)

HOLLYCOMBE STEAM COLLECTION
See Unusual Outings: Hollycombe
Steam Collection

EAST HILL CLIFF RAILWAY
Map 4 Ac/p 53
Rock-a-Nore to East Hill (Hastings)
Open: end May-end Sep, daily 10.00-
12.30 & 13.30-17.45
Charge: 25p (ch15p), return fare 20p
(10p)

VOLKS ELECTRIC RAILWAY
Map 2 Bc/p 29
Brighton (0273) 681061
Brighton
Open: April-Oct, daily 10.00-18.00
(closed speed trial day)
Charge: 35p (20p), group reductions
(30) by arrangement

WEST HILL CLIFF RAILWAY
Map 4 Ac/p 53
George St to West Hill (Hastings)
Open: end March-end Sep, daily
10.00-12.30 & 13.30-17.45
Charge: 25p (ch 15p), return fare
20p (ch 10p)

Riding

This list includes stables offering riding instruction and hacking (country rides). Most lessons are in classes or groups but private tuition is often available. Hacking is not usually allowed unaccompanied unless the ability of the rider is known. Stables which provide livery or stud services are not included. Exact locations of stables are not given since it is always advisable to telephone in advance.

ARUNDEL RIDING STABLES
Arundel (0903) 882061
Park Place, Arundel
Open: daily (except Mon)
Hack: £3.50 hour (ch £3.25), £6.50 2 hours (ch £6), day rides over South Downs £15 (ch £12)
Lessons: £2.75 half hour (ch £2.25), private £6.75 hour (ch £6.50)
19 mounts, residential & non-residential holidays with instruction, all standards

ASHDOWN FOREST RIDING STABLES
Nutley (082571) 2738
Whitehouse Farm, Duddleswell, off B2026
Open: all year, daily (except Mon)
Lesson: £5 45 min, private lesson £7 45 min
25 mounts, riding holidays for children & adults by arrangement, training by BHS instructors

AUDIBURN RIDING STABLES
Lewes (07916) 4398
Kingston, Lewes
Open: anytime
Lesson/Hack: £3 hour, private lesson £5 half hour
12 mounts, jumping, livery

BAILIFFS COURT RIDING STABLES
Littlehampton (09064) 6094
Slonkhill Farm, New Barn Rd,
Climping off A259/B2233
Open: daily
Lesson: £4.50 hour, private lesson £6 hour
Hack: £4
10 mounts, carriage driving, dressage & cross country

BEAUPORT PARK
Hastings (0424) 51424
St Leonards-on-Sea, off A21
Open: daily (except Mon)
Lesson/Hack: £4 hour, private lesson £7.50
30 mounts, instruction & eventing

BRENDON RIDING SCHOOL
Hassocks (07918) 2158/4508
Haresdean Farm, Pyecombe on A281
Open: anytime
Lesson/Hack: £5 hour (ch £4.50), private lessons from £3.50
20 mounts, day rides on BHs, riding w/ends, holidays, shows

BRIDGE HOUSE RIDING SCHOOL
Slinfold (0403) 790163
Five Oaks Rd, Slinfold, Horsham
Open: daily (except Tue)
Lesson/Hack: £4.10 hour (ch £3.70), private lesson approx £7 hour
15 mounts, all aspects of riding

CANTERS END
Hadlow Down (082585) 213
Hadlow Down, Uckfield
Open: daily (except Thur)
Lesson/Hack: £1.80-£3.75 (according to age and experience)
8 mounts, indoor riding school, mainly for children

CHESTNUTS RIDING STABLES
Brighton (0273) 503842
London Rd, Pyecombe on A 281
Open: Mon-Fri dawn to dusk (w/end rides 10.00, 11.30 & 14.00)
Lesson: £4 hour, private lesson £7 hour
10 mounts (not suitable for heavy people), showjumping, elementary dressage

COLDWALTHAM HOUSE
Bury (079881) 418
Coldwaltham, S Pulborough
Open: daily 10.00-17.00
Lesson: private lessons only by arrangement from £5.50
5 mounts, dressage & jumping

COPHALL FARM STABLES
Polegate (03213) 3975
Polegate, East Sussex
Open: anytime
Lesson: £5 hour (telephone for details of private lessons)
Hack: £4.50 hour
25 mounts, mainly for children

CRABBET PARK EQUITATION CENTRE
Crawley (0293) 882601
Worth, 4m S Gatwick off M23
Open: anytime
Lesson: £6.50-£8.25 hour (ch £4-£5.50), private lesson £8.25-£12.10 hour (ch £7.70-£8.50)
2 indoor schools, outdoor manege, showjumping, cross country, week/day & w/end courses, holidays

EASTERGATE EQUESTRIAN CENTRE
Eastergate (024368) 3980
Wandleys Lane, Eastergate
Open: daily
Lesson: £5 hour (ch £4), private lesson £8 hour(ch £7)
Hack: £8 2 hour hack (Sun afternoon)
Elementary & general standards, dressage, cross country, showjumping, equine science & children's courses.

FERRING RIDING STABLES
Worthing (0903) 45078
Rife Way, Ferring, W. Worthing off A259
Open: anytime
Lesson/Hack: £4.50 hour (ch 9 £2.75 half hour)
7 mounts, 10 ponies, livery, showjumping, cross country

GATEWOOD FARM RIDING STABLES
Polegate (03212) 3709
Wilmington, W Polegate off A27
Open: daily
Lesson/Hack: £3.50 hour
10 mounts, only experienced riders, indoor school, picnic rides Mon & Thur, dressage meetings

HAPPY VALLEY RIDING STABLES
Shoreham (07917) 64537
Slonkhill Farm, New Barn Rd, Shoreham
Open: w/ends only
Lesson: £4.50 hour
6 mounts, mainly for children, livery

KINGSFOLD RIDING STABLES
Billingshurst (040381) 2458
Marringdean Rd, Billingshurst
Open: Mon-Fri
Lesson: £4 hour (ch £3), private jumping lessons £10 hour
6 mounts, showjumping

LAZY 'W' RANCH
Yapton (0243) 551409
Yapton Lane, Walberton, 1½m W Littlehampton on B2132
Open: all year, daily
Hack: £6.50 half day (9.45-12.15 & 13.30-16.00 w/days); £12 full day (9.45-15.30 w/ends)
Treks over South Downs 'Western Style'

OFFINGTON HALL RIDING SCHOOL
Worthing (0903) 62342
Offington Lane, Worthing
Open: anytime
Lesson: £4.50 hour, private lessons by arrangement
Hack: £4 hour
10 mounts, livery

ROYAL RIDING STABLES
Henfield (0273) 492523
Oreham Manor Farm, Horn Lane, Henfield
Open: daily 9.00-20.00
Lesson: £3.50, private lesson £4 half hour (ch only)
Hack: £6 (ch £4)
35 mounts, ponies, hunters

SEFTER LODGE
Pagham (02432) 3767
Sefter Rd, Bognor Regis, W of town off B2166
Open: daily (except tue)
Lesson: £4 (ch £3.50)
Hack: £5.50 hour
26 mounts, indoor school, dressage, showjumping & cross country

SNOWHILL STABLES
West Wittering (024 366) 2304
Coastguard Lane, West Wittering off B2179
Open: daily
Lesson/Hack: £4 hour, private £4 half hour
12 mounts, jumping

SOUTHDOWN RIDING SCHOOL
Brighton (0275) 680953
Race Hill, Bear Road, Brighton
Open: daily 10.00-18.00
Lesson: group lessons from £4.20-£6.50 hour, private £5 half hour.
12 mounts, indoor school, qualified instructors

THREE GREYS RIDING SCHOOL
Hassocks (07918) 3536
2 School Lane, Pyecombe, off A 281
Open: daily (except Mon)
Lesson/Hack: £3.60 (ch £3.30), day treks £11.50 (ch £10.50)
20 mounts, specialises in hacking

WEST WOLVES RIDING CENTRE
Ashington (0903) 892798
Billingshurst Rd, Ashington off B2133
Open: daily
Lesson: from £4 (ch £3.50), private £6 half hour
Hack: half day £5.75 (ch £5.25)
20 mounts, pony & trap drives, picnic & pub rides

WINTONS EQUESTRIAN CENTRE
Burgess Hill (044 46) 2040
44 Folders Lane, Burgess Hill
Open: daily (except Wed)
Lesson: £2.50 half hour, £4.25 hour
Hack: £4 hour
20 mounts, indoor school, outside manege, cross country, jumping, riding holidays

WHYDOWN PLACE
Battle (04246) 2334
Open: evenings after school & w/ends
Lesson: £4 hour
Indoor school, for children only

Roman Sites

BIGNOR ROMAN VILLA
Map 1 Bb
Sutton (07987) 259
Bignor, 6m S Pulborough on A29
Open: April-June, Tue-Sun & BH
Mon; July-Oct, daily 10.00-17.00
Charge: 90p (ch 40p, OAPs &
disabled 60p); reductions for groups
(15) by arrangement
P 🅿 ♿ ⛽ 🚻🎇

FISHBOURNE ROMAN PALACE
Map 1 Ac/p 35
Chichester (0243) 785859
Fishbourne, ½m W Chichester off
A27
Open: March, April & Oct, daily
10.00-17.00; May-Sep 10.00-18.00;
Nov-Feb, Sun 10.00-16.00
Charge: £1.10 (ch 40p, OAPs &
students 70p); groups (20) by
arrangement 70p; school groups
contact secretary
Largest Roman residence found in
Britain, remains of North Wing
including mosaic floors, courtyards,
hypocausts & bath suite, reconstructed
dining room, garden replanted to 1st
century AD plan, museum

Sailing

ROYAL YACHTING ASSOCIATION
London & SE Region
Medway (0634) 76309
Secretary: Mrs D. Whittaker
120 Broom Hill Rd, Strood, Rochester
The Association is the co-ordinating
organisation for the sport and organises
proficiency schemes. The following
clubs are all members of the Royal
Yachting Association.

Sailing Clubs

ADUR CENTRE BOAT CLUB
Secretary: E G Tuckmott
133 Brighton Road, Lancing

ADUR CRUISING ASSOCIATION
Secretary: Mrs V A Reed
5 Maple Walk, Sompting, Lancing
BN15 ODS

ARUN YACHT CLUB
Secretary: Lt Cdr T Cooper RN (RTD)
MBE
Riverside West, Littlehampton BN17
5DL

BEXHILL SAILING CLUB
Secretary: Gordon Viner
10 New Park Avenue, Bexhill-on-Sea

BRIGHTON MARINA
Brighton (0273) 693636

BOGNOR REGIS YACHT CLUB
Secretary: E Hopkins
The Esplanade, Bognor Regis PO21
2NA

BRIGHTON COLLEGE SAILING CLUB
The President
Brighton College, Eastern Rd, Brighton
BN2 2AL

BRIGHTON MARINA YACHT CLUB
Secretary: G Gilbert
Brighton Marina, Brighton BN2 5UF

BRIGHTON SAILING CLUB
The Sailing Secretary
109 Kings Road ARches, Brighton,
Sussex

CRAWLEY MARINERS YACHT CLUB
Secretary: K Buckton
6 Grebe Crescent, Horsham

EASTBOURNE SAILING CLUB LTD
The Secretary
The Redoubt, Eastbourne

FELPHAM SAILING CLUB
The Secretary
Blakes Road, Felpham, Bognor Regis
PO22 7EF

**HASTINGS MOTOR BOAT &
YACHT CLUB**
Secretary: A Barnard
The Clubhouse, Rock-a-Nore Parade,
Hastings

**HASTINGS & ST LEONARDS
SAILING CLUB**
Commodore: N D Scruys
Flat 2, 24 Quarry Rd, Hastings

HORSHAM CRUISING CLUB
Secretary: Mrs C E Austin
1 Little Grebe, Horsham RH12 2NG

LANCING SAILING CLUB
Secretary: M B Bacon
Warrie, 17 West End Way, Lancing

**LEWES ROWING CLUB-POWER &
SAIL**
Secretary: R Grandis
1 De La Warr Green, Lewes BN7 2TG

**LITTLEHAMPTON SAILING &
MOTOR CLUB LTD**
Secretary: C W Pierce
90-91 South Terrace, Littlehampton
BN17 5LJ

THE MARABU SYNDICATE
Secretary: M A Hetherington
46 Phyllis Ave, Peacehaven BN9 7PW

**NEWHAVEN & SEAFORD SAILING
CLUB LTD**
Secretary: R S G Cawse
40 Upper Belgrave Rd, Seaford BN25
3AP

NEWHAVEN YACHT CLUB
Commodore: Capt J D Bolt
Fort Road, Newhaven BN9 8ND

PAGHAM YACHT CLUB
The Secretary
1 West Front Rd, Pagham, Bognor
Regis PO21 4SY

PEVENSEY BAY SAILING CLUB
c/o L Montagu
71 Bedwardine Rd, Upper Norwood,
London SE19

**ROYAL MILITARY POLICE YACHT
CLUB**
The Secretary
RAP Training Centre, Chichester

**RYE HARBOUR BOAT OWNERS
ASSOCIATION**
Secretary: John F Sivier
200 Harley Shute Rd, St Leonards
TN38 9JH

SOVEREIGN SAILING CLUB
Secretary: D R Johnson
Norbrian Cottage, Butts Lane,
Willingdon, Eastbourne

ST ANDREWS CRUISING CLUB
Secretary: Miss J M Payne
22 Muster Court, Haywards Heath
RH16 4AW

SUSSEX MOTOR YACHT CLUB
Secretary: T N McKernan
7 Ship Street, Brighton BN1 1AD

**SUSSEX MOTOR YACHT CLUB
SAILING DIVISION**
The Secretary
223 Harbour Way, Shoreham-by-Sea

SUSSEX YACHT CLUB
The Secretary
85-89 Brighton Rd, Shoreham-by-Sea

WEIR WOOD SAILING CLUB
Secretary: M Barton-Smith
Freshmill Cottage, Sloop Lane,
Scaynes Hill, Haywards Heath

**W SUSSEX SCH & YOUTH SAIL
ASSOCIATION**
Sec/Treasurer: R Pichard
Youth & Community Office, Ed Dept,
Geoffs Park, Crawley

WORTH SCHOOL SAILING CLUB
President: Revd B Sankey, OSB MA
Worth School, Paddockhurst Rd,
Turners Hill, Crawley RH10 4SD

WORTHING YACHT CLUB
Secretary: L G H Cullen
6 Valencia Rd, Worthing BN11 4QB

Show Jumping

**HICKSTEAD ALL ENGLAND SHOW
JUMPING COURSE**
Map 2 Bb/p 59
Hurstpierpoint (0273) 834315
11m S Crawley on A23
Open: end April-Sep, w/ends, national
& international championships held
Charge: varies, approx. £2-£5 (ch
£1); club enclosure £5-£10 (ch £2-
£6); public grandstand £1-£2; 3 or 4
day membership £12-£20 (ch 50%
reduction); group reductions by
arrangement (telephone secretary)
🅿 ⛱ ♀ ✕

Sports Centres

ARUN LEISURE CENTRE
Bognor Regis (0243) 826612
Felpham Way, Bognor Regis
Open: all year, daily 9.00-23.00
(restrictions during school term, BHs
15.00-22.00)
Facilities: badminton, squash, table
tennis, tennis, 5 a side football,
gymnastics, volleyball, basketball,
Martial Arts, ladies' health & beauty,
keep-fit, weight training, rollerskating
(Sat eve & hols)
Courses: various
Charges: squash £2.20 45 min,
£1.45 30 min; badminton £2.40
hour; football £9.60
Membership: £15 family (over 16
£7.50; OAPs, ch 16, disabled £3.75)
Special events, supervised activities for
children
🅿 ♿ ⛱ ♀

BEWBUSH LEISURE CENTRE

Crawley (0293) 0546477
Breezehurst Drive, Bewbush, Crawley
Open: all year, Mon-Fri 9.00-23.00,
Sat 10.00-18.00, Sun 10.00-23.00
(closed 25 & 26 Dec, BHs)
Facilities: squash, badminton, table
tennis, basketball, football, keep-fit,
gymnastics, trampoline, judo
Courses: squash, archery, golf,
trampoline, cricket
Charge: squash £1.70 30 min;
badminton £2.70 hour; table tennis
£1.10 hour; weight training 55p;
keep-fit 60p session; courses £6-£8
Folk club selected Sun eve, over 50s
health club
🅿 ♿ 🚻 ♀

CRAWLEY LEISURE CENTRE

Crawley (0293) 37431
Haslett Ave, Three Bridges, Crawley
Open: all year, Mon-Sat 9.00-23.00,
Sun 9.00-18.00
Facilities: squash, badminton,
swimming, netball, gymnastics,
archery, trampoline, yoga, judo, keep-
fit, sauna, bowls, creche, table tennis
Courses: squash, archery, weight
training, badminton
Charges: daily membership 20p;
squash £1.70 30 min; badminton
£2.70 hour; volleyball court £8
(residents) hour; yoga 90p 2 hour
session
Athletics arena, lecture room, floodlit
games area
🅿 ♿ 🚻 ✕ ♀

FOREST RECREATION CENTRE

Horsham (0403) 68561
Forest School, Comptons Lane,
Horsham
Open: all year, Mon, Wed & Fri
21.00-23.00, Thur & Fri
17.30-23.00, w/ends & school
holidays 10.00-23.00
Facilities: badminton, table tennis, 5-
a-side football, netball, basketball
(mostly clubs)
Membership: £5 (ch £2.50), family
£12.40
Non-members: entrance fee 15p
(bookings at reception, Park
Recreation Centre)

THE GRANGE CENTRE

Midhurst (073081) 2606
Bepton Rd, Midhurst
Open: all year, daily 7.00-21.00
Facilities: badminton, squash,
volleyball, gymnastics, Martial Arts,
aerobics, pop mobility, 5-a-side
football, health studio, yoga
Courses: Jane Fonda Workout
introduction, health studio, racquet
games
Charges: squash £2.30 45 min,
£1.60 (off peak); badminton £2.30
(£1.70) hour; table tennis 80p (60p);
football area £6 (£5); gymnastics
£2.50 (£2.25)
🅿 🅿 ♿ 🚻 ♀

KING GEORGES HALL SPORTS CENTRE

East Grinstead (0342) 21096
Moat Rd, East Grinstead
Open: all year, Mon-Fri 9.00-22.30
Facilities: squash, badminton,
basketball, football, table tennis, keep-
fit, children's gymnastics
Courses: gymnastics & special
holiday activities
Charges: main hall £14 hour,
badminton £3.50 hour, squash £2.20
hour, table tennis 75p (ch 40p)
Disabled swimming club (Thur
morning), community recreation (Wed
& Fri morning) £1
🅿 🅿 ♿ 🚻 ♀

MARESFIELD LEISURE CENTRE
Crowborough (08926) 3311 ext 233
Batbridge Rd, Wealden, 2m
N Uckfield
Renovated hall suitable for indoor
sports, shows & exhibitions
exclusively for private use through
Uckfield Leisure Centre
Charges: £6-£7 hour for sports, rate
negotiable for shows etc; outdoor
tennis courts 80p hour

PARK RECREATION CENTRE
Horsham (0403) 68561
Horsham Park, Horsham
Open: all year, Mon-Thur 10.00-22.30,
Fri & Sat 11.00-23.00, Sun
10.00-22.30
Facilities: table tennis, weight training,
trampoline, badminton, ladies' keep-fit,
pop mobility, yoga
Courses: badminton, judo, trampoline,
dance & movement
Membership: £5 (ch £2.50), family
£12.40
Non-members: entrance fee 15p
Charges: badminton £2.45, £1.55
(off peak); £8.65 (£7.65) hire of
tennis hall; pop mobility 60p members
(76p non-members)

PORTSLADE COMMUNITY COLLEGE
Brighton (0273) 411100
Chalky Rd, Portslade
Open: all year, Mon-Fri 9.00-23.00,
Sat 9.00-22.30, Sun 10.00-22.30
Facilities: badminton, basketball, 5-a-
side football, cricket, trampoline,
archery , judo, keep-fit, gymnastics,
squash, floodlit red gra area
Courses: squash, badminton
Membership: £10.50, family £21,
under 18 £3.50
Non-members: 35p (day)
Charges: badminton £2 hour,
basketball/volleyball £9 hour, squash
£1.80 40 min, £1.40 (off peak),
cricket nets £6.50 hour, red gra £4
half area unlit (£9 lit), whole area £8
unlit (£13 lit)
Telephone bookings from members,
non-members in person
🅿 ⌁ 🍸

SOUTHWICK SPORTS CENTRE
Southwick (0273) 593202
Open: all year, daily 10.00-22.30
Facilities: badminton, squash, tennis,
table tennis, football, hockey, volley
ball
Membership: £7.20
Non-members: 20p (day)
Charges: badminton £2.20 hour,
squash £1.65 half hour, table tennis
65p hour
🚹 ⌁ ✕

SUMMERFIELD SPORTS CENTRE
Hastings (0424) 438166
Open: all year, daily 9.30-22.30
Facilities: squash, badminton,
archery, volleyball, trampoline, keep-fit,
swimming, sauna, solarium
Courses: swimming, archery,
badminton
Membership: £3.50 half year (ch
£1.75), family £7.50
Non-members: 25p (ch 15p)
entrance fee
Charges: squash £3.50 hour (off
peak £2.50), badminton £2.70 hour
(£1.90), table tennis £1 hour (90p),
keep fit 95p per session (50p)
🅿 ⌁ 🚹 🍸

UCKFIELD LEISURE CENTRE
Uckfield (0825) 5518
Downsview Crescent, Uckfield
Open: all year, daily 17.30-23.00;
w/ends & school hols 9.00-23.00
Facilities: swimming (summer),
badminton, squash, volleyball, cricket,
Martial Arts, aerobics, gymnastics
Courses: various, swimming, judo,
gymnastics
Charges: squash, badminton £2,
others 70p per session
🅿 🚻 🚹 🍸

WHEEL RECREATION CENTRE
Billingshurst
Under construction for autumn 1983,
specially for disabled people;
further information: Mr Bridges,
Horsham District Council,
Horsham (0403) 64191 ext 278

WORTHING SPORTS CENTRE
Worthing (0903) 502237
West Park, Shaftesbury Ave, Goring-
by-Sea
Open: all year, daily 9.30-22.30
Facilities: badminton, basketball,
tennis, volleyball, archery, table tennis,
gymnastics, weight training, judo
Courses: weight training, keep-fit, pop
mobility, yoga
Membership: £10.50 (full), £5.50
(off peak), £7.50 (17 weeks)
Non-members: entrance fee 25p day
Charges: badminton £2.75 (£1.90
off peak), squash £1.80 half hour
(£1.40), weight training 60p (90p),
main hall £27 (£19), gymnastics area
£3.40 (£2.70), reduction for schools
& OAPs, lunchtime yoga £1.10,
red gra pitch (markings) £17.75,
£9.25 (no markings)
Telephone bookings from members,
non-members in person
P & ⊑ ⏰

Swimming Pools

Brighton

JUBILEE STREET POOL
Jubilee St, Brighton
Main pool 33.3m x 12.3m; learner
pool; specialist diving pit 1m x 3m

KING ALFRED SPORTS CENTRE
Brighton (0273) 734422
Kings Way, Hove
Main pool 75ft x 30ft area, 3ft 6in-6ft
depth; room for 200 spectators

Burgess Hill

BURGESS HILL SWIMMING CENTRE
St John's Park, Burgess Hill (04466)
43735
Main pool 25m x 7.2m area, 0.9-
2.0m depth

Chichester

CHICHESTER SWIMMING POOL
Chichester, (0243) 86587
Eastgate Square, Chichester
Main pool 33.3m, diving boards
1m, 3m & 5m; room for 250
spectators

Crawley

CRAWLEY LEISURE CENTRE
Crawley (0293) 37431
Haslett Ave, Crawley
Main pool 33.3m, diving boards 1m,
3m & 5m

Tennis

Eastbourne

EASTBOURNE LEISURE POOL
Princess Park, Eastbourne
Main pool 33.3m x 15m area, 0.9-1.9m depth; 6 international lanes 2.5m; diving, 1m & 3m spring boards, 0.5m & 5m fixed boards; deep water tank 10m x 10.5m x 3.5m; learner pool 20m x 8.85m; room for 28 spectators

Hastings

SUMMERFIELD SPORTS CENTRE
Hastings (0424) 429677
Main pool 33.3m x 12.5m; 0.9m deep at each end, falling to 1.8m with central trough 2.25m deep, 3m wide (learner bay 7m x 4.5m); room for 200 spectators

Haywards Heath

THE DOLPHIN LEISURE CENTRE
Haywards Heath (0444) 57337/8
Pasture Hill Rd, Haywards Heath
Main pool 33.3m x 12.5m; diving, 1m spring board, 1m; 1.5m & 2m fixed boards; deep water pool 10.5m x 9.5m x 3m; instructional pool 12m x 9.5m x 0.75m; room for 100 spectators

Horsham

PARK SWIMMING CENTRE
Horsham (0403) 58078

Littlehampton

LITTLEHAMPTON SWIMMING CENTRE
Sea Rd, Littlehampton (east end of seafront)
Main pool 25m x 13m, 0.9-1.8m depth; shallow pool 12.5m x 8.5m

Worthing

THE AQUARENA
Worthing (0903) 31797
Brighton Rd, Worthing
Main pool 33.3m, diving boards 1m, 3m & 5m; room for 400 spectators

Tennis

Sussex has over 75 tennis clubs affiliated to the Lawn Tennis Association, the governing body for sport in this country. In addition there are hundreds of public tennis courts and information on these can be obtained from local council offices.

For any information on the sport and for details of local clubs, too numerous to mention herein full contact:

LAWN TENNIS ASSOCIATION
01-385 2366
Barons Court, West Kensington, London W14 9EG

SUSSEX LAWN TENNIS ASSOCIATION
Hon Secretary: Mrs W E Peall
Littlehampton (09062) 73023
25 Golden Ave, East Preston, Littlehampton BN16 1QY

Tourist Information Offices

Tourist Information Offices can be helpful whether you are a visitor to Sussex or a resident. They have a wealth of information on local attractions, places to stay and eat, events, activities, history and much more. For example if you have trouble in contacting any of the places listed in this directory contact the local information office for help. If you want to find out what you can do in your area contact your local information office and always make a point of contacting the information office at any place you are intending to visit.

They can usually provide leaflets on hotels and restaurants, town plans and brochures about attractions in the area.

SOUTH EAST REGIONAL TOURIST OFFICE
Tunbridge Wells (0892) 40766
Cheviot House, Tunbridge Wells TN1 1NH
This is the coordinating office for all tourist information in the South East of England and it covers Kent, Surrey, East & West Sussex.

ARUNDEL
Arundel (0903) 882268
61 High Street, Arundel

BATTLE
Battle (04246) 3721
88 High Street, Battle

BEXHILL-ON-SEA
Bexhill (0424) 212023
De La Warr Pavilion, Marina, Bexhill

BOGNOR REGIS
Bognor Regis (0243) 823140
1-2 Place St Maur des Fosses, Belmont St, Bognor Regis

BRIGHTON
Brighton (0273) 23755
w/ends (0273) 26450
Marlborough House, 54 Old Steine, Brighton (winter)

Brighton (0273) 26450
Sea Front, Kings Road, Brighton (summer only)

CHICHESTER
Chichester (0243) 775888
The Council House, North Street, Chichester

EASTBOURNE
Eastbourne (0323) 27474
3 Cornfield Terrace, Eastbourne

Eastbourne (0323) 27474
Shopping Precinct, Terminus Road, Eastbourne

Eastbourne (0323) 27474
Lower Promenade, Grand Parade, Eastbourne (summer only)

GATWICK AIRPORT
Crawley (0293) 502042
South East England Tourist Board, Arrivals Concourse, 2nd Floor, Terminal Building, Crawley

HAILSHAM
Hailsham (0323) 840604/P Western Rd, Hailsham

HASTINGS
Hastings (0424) 424242
4 Robertson Terrace, Hastings

Portakabin, Adjacent Fountain, Castle St, Hastings (summer only)

HOVE
Brighton (0273) 775400
Town Hall, Norton Rd, Hove

LEWES
Lewes (07916) 71600
Lewes House, High Street, Lewes

LITTLEHAMPTON
Littlehampton (09064) 3480
Windmill Complex, The Green,
Littlehampton (summer only)

NEWHAVEN
Newhaven (07912) 7450
South East England Tourist Board, Car
Ferry Terminal Car Park, The Harbour,
Newhaven (summer only)

PEACEHAVEN
Peacehaven (07914) 2668
Meridian Centre, Roderick Ave,
Peacehaven

PEVENSEY
Eastbourne (0323) 761444
Castle Car Park, High Street,
Eastbourne (summer & w/ends in
March & Oct)

County Planning Department
East Sussex County Council,
Southover House, Southover Rd,
Lewes (winter)

RYE
Rye (07973) 2293
Council Offices, Ferry Rd, Rye

SEAFORD
Seaford (0323) 892224
The Downs, Sutton Rd, Seaford

WORTHING
Worthing (0903) 39999 ext. 132/3
Town Hall, Chapel Rd, Worthing

Worthing (0903) 39999 ext. 372 or
(0903) 210022
Marine Parade, Worthing

Unusual Outings

BUTTERFLY CENTRE
Map 3 Bc/p 43
Eastbourne (0323) 645522
Royal Parade, Eastbourne
Open: end April-end Oct daily 10.00-
17.30
Charge: £1.20 (ch & OAPs 70p),
family rates 2 adults 2 ch £3.50 (3
ch £4); school groups 50p each (by
arrangement)
Semi tropical landscaped gardens,
waterfalls, exotic plants, tropical
butterflies
No dogs
🅿 💺

THE FORT
Map 3 Ac/p 70
Newhaven (07912) 3600
Open: all year, daily 9.00-18.00
Charge: £1.50 (ch £1); group
reductions by arrangement
Coastal fort built 1864 by Lord
Palmeston, training base & garrison
until 1914, museum, largest
fortification of its type in Sussex
Guided tours
🅿 💺 ♿ ⛲🍴✕

THE HASTINGS EMBROIDERY
Map 4 Ac/p 52
Hastings (0424) 424242
Town Hall, Queen's Rd, Hastings
Open: all year; Oct-May, Mon-Fri
11.30-15.30 (last admissions 15.00),
early June-late Sep, Mon-Fri
10.00-17.00 (last admissions 16.30),
Sat 10.00-13.00 & 14.00-17.00;
groups by arrangement
Charge: 50p (ch & OAPs 25p);
reductions for groups (20) by
arrangement (apply: Publicity &
Entertainment Officer, Tourist
Information Office)
27 embroidered panels of
chronological historic events,
embroidery hall, dispaly of dolls &
scale model of Battle of Hastings with
2,500 model soldiers
&

HASTINGS MODEL VILLAGE
Map 4 Ac/p 53
Hastings (0424) 427861
White Rock Gardens, Hastings
Open: end May-mid Sep, daily 10.00-
18.00
Charge: 30p (ch 20p)
Miniature Tudor village in landscaped
gardens
P ⛱

HOLLYCOMBE STEAM COLLECTION
Map 1 Aa/p 68
Liphook (0428) 723235
1½m S Liphook off A3
Open: Easter-Sep, Sun & BH Mons
14.00-18.00 (garden 12.00)
Charge: £1 (ch & OAPs 70p);
reductions for groups (20) by
arrangement
2 railways (7¼ standard & 7¼
gauge), steam saw mill, tractor, steam
farm with implements, steam driven
projector showing first film (1896)
Children's play area, nature walks,
aborteum, dogs to remain in car park
P ♿ ⛱🍴

RAYSTEDE CENTRE FOR ANIMAL WELFARE
Map 3 Ab/p 80
Halland (082584) 252
Raystede, Ringmer, 2m NE Lewes off
B2192
Open: all year, daily 10.00-16.00
(closed 13.00-14.00)
Charge: 10p
25 acres of home & wildlife sanctuary
for discarded & unwanted animals
P ♿ & 🍴

ROYAL GREENWICH OBSERVATORY
Map 3 Bc/p 56
Herstmonceux Castle, Herstmonceux,
6m E Hailsham off A271
Open: Good Fri-Sep, Mon-Fri 12.00-
17.30 (grounds & tea shop); 14.00
(exhibition); Sat, Sun & BHs 10.30-
17.00; groups by arrangement
Charge: 90p (ch & OAPs 45p)
Housed in Herstmonceux Castle (not
open), exhibition & astronomer to
answer questions (July-Aug 14.00-
15.00), audio visual history of castle;
set in 200 acres, gardens, moat,
nature trail
Dogs on leads
P ♿ & 🍴

RYE TOWN MODEL LIGHT SHOW
Map 4 Bb
Rye (0797) 223902
Mermaid St, Rye
Open: Easter-Sep, daily 10.30-17.00
Charge: 60p (ch 30p) half hour
show, 40p (ch 20p) 10 min show;
group reductions by arrangement
Authentic scale model of Rye with
directional sound & subtle lighting
telling story of Rye
No lavatories
P ♿

THE SUSSEX SHIRE HORSES
Map 4 Ab/p 45
Etchingham (058081) 501
½m N Etchingham on A265
Open: late March-early Nov, Tues-Sun & 10.30-17.00; shows at 11.00 & 15.00, other times by arrangement
Charge: £1.25 (ch14 75p, OAPs £1), group by arrangement £1 (ch & OAP 70p)
17th century manor house in 140 acres; breeding centre for French Ardennes, Welsh Cobs, Suffolk Punch, Colliers & Cart Horses; cart rides for children, horse demonstrations & working horse course during winter
No dogs
See also Historic Homes: Haremere Hall
🅿 🍴 ⅙ ⌗

ST CLEMENTS CAVES
Map 4 Ac/p 61
Hastings, Tourist & Recreation Dept (0424) 424242
West Hill, Hastings
Open: late March-mid Sep, daily 10.15-17.15 (closed 12.30-13.30); winter Sat & Sun only
Charge: 60p (ch 30p), group reductions (20) by arrangement 50p (ch 25p); contact External Entertainments Officer, Tourist & Recreation Dept
Guided tours 30 min
4 acres cut into slopes of West Hill used by smugglers in 18th century

THOMAS SMITH TRUGS
Map 3 Bb/p 56
Herstmonceux (0323) 640071
Gardner St, Herstmonceux, 3½m NE Hailsham on A271
Open: all year, Mon-Fri 12.00-16.00
Free
30 min guided tour
Founded 1858; highly skilled craftsmen manufacture traditional boat shaped baskets (trugs)
🅿 🍴 ⅙

Vineyards

Vines were first brought to the South East by the Romans, but the production of the now famous dry white wine declined for many centuries until its recent revival. Yearly the acreage and variety of vineyards increases and wines of reasonable quality are being produced.

BARNSGATE MANOR VINEYARD
Map 3 Ab
Nutley (082571) 2854
Herons Ghyll, 4m N Uckfield on A26
Magnificent manor house with wonderful views, 21 acres, small museum & all aspects of wine production
Open: all year, daily; groups by arrangement
Tours: £1.65 (£5.50 includes food)
🅿 🍴 ✕ 🍷

BREAKY BOTTOM VINEYARD
Map 3 Ac
Lewes (07916) 6427
2m SW Rodmell, 1½m off A26
4 acres, winery in old shepherd's cottage
Open: June-Sept by arrangement only
Charge: £1.50, includes wine tasting; groups (15) welcome
🅿

CARR-TAYLOR VINEYARDS
Map 4 Ab
Hastings (0424) 752501
Yew Tree Farm, Westfield, 5m N Hastings on A28
Open: May-Sep, Wed-Sun 10.00-17.00 (other times by arrangement)
Charge: £1.50 (ch 50p) includes tour & tasting (1-1½ hours)
Refreshments for groups by arrangement
🅿 🍴

CHILSDOWN VINEYARD
Map 1 Ab
Singleton (024363) 398
Singleton, 6m N Chichester of A286
13 acres located on site of 100 yr old
railway station run by family
Open: early May-late Sep, daily
10.30-17.00
Charge: 90p (ch 30p); groups (20)
£1.75 by arrangement, includes
guided tour and 1½ glasses wine;
leaflets 10p
Off licence
🅿 ⅃

DOWNERS VINEYARD
Map 2 Bb/p 78
Poynings (079156) 484
Clappers Lane, Fulking, Henfield, 3m
SE Henfield off A281
6 acres (to be extended) of Meullar-
Thurgau vines; spectacular views of
South Downs from Wolstonbury Hill
to Chanctonbury Ring
Open: anytime for wine buyers, June-
Sep tours by arrangement
Charge: £1 (ch 60p) includes tour &
wine tasting
'Downers' wine on sale
🅿 ⅃

MERRYDOWN WINE CO
Map 3 Bb
Horam Rd (04353) 2254/2401
Horam, 5m N Hailsham off A267
Open: mid May-early Oct, daily tours
10.00, 11.15, 14.00 & 15.15
Tours: by arrangement, maximum 40
£1, includes audio visual about cider
process, tour, cider & wine tasting
🅿 ⅃

ROCK LODGE VINEYARD
Map 2 Bb
Scaynes Hill (044486) 224
Scaynes Hill, 5m N Lewes on A272
Open: July-Sep, Sun 11.00-16.00
Charge: £1.50 (ch 50p); groups (20)
by arrangement
Tours: each lasts 1½-2 hours
Own wine available, advice on
viniology
Dogs on leads, lavatories
🅿 ⅃

VALLEY WINE CELLARS
See Zoos: Drusilla's Zoo Park

Walking

Sussex derives much of its character
and charm from a combination of the
wooded Weald, downland, marsh and
sea, providing a wealth of choice for
the serious walker, rambler and family
alike. The South Downs in particular
with its ancient pathways is rich in
prehistoric earthworks and Roman
remains.

There are many walking groups in
the county and a great deal has been
achieved through their efforts in
keeping the paths open and reclaiming
public rights of way.

For the enthusiast there are many
long walks to be taken but those
interested in a casual stroll are also
well catered for. To begin this
section, here are some suggestions for
shorter walks along marked trails and
walks set out in leaflets. Details can be
found in other sections of the
Leisure A-Z.

MARKED TRAILS

Many organisations have marked walks and produce leaflets to accompany walks which explain the landscape and describe the plant life and wildlife encountered. These walks are often through Forestry Commission woodland, country parks, farms, nature reserves, locations offering good views and areas of outstanding beauty. Many start from picnic sites or car parks.

See: Woodland, Country Parks, Picnic Sites, Nature Reserves, Farms

West Sussex County Council has prepared a few walk cards, available from:

West Sussex County Council, County Hall, Chichester, West Sussex

Organisations

RAMBLERS' ASSOCIATION

Southern Area
1-5 Wandsworth Rd, London SW8
SW8 2LJ

The Ramblers' Association campaigns for public access to all rural areas. Its members keep paths clear and fight any development which hinders access to public footpaths. They also waymark paths to make them easier to follow and work to protect the countryside.

The RA also organises excursions and group walks, including trips to different areas of the country. There are hundreds of RA groups throughout Britain, keeping a close watch on footpaths and ensuring they are well maintained, as well as enjoying walking together. Even those who prefer to walk alone may consider joining the RA, since it is responsible for enabling lone walkers to have unhindered access to the countryside.

If you come across a public footpath which is closed, is not accessible or is in any way impassable you should contact the Sussex Area RA (see below) and report this.

The RA also publishes many leaflets on all aspects of its work as well as a Bed & Breakfast Guide for walkers and a regular journal (free to members).

Membership: £6; couple £7.50; couple retired £3.75; ch 18, students, unemployed & OAPs £3; life membership £210, members get free copy Bed & Breakfast Guide (each year), free journal 'Rucksack' (3 each year), local area news, access to Ordnance Survey 1:50,000 map library; special offers & reductions on publications from shops

RAMBLERS' ASSOCIATION SUSSEX AREA

Hon Secretary: Mr M F H Gray
Chichester (0243) 776991
67 Windsor Rd, Chichester
PO19 2XG
(please enclose SAE for reply)

See also: RA Local Groups (below)

Long Distance Pathway

THE SOUTH DOWNS WAY

Route: 80m from Eastbourne on the Sussex coast to the Hampshire border south of Petersfield. It follows the coast to Beachy Head, along the clifftops of the Seven Sisters to Cuckmere Haven, then inland across rolling downland. There are magnificent views from vantage points such as Ditchling Beacon (248m), where warning fires were once lit. Places of interest along the Way include the 14th century Clergy House at Alfriston and the hill-fort at Chanctonbury Ring.

Shorter Walks

The Coast and Countryside Committee of the West Sussex County Council have produced a leaflet of guided walks for the family ranging from 1 to 12 miles. They aim to provide those who are not necessarily regular walkers with the opportunity to walk in the countryside with a guide who knows the area. Also some specially designed walks for children.

The Chichester Harbour Conservancy have also produced a leaflet comprising 10 walks around Chichester Harbour Leaflets available: West Sussex County Council, County Hall, Chichester, West Sussex

The Downsman Rambler Bus 222 provides a 30 mile circular bus route of the Downs

For details telephone:
Brighton (0273) 606600, contact Tourist Information Centre, High Street, Arundel or your local Southdown Travel Office

FOREST WAY
See Country Parks

WORTH WAY
Route: 6m from Three Bridges to East Grinstead mostly in the Parish of Worth, following the old railway line

R.A. Local Groups

ARUN-ADUR R.A.
Secretary: Miss J Smith
Rustington (09062) 4712
41 Foxdale Drive, Angmering,
Littlehampton, W Sussex BN6 4HF

BRIGHTON & HOVE R.A.
Secretary: Miss J Reynolds
Brighton (0273) 558181
41 Reigate Rd, Brighton, E Sussex
BN1 5AH

HEATHFIELD (WEALDEN CUCKOOS)
Secretary: Mr S Bayliss Smith
Heathfield (04352) 3009
35 Downsview, Heathfield, E Sussex
TN21 8PF

MID-SUSSEX R.A.
Secretary: Mrs J P White
Burgess Hill (04446) 6833
29 Greenlands Drive, Burgess Hill,
W Sussex RH15 OAZ

NORTH SUSSEX R.A.
Secretary: Mrs M Rich
49 Brantridge Rd, Furnace Green,
Crawley, W Sussex RH10 6HT
Crawley (0293) 26534

SOUTH-WEST SUSSEX
Secretary: Mrs J Denton
21A Cleveland Rd, Chichester,
W Sussex PO19 2HF
Chichester (0243) 784216

Water Skiing

Water skiing is best undertaken as a member of a recognised club. The British Waterski Federation (BWF) is the governing body for the sport in Britain and most clubs are affiliated to it, including all those listed below.

If you wish to learn how to water ski contact a club near you. Clubs with vacancies may be able to provide equipment and instruction. The BWF run many courses and should be contacted for details.

Most clubs will hire equipment such as wet suits and usually provide boats. In many cases members are not allowed to use their own boats since the number of boats operating in any one area of water must be carefully controlled.

For any information contact:

BRITISH WATER SKI FEDERATION
Secretary: Gillian Hill
01-387 9371
16 Upper Woburn Place,
London WC1H OQL

Water Ski Clubs

BRIGHTON MARINA
Brighton (0273) 693636
Telephone in advance
Charge: jet ski hire, June-Sep, Tue-Sun, £50 per day, £25 half day
See also Marinas: Brighton Marina

CHICHESTER WATER SKI CLUB
Chichester (0243) 787715
Southern Leisure Centre, Vinnetrow Rd, Chichester
Secretary: Tony Mortimer
Horsham (0403) 58902
15 Bethune Rd, Horsham
Membership: £135 (boat owners), £58 (non boat owners)

HASTINGS MOTOR BOAT & YACHT CLUB
Hastings (0424) 429779
Rock-a-Nore Parade, Hastings
Secretary: Mr D Renno
H.M.B.Y.C.

RYE WATER SKI CLUB
Rye (07973) 2181
Rye Harbour, Rye
Secretary: Mr A Rabbitt
Hadlow (073279) 662
Plaxtol (073276) 338
23 Tainter Rd, Hadlow, Tonbridge, Kent
Membership: £7.50

Windsurfing

If you are a capable windsurfer and have your own sail board you can use it on much of the coastal waters of Sussex (weather permitting). Most inland waters are controlled and only private clubs have access to them for sports such as windsurfing. This section gives details of these clubs (many of which have exclusive access to inland waters) and of courses for learning windsurfing. Some of the clubs are sailing clubs with windsurfing members. Other clubs are purely for windsurfing. Some clubs, particularly the sailing clubs, offer a wide range of facilities from bars and restaurants to dressing rooms and showers. It is usually necessary to wear a wetsuit when windsurfing in this country and they can often be hired, as can the sailboards.

BOGNOR REGIS YACHT CLUB
Bognor Regis (0243) 865735
The Esplanade, Bognor Regis

BRIGHTON MARINA
Brighton (0273) 693636
Marina Watersports
Open: June-Sep, daily
Courses: elementary £30, open sea
£20 (equipment included), telephone
in advance
Board hire: £15 per day, £25 per
w/end, £50 per week

BEWL BRIDGE WINDSURFER SCHOOL
Eastbourne (0323) 22595
Surf 'n Sail lake school at Bewl Bridge
Reservoir
Courses: w/days, 10.00-17.00
(closed 13.00-14.00); full course (for
certificate) 6 hrs £28, 3 hrs £14, group
rates by arrangement; equipment
supplied, ideal for children, changing
rooms, showers
IWS & RYA approved, beginners &
advanced
🅿 ⛭

CHICHESTER SEA SCHOOL
Chichester (0243) 512557
Chichester Yacht Basin, Chichester

EASTBOURNE WINDSURFER SCHOOL
Eastbourne (0323) 22395
Surf 'n Sail, 66 Susans Rd, Eastbourne
Courses: daily, 10.00-17.00 (closed
13.00-14.00); 5 lessons divided into
2/3 hr sessions £28, group rates by
arrangement; supervised by Barry Stuart
IWA & RYA qualified instructor
Board hire: £4 hour, £10 half day, £15
day (includes rescue), wet suits £1
extra; positive identification required &
deposit of £50; board hire includes
temporary membership of Eastbourne
Sailing School & use of club facilities
Demonstrations every Sat morning at
Eastbourne Windsurfer school beach

FELPHAM WINDSURFING SCHOOL
Bognor Regis (0243) 863899
White Lodge, Sea Rd, Felpham
Courses: £10 half day, £15 full day
(beginners)
Board hire: £6 hour including wetsuits
Olympic courses, some slalom & fun
events arranged
Changing rooms & shower
🅿 ⛭ 🗔

HASTINGS WINDSURFING CLUB
Hastings (0424) 430601
Crown House, 57 Marina,
St Leonards-on-Sea
Membership: £20 per year, £23
family, board storage free
Racing & fun events Suns & Weds
evenings, regular social functions
& disco
🅿 🗔 ♇

HOVE LAGOON WINDSURFING SCHOOL
Brighton (0273) 692165
Courses: 3 hr introductory course
w/days £14.75, w/ends £15.75 ;6 hr
elementary course £28.75 & £30.75
(ch16 £18.75 & £21.75); group rates
by arrangement, equipment provided
Advanced courses, RYA boardsailing
certificate, RYA open sea award
(telephone for details)
Board Hire: lagoon w/days £3 hour,
w/ends £3.75 (2 hrs £5, £6.50)
Sea w/days £3.50 hour, w/ends £4.25
(2 hrs £5.40, £7)
Wet suits w/days £1.50
 w/ends £2; boots 2 hrs w/days 50p,
w/ends 75p
Special offers w/days, changing rooms,
children's play area, cafe and pub nearby

SOUTHDOWN SAILBOARDS

Chichester (0243) 776439
Westhampnett Lake, Coach Rd,
Chichester
50 acres lake for all levels proficiency
Open: Wed-Mon 10.00-18.00
Courses: 4 hour introductory course
£15, £25 per day, group reductions
(equipment included)
Charge: daily membership £2, board
storage £15 year (members only)
Board hire: £3 first hr, £2 every hr after,
full day £10; wetsuits with board
£2 day, 75p with own board
Membership: £35 year

SUNSPORTS

Tuition on Piddinghoe Lake (private)
Courses: 5hr course £20
(RYA approved)
Changing rooms

SUSSEX WINDSURFING

Worthing (0903) 47174
37-39 Eirene Rd, Sea Place, Worthing
Courses: elementary, w/days £10,
w/ends £12; intermediate & advanced
£10; group sailing, w/days £13,
w/ends £15; all equipment included,
RYA & IWS approved
Membership: £20 per year,
family £30
Board hire: £3 per hour, wetsuits £1

WATER INDULGENCE

Eastbourne (0323) 766852
11 Pevensey Court, Collier Rd,
Pevensey Bay
Courses: 'Taster' £5 hour; 3 hrs £12;
certificate level £21
Board hire: £3 hour, £8 day
IWS & RYA approved, wetsuits
compulsory
Shower

Women's Institute

The Women's Institute is a completely
independent voluntary organisation,
with a total membership of about
400,000 women in England, Wales,
the Channel Islands and the Isle of Man.

The broad purpose of the WI is to give
countrywomen the opportunity of
working together to improve the quality
of life in rural areas; and to provide a
wide variety of educational and leisure
activities. New members are always
welcome. WIs usually meet once a
month in a hall, parish room or perhaps a
school.

If you want to find out more about the
WI in your area contact the NFWI or one
of the local secretaries in Sussex
listed below.

THE NATIONAL FEDERATION OF WOMEN'S INSTITUTES

Membership Secretary
01-730 7212
39 Eccleston Street
London SW1W 9NT

EAST SUSSEX FEDERATION OF WOMEN'S INSTITUTES

Secretary: Mrs Rosemary Gillett
Lewes (07916) 2616
Westgate Street, Lewes, East Sussex
BN7 1YR

WEST SUSSEX COUNTY FEDERATION OF WOMEN'S INSTITUTES

Secretary: Mrs Doreen B Deeley
Chichester (0243) 83134
North Lodge, Northgate, Chichester

Woodland

This section includes forests, woods, arboretums. Many of them are owned and managed by the Forestry Commissions (FC). Woodlands mentioned are open at all times and access is free unless otherwise stated.

ABBOTS WOOD
Map 3 Bc
Alfriston, West Dean Forest Office (0323) 870301
1 m E Arlington, 3 m SW Hailsham
Broadleaved, coniferous & larch trees
1¼ m walk, leaflet available, special 400 yd trail for the disabled, lavatories
FC 🅿 ⛱

ASHDOWN FOREST
Map 3 Aa
1 m S of Forest Row Town Centre, off A22
6,500 acres unspoilt & unenclosed countryside open to the public for quiet enjoyment, walking & picnicking; largely heathland with areas of oak, beech woods, naturally regenerating birch & Scots pine trees; 60 car parks around the Forest; outstanding views of North & South Downs; privately owned, managed by Conservators of Ashdown Forest
🅿 ⛱

BLUEBELL WALK
Map 3 Bc
Polegate (03212) 2039
Bates Green Farm, Arlington, NW Polegate off A27
Open: early-late May, daily dawn to dusk
Charge: fixed annually, proceeds to local organisations
Leaflet available, dogs on leads
🅿 ♿ ⛱

FLATROPERS WOOD
Henfield (0273) 2630
5 m NW Rye off A268
87½ acres on Tunbridbge Wells sandstone; mixed wood, mainly oak birch, sweet chestnut & Alder Buckthorne
Managed by STNC

FORE WOOD
See Bird Parks: Fore Wood

FRISTON FOREST
Map 3 Bc
Alfriston, Warden, (0323) 870301
Between Seaford & Eastbourne, N of A259, adjacent to Seven Sisters Country Park
FC establishing new broadleaved forest here; exposed to strong winds off the sea and pine trees have been used to nurse other species; 2¾ m circular trail; leaflet available (small charge)
🅿

MALLYDAMS WOOD
Map 4 Ab
Hastings, Warden, (0424) 862055
3¼m NE Hastings off A259
Open: by arrangement only (closed April-June); groups can be escorted
Remnant of Ancient Wealden Forest, wildlife, field study centre for school use; owned & managed by RSPCA
🄿

NAP WOOD
Map 3 Ba
**5m NE Crowborough, 4m
S Tunbridge Wells off A267**
Open: April-Oct, Suns (other times permit required STNC)
Oak, woodland, birch & pine trees, wildlife; magnificent bluebell display May; owned by NT & leased by STNC, leaflet available

SELWYNS WOOD
Map 3 Bb
Henfield, STNC (0273) 2630
1½M SW Cross-in-Hand, S Heathfield off B2102
Small wealden wood on Ashdown Sand, mature beech, oak, conifers, brush scrub, coppice of sweet chestnut; owned & managed by STNC

Yoga

Many Adult Education Centres run regular yoga classes, contact your local council for details. There are also private yoga teachers in Sussex. For details on private classes and any other information on yoga contact:
Mary Loader
(0424) 222301
5 St Peters Crescent
Bexhill
TN24 2EH

Zoos

BRIGHTON AQUARIUM & DOLPHINARIUM
See Aquarium: Brighton Aquarium & Dolphinarium

DRUSILLAS ZOO PARK
Map 3 Ac
Alfriston (0323) 870234
Alfriston, N of village, 4m N Seaford off A27
Open: April-Oct, daily 11.00-18.00
Charge: £1.25 (ch12 & OAPs 65p); group reductions by arrangement
Garden centre, thatch barn restaurant, farmhouse lunches, cream teas & valley wine cellars
🄿 ⬛ �& ⛄ ⅃ ✕

RAYSTEDE CENTRE FOR ANIMAL WELFARE
See Unusual Outings: Raystede Centre for Animal Welfare

TILGATE PARK NATURE CENTRE
See Country Parks: Tilgate Park
Wide variety of animals & birds including rare breeds & species

ZOOTOPIA
Map 1 Bc/p 20
Bognor Regis (0243) 824858
Open: all year, daily 10.00-18.00 (summer); 10.00-17.00 (winter)
Charge: £1.20 (ch & OAPs 60p, ch3 free); group reductions (telephone for details
'Wonderful World of Magic' paradise for children, exotic & domestic animals, tableaux of fairy stories & legends with sound & animation
⬛ ⛄ ⅃ ⅃ ⅃

Acknowledgments

The author and publishers would like to thank the following individuals and organisations for their help and co-operation in providing information for this book:

The Department of the Environment; East Sussex Planning Department; Forestry Commission; Anne Griffiths, West Sussex Planning Department; John Houghton, Sussex Archaeological Society; South-East Arts; Nature Conservancy; National Gardens Scheme; National Trust; Dr Perring, Royal Society for Nature Conservation; Ramblers Association; Royal National Lifeboat Institute.

Thanks also go to the many individuals who provided information through tourist information offices and through other societies and organisations too numerous to mention.

Notes